FRANCE

Guillaume Apollinaire

(TWAS 14)

TWAYNE'S WORLD AUTHORS SERIES (TWAS)

The purpose of TWAS is to survey the major writers —novelists, dramatists, historians, poets, philosophers, and critics—of the nations of the world. Among the national literatures covered are those of Australia, Canada, China, Eastern Europe, France, Germany, Greece, India, Italy, Japan, Latin America, New Zealand, Poland, Russia, Scandinavia, Spain, and the African nations, as well as Hebrew, Yiddish, and Latin Classical literatures. This survey is complemented by Twayne's United States Authors Series and English Authors Series

The intent of each volume in these series is to present a critical-analytical study of the works of the writer; to include biographical and historical material that may be necessary for understanding, appreciation, and critical appraisal of the writer; and to present all material in clear, concise English—but not to vitiate the scholarly content of the work by doing so.

Guillaume Apollinaire

By SCOTT BATES

University of the South

Twayne Publishers, Inc.   ::   New York

To Phoebe

APOLLINAIRE

Preface

J'ai bâti une maison au milieu de l'Océan de terre.

Like Christians of the first or tenth centuries we live in an eschato-logical age; it is no more news to anyone who reads the news-papers that the world could end shortly from atomic destruction than it is that he could die in an automobile accident or from cancer. It is therefore relevant to recall that certain poets, novel-ists, cranks, priests, and scholars have been concerned with the arrival of the ultimate catastrophe for more than a hundred years now. In their analyses and prophecies our present situation has been anticipated and even oriented; so that a serious study of modern literature and art today cannot any more ignore the *end of the world* theme than it can ignore, say, myth, Freud, or literary ambiguity.

In secular literature the theme has been with us since Grain-ville and Mary Shelley wrote works on *the last man* in 1805 and 1826, respectively, and since Poe and Baudelaire gave currency to an accelerating wave of science fiction known to the trade as the "anti-utopia theme." During the same years the theme con-tinued to be a predominant one in religious works and utterances, with, however, a Romantic intensification: Paul Vulliaud notes in his comprehensive study of its course from ancient India to the present, "The nineteenth century was one of the ages most fraught with predictions of the end of the world, which constitute, it might be said, a specialty of its [religious] literature" (*La Fin du monde*, 1952). In poetry, we are familiar with the multiple prog-nostications from Baudelaire's "the world is going to end" (in *Fusées*) and Rimbaud's "the earth is melting" to Yeats' rough beast and Eliot's final whimper.

Before August 6, 1945, however, there was a major difference between secular and religious visions of Armageddon. While various fundamentalist sects and heretics saw it as immediate and called upon the world to repent before it was too late, secular prophets, literati, scientists, and socialists either postponed an ultimate scientific calamity to a vague distant date when the comet would strike, the sun explode or burn out, and the world ignite or freeze, or they foresaw a relative human ending in which the yellow horde would sweep in from the East ("over the new Transsiberian railway," ironized Apollinaire), nations would exterminate each other, or the downtrodden Occidental masses would rise and wash the earth with blood. In these last predictions, particularly numerous in the last half of the nineteenth century, the imminent catastrophe was only occasionally seen as absolute; usually some millennium, esthetic, socialist, and/or scientific, would rise from the smoking ruins to establish itself as the Crystal City, the eternal New Jerusalem.

The idea of revolutionary death and rebirth, a kind of poetico-religio-socialist phoenix theme, will be one that will concern us most in the works of the poet Guillaume Apollinaire and his friend the painter Pablo Picasso. The two artists chanced on the globe during the turn-of-the-century apogee of all these eschatological currents and made a specialty of bringing them to the attention of the twentieth century. In the case of Apollinaire, fundamentalist Catholic dogma concerning the Biblical prophets, the Antichrist, and the Messiah played a major role in orienting his secular thought—and thereafter the thought of his numerous heirs.

When he wrote in the first decade of the century, for example, "I used to hope for the end of the world" ("The Betrothal"), he was probably referring to his earlier utopian anarchist leanings; yet the plot of his first novel, *The Glory of the Olive*—or at least what may be perceived of it in the remaining fragments of the book—follows more or less traditional religious beliefs in its description of the Antichrist's attempt to avert the end of the world by preventing the accession to the Roman See of the last pope, called "The Glory of the Olive." In his most violent anticlericalism he believed in the inevitable death and resurrection cycles of nations and masses, as did his mentors of anarchist thought Sébastien Faure, Laurent Tailhade, Octave Mirbeau, Georges de Bouhélier, and Mécislas Golberg, several of whom had undergone a similar Catholic upbringing. Out of this witches' brew of the sacred and profane came much of our modern art and literature, that, for example, of Picasso, Yeats, Rilke, Kafka, Gide, Lawrence, Joyce, and Sartre. Also the new gods of the century, Mussolini (a revolutionary anarchist), Hitler (Mussolini's disciple), Lenin, and Mao Tse-tung. "The more carefully one compares the outbreaks of militant social chiliasm during the later Middle Ages with modern totalitarian movements the more remarkable the similarities appear," writes Norman Cohn in *The Pursuit of the Millennium.*

An eschatological age, therefore, our age, with its anxiety and its desperate search for religious and secular solutions, for gods, for mere survival. An age similar to that approaching the year 1000, wrote Apollinaire in 1915:

If we aren't in an early medieval age of mental licence, of lyrical irony, of the *danse macabre* and the terrors of the year 1000, we are in an age roughly equivalent to it, today is the time of Anguish (*le temps de l'Angoisse*).—(Letter to Lou, Feb. 2, 1915.)

An age in which, thought both he and Picasso, God was dead and the artist was obliged either to assert his prerogative as a microcosm of the universe, become the macrocosm and save the world for art, or else perish miserably in anonymous masses. In short, an age in which at least two of our leaders of modern taste were early acquainted with existential anguish, the terrible responsibility of re-creating the world in one's own image before it die in natural or supernatural agony. It is a tribute to them and perhaps a lesson to use that they were able to formulate and impose their image in Dionysian energy and joy ("the anguish of my delight," wrote Apollinaire) with full Apollonian awareness of the proximity of the danger.

Until recently, this picture of a committed Apollinaire dedicated to the task of bringing light to chaos and, if not to replace God in person, at least to become a sort of illegitimate Christ saving the world through the Verb, would not have been accepted by many admirers of the poet. Given the surface dilletantism, the cultivated mystery, the charm and fantasy of the person Apollinaire, this is completely understandable. By friends and enemies alike he has been variously described as the delightful impresario of the avant-garde, the pontiff of cubism (who really knew very little about art), the continuator of France's lyrical traditions from Villon through Verlaine (whose poems were intuitively created almost in spite of himself), the inventor of the word *surrealism,* who used it without full knowledge of its implications, the man who would embrace anything if it were new, who was a slave to love, who bridged the gap between two centuries of great literature and art by a miraculous combination of luck, ubiquitousness, enthusiasm, audacity, and lyrical intoxication.

Some of this is true; but it is superficial truth at best. As in the earlier case of Rimbaud, much influence was here united to much misunderstanding, as some of Apollinaire's closest friends, followers, and critics failed to catch the largest import of his communication and to understand what he was saying—what his works "meant." In the last twenty years, the picture has substantially changed. The large number of documents that have been made available for the first time following World War II rendered possible a close look at Apollinaire's esthetics and philosophy and brought many obscure references to light. The present study, which is the first comprehensive survey of Apollinaire's symbolism and ideas, is especially indebted to works of Michel Décaudin, Marcel Adéma, L. C. Breunig, Roger Shattuck, and Marie-Jeanne Durry, all of them written during the golden age of Apollinaire scholarship between 1950 and 1965. Michel Décaudin's careful *Dossier d'Alcools* (1960) and L.-C. Breunig's *Chroniques d'Art* (1960) have provided essential documents and information, and Marcel Adéma's *Guillaume Apollinaire le Mal-aimé* (1952), the first biography to penetrate through the great quantity of legendary material accumulated about the poet to the facts of his existence, has given many valuable insights. Finally, special thanks are due Jacqueline Apollinaire, the poet's widow, for graciously allowing access to manuscripts and her husband's library, and Mme. Onimus-Blumenkrantz for communicating a copy of a heretofore unknown work of Apollinaire, *French Grace and Manners* (*La Grâce et le Maintien Français*).

In my study I have endeavored to help the reader arrive at an understanding of the meaning of the major works of Apollinaire by (1) considering in a schematic way principal themes and symbols; (2) analyzing key works of poetry, fiction, and criticism; (3) surveying chronologically the philosophical and esthetic ideas of the poet in relation to those of his period; and (4) listing the sources and meanings that have been discovered to date of the obscurer references. Apart from a brief chronology of external events of the poet's life, the study does not cover biographical or historical events except insofar as they are pertinent to an understanding of the writings. Inevitably, because of the complexity of symbolism, breadth of cultural reference, and extreme subjectivity of Apollinaire's work, many of my interpretations are different from those of other critics; wherever possible, I have presented the other points of view and the reasons behind the discrepancies. In all, I hope this study will serve as a guide and reference work for an important, very concerned body of literature which traces at least one major path for the twentieth century to follow along its by now all-too-familiar precipice.

SCOTT BATES

Acknowledgments

For permission to quote from the works of Guillaume Apollinaire, the following acknowledgments are due. To Editions Gallimard for "Un soir," "Le Vent nocturne" (*Alcools*), "La Colombe" (*Le Bestiaire*), "La Nuit du 14 avril" (*Calligrammes*), "Peu de chose," "Endurcis-toi vieux coeur" (*Oeuvres poétiques*), and extracts from "Le Larron," "L'Ermite," "La Chanson du malaimé," "Automne malade," "Le Voyageur,' "L'Emigrant de Landor Road," "Lul de Faltenin," "Le Brasier" (*Alcools*), "La Victoire" (*Calligrammes*), and "Le Quatrième Poème secret" (*Oeuvres poétiques*). To Editions Messein for an extract from "Ispahan" (*Il y a*). And to New Directions for extracts from "Les Fiançailles," Cortège," "Zone," "Vendémiaire," "Le Musicien de Saint Merry," "La Jolie Rousse," and "Les Collines" (*Selected Writings of Guillaume Apollinaire* [ed. Roger Shattuck, N. Y., 1949]).

Contents

GUILLAUME APOLLINAIRE

by

SCOTT BATES

Since the death of Guillaume Apollinaire in 1918, the extent of his influence on modern poetry and art has become increasingly evident. The steady growth of his reputation may be traced in works of poets and painters throughout the world; and the leading role that his critical ideas and creative example played in bringing about a twentieth-century revolution of the arts is now almost universally recognized. The present study is the first in any language to make a comprehensive analysis of the writings that gave rise to this world-wide recognition and is the first to use three of Apollinaire's works heretofore unknown to scholars, fragments of an early "lost" novel, a ghost-written dance manual and an unpublished volume of correspondence written during World War I. Throughout the study Apollinaire's role as a revolutionary, apocalyptic poet is emphasized, as is the significance of his existential efforts to transform the world into his lyrical vision of it. The author has tried to remain faithful to Apollinaire's vision; he sees him as he wishes himself to be seen by future generations, as one of the major poetic prophets of our time.

Chronology

1880   August 26: Born Guillaume-Albert-Wladimir-Alexandre-
        Apollinaire Kostrowitzky, natural son of Angelica Kostro-
        witzky and Francesco Flugi d'Aspermont (?) at Rome.
1883   Comes to France for the first time.
1887   March: In earthquake on French Riviera.
1889   Travels to Paris Exposition. Enters Catholic parochial
        school at Monaco.
1892   May 8: First communion. Fall: Writes first poetry.
1895   First love affair. Enters parochial school at Cannes.
1897   February: Enters high school at Nice. June: Leaves high
        school without receiving diploma.
1898   Is a strong partisan of Dreyfus.
1899   April: Arrives at Paris with mother and brother. July: Takes
        lodgings at Stavelot, Belgium, in the Ardennes; love for
        Maria Dubois. October 6: Leaves lodgings secretly to avoid
        payment of rent; returns to Paris.
1900   Spring: Collaborates anonymously on serialized novel
        What to Do? Difficult existence at Paris. Love for Linda
        Molina da Sylva; writes dance manual for her father,
        French Grace and Manners.
1901   August: Employed as tutor for the daughter of the Vis-
        countess de Milhau; Annie Playden employed as governess.
        Leaves for the properties of the Viscountess in the Rhine-
        land.
1902   Spring: Travels extensively in Germany, Austria, and
        Czechoslovakia. August: Terminates employment for the
        Viscountess de Milhau. September: Becomes bank clerk
        at Paris.
1903   Meets André Salmon, Alfred Jarry, Jean Moréas. Novem-
        ber: Travels to London to see Annie Playden. Edits small
        review *Le Festin d'Ésope.*

1904   Works on financial paper. May: Second trip to London; Annie leaves him. Meets Max Jacob, Pablo Picasso. August: Discontinues *Le Festin d'Ésope.*

1905   Spring: Edits the *Revue Immoraliste* (two issues).

1906   Writes pornographic novels.

1907   Meets Marie Laurencin. Introduces Picasso to Braque.

1908   Spring: Lectures on young poets. Collaborates with Jean Royère on *La Phalange.* Meets Jules Romains. Summer: Travels to Belgium, Holland; visits Gustave Kahn, Théo Varlet.

1909   Publishes *The Putrescent Enchanter.* October: Moves to Auteuil, near Marie Laurencin.

1910   Publishes *The Heresiarch and Company.*

1911   Begins writing chronicle for the *Mercure de France.* Publishes *The Bestiary,* or *The Cortege of Orpheus.* September 7: Arrested for theft of the "Mona Lisa" from the Louvre, imprisoned at the Santé. September 12: Released from prison as innocent.

1912   Summer: Marie leaves him. Friendship with Blaise Cendrars. October: Moves from Auteuil to the Latin Quarter.

1913   February: Assumes editorship of *Les Soirées de Paris.* Publishes *Alcools, The Cubist Painters,* and *The Futurist Antitradition.*

1914   August: War declared; tries to in vain to enlist. September: Leaves Paris for Nice; meets the Countess Louise de Coligny. December 6: Joins the artillery at Nimes.

1915   January 2: Meets briefly Madeleine Pages. March 29: Lou ends liaison. April: Moves from Nimes to front near Reims. August: Becomes engaged to Madeleine. Is made gunnery sergeant. November: Joins infantry to become second lieutenant. December: Travels to Oran on leave to see Madeleine.

1916   March 17: Wounded in the head by shrapnel. May 9: Trepanned. Fall: Publishes *The Assassinated Poet.*

1917   June 21: Produces *The Breasts of Tiresias.* November 26: Lectures on the *new spirit.*

1918   May 2: Marries Jacqueline Kolb. Summer: Publishes *Calligrammes.* November 9: Dies of grippe.

Tentative Chronology of the Poems of Alcools (1913)

Pre-Rhineland to Post-Rhineland Period, 1898–1903

The Thief

The Hermit

Merlin and the Old Woman

Claire de lune

Hotels (?)

The Door (?)

Sign

Rhineland and Post-Rhineland Period, 1901–1903

Rhenish Night

The Night Wind

The Synagogue

Marizibill

Autumn

Adieu

The Lady

Rhenish Autumn

 (*Rhénane d'Automne*)

The Saffron

Sick Autumn

The Pines

The Women

Snow White

The Gipsy

The House of the Dead

May

The Bells

Schinderhannes

The Lorelei

1903–1907

One Evening (?)

The Emigrant of Landor Road

The Song of the Poorly

 Beloved (parts)

Annie (?)

Palace

Salome

Lul de Faltenin

1908–1910

The Brazier

Rosemonde (?)[1]

The Betrothal

1909

Poem Read at the Marriage

 of Andre Salmon

Cortege

Vendemaire

1910–1912

Saltimbanques (?)
Twilight (?)
At the Sante
Marie
The Mirabeau Bridge

Clotilde (?)[2]
Hunting Horns
The Traveler
Zone
Cantor (?)

CHAPTER 1

Christ and Antichrist

Patriarche, qui donc n'est pas un sauveur?—
L'Enchanteur pourrissant

I *"One Evening"*

SOME of Apollinaire's primary themes and symbols are found in the following poem from his important collection *Alcohols* (*Alcools*, 1913).

One Evening (*Un soir*)

An eagle descended from the sky white with archangels
    Help me to bear
Will you permit all these lamps to tremble for long
    Pray pray for me

The city is metallic and the only star is drowned
    In thy blue eyes
When the trolleys were rolling casting pale fires
    On mangy birds

And all that was trembling in thine eyes of my dreams
    Drunk by one man
Under the gaslights russet as the false agaric
    O clothed-one (*vêtue*) thine arm coiled (*se lovait*)

See the mountebank sticks out his tongue at the women waiting
    (*attentives*)
    A phantom has committed suicide
The apostle on the fig tree hangs slowly salivating
    Let's play for this love then with dice

Thy birth was proclaimed by the clear bells ringing
    See
The ways are in flower and the palms are moving
    Towards thee

At first glance "One Evening" seems a jumbled résumé of New Testament history. The narrator is first present at the end of the world as he witnesses the eagle and the archangels of the Book of Revelation (8:13 in the Revised Standard Version); he spies the star of Bethlehem in blue eyes, watches the suicide of the apostle Judas—apocryphally supposed to have hanged himself on a fig tree—and finally hails the birth and entrance into Jerusalem of the Messiah. On closer examination, however, the poem takes on a diabolical turn. The feminine "clothed-one" (*vêtue*) and the pun *se lovait* at the end of the third stanza reveals the *thee* of the poem to be a woman, associated with a serpent, "love," and thus fallen Eve; moreover, *vêtue* is an adjective which was used in the thirteenth century for a female heretic.[1] Apollinaire's placing of the exclusive guiding star in her blue eyes would suggest that she is both his beloved and his new Messiah, a kind of a female Antichrist; she will reign transcendent only after the deaths of a phantom Judas hanged on the phallic fig tree and of Christ Himself, whose death turns love into a game of chance—just as Roman soldiers gambled for His robe.[2] The images at the beginning of the fourth stanza, mountebank, projected tongue, and waiting women, are used elsewhere by Apollinaire to symbolize the death of love; here the mountebank ("histrion" or Italian buffoon, as contrasted to the serious saltimbanque-artist) undergoes a phantom death like that of Judas and puts out his tongue like a fool or a hanged man at "attentive ones" (*attentives*)—a noun created by the Symbolists and always used by our poet to signify female lovers. Indeed, the mountebank, Judas, and love may be one and the same phantom; this follows the thesis of Rémy de Gourmont's novel *The Phantom* and anticipates Proust's similar ideas.

Certain biographical precisions clarify the poem's experience. Apollinaire's blue-eyed beloved was Annie Playden, a frustrating young English governess who ultimately fled him to America. Her love was a poison in other poems—like the poisonous false agaric (fly-agaric) in this one, with its color of Christ's red hair[3] —and he loved her sensual arms (*all* women's arms were sensual to him and to Rémy de Gourmont). She was his divinity: before leaving the Catholic faith in school, he had celebrated a cult of hyperdulia for the Virgin Mary, the nostalgia for which was to haunt him the rest of his life and change his mistresses into madonnas and goddesses. On the other hand, the influence exerted upon him during his early years in Monaco by a gambling, passionate mother caused him to associate the cycles of profane love, particularly its downward trend of frustration, cruelty, and death, with the wheel of fortune, defeat at the gaming table, and suicide. For one example out of many, François des Ygrès in his novel *The Assassinated Poet* gambles his money away at Monte Carlo, loses his love, and commits suicide—all on Palm Sunday.

"One Evening" serves as an introduction to Apollinaire's nature myths. On a visual level, the eagle descending seems to represent the setting sun, which in turn suggests the eclipse of Christ the sun god and Christian faith. In keeping with an ancient poetic tradition, Apollinaire usually represented the death of love as taking place in evening (and autumn) whereas spring was often his time of creation and rebirth.

A great mastery of poetic technique is revealed in the poem. The abrupt changes from the past tense to the present of the first and fourth stanzas give a dramatic suddenness to the corresponding changes of emotion. The second stanza retains the present tense found in the formal prayer of the first, but then slips into the imperfect and the intimate form of address to translate a depth of nostalgia which remains contemporary through an adroit combination of tenses ("the only star *is* drowned/ . . . ./When the trolley cars *were* rolling"). In the last stanza, a less abrupt change of tense keeps the emotion muted, and the soft monosyllables, "Vois" ("See") and "Vers toi" ("Towards thee"), quietly indicate the poet's beloved. The vocabulary is sharp and modern except for the Symbolist *se lover*, which finds new freshness in a striking image; and the romantic, elegiac line of the third stanza, "And all that was trembling in thine eyes of my dreams," is abruptly broken by the short line following it yet sets the tone for the worshipful last stanza. In the French version the first and last stanzas contain the same basic vowel rimes, (*-anges-moi-lampes-moi; -ssance-vois-vancent-toi*), dissonant and assonant at the beginning, homophonous and resolved at the end. The images are direct and carefully linked: the movement from the present world to the beloved is kept in each stanza and between stanzas until the entire poem follows this rhythm, directed at first towards the suffering poet—"for me"—and cumulating in his Love—"towards thee." The lyrical techniques of repetition ("Pray pray") and exclamation ("O clothed-one"), both often used to excess by Apollinaire, here do not force the power of the emotion and become part of it; and the two "See's" transmit a sense of quiet urgency which corresponds to the suppressed excitement of the mood. Finally, the imagery, intentionally ambiguous, is directed towards a single, unique perspective in the mind's eye of the poet.

In summary, the main themes of "One Evening" are the end of the old world and Christian faith; the secular second coming with its divinization of beauty and love and its canonization of the poet-prophet-worshiper; and the presence of a marvelous iron pastoral of modern urbanity full of despair and hope, death and resurrection, and the legendary ghosts of the past. In a later poem, Apollinaire will transfer his beloved's messiahship to a soaring twentieth century and send up an eagle and a phoenix to accompany it.

II *The End of the World*

Apollinaire's interest in the end of the world very likely began on the Riviera at the age of six when he spent a month in a tent because of a serious earthquake, a natural calamity which the panicked populace—including, probably, Mme. de Kostrowitzky —immediately took to be the beginning of world destruction. It was symbolic of his future philosophy that he on the contrary enjoyed the shocks and was sorry when they were over.[4] Soon after, he was enrolled in a private religious school in Monaco run by nuns and Marist fathers who, judging by the amazing knowledgeability he showed in later life in hagiography and Church history and ritual, must have well indoctrinated him along the lines of the most orthodox Roman Catholic belief, much concerned with the final questions. During his school years more interest in the millennium was manifested throughout Western civilization than had been shown since the sixteenth century, and if his teachers were not acquainted with the numerous little pamphlets predicting the end of the world for 1900 or early in the next century, they must have known many of the summaries of orthodox belief in the Antichrist, popularizations and tracts which often cited the latest secular scholarship of Conway (1881), Huntingford (1891), Gunkel (1895), and particularly Bousset (1895). Apollinaire may have read them, too; in any event, his writings

[22]

prove he knew the finer points in the legend of the Last Judgment, both from the writings of Church Fathers like Saint Jerome,[5] Saint Augustine, and Saint Thomas Aquinas, and from the anthropologists' rationalizations. When he lost his faith around 1894 at the age of fourteen, he was already well versed in Symbolist literature, full of eschatological speculation.

Poetically, decadent writers like Léon Dierx, Catulle Mendès, Maurice Rollinat, Jean Lorrain, and Maurice Maeterlinck were suffocating in civilization's claustrophobic ennui and bloody dreams of self-destruction; politically, in the climactic years of French anarchism (1880–1900), poets like Laurent Tailhade, Félix Fénéon, Adolphe Retté, and Pierre Quillard were hailing the idealistic bombers Ravachol, Vaillant, and Henry, and anticipating a forthcoming purge of blood. In the novel, the apocalyptic Russians were all the rage, Dostoevski and Tolstoy as well as those prophets of new Antichrists Soloviev and Merejkovski; Wagnerism and "the twilight of the gods" were everywhere; Nietzsche's denunciations were becoming popular; Ibsen translations abounded; Sar Péladan was describing the decline and fall of latinity in an interminable flood of gnostic fiction; and Des Esseintes' weary "Oh, go ahead and die, old world!" in Huysman's *À Rebours* (1884) was being echoed by many an esthete, including Dorian Gray:

"*Fin de siècle*," murmured Lord Henry.
"*Fin du globe*," answered his hostess.
"I wish it were *fin du globe*," said Dorian with a sigh. "Life is a great disappointment." (*The Picture of Dorian Gray*—1890)

Esthetic Byzantinism was the order of the day: "the period of antiquity with which these artists of the fin de siècle liked best to compare their own," writes Mario Praz, "was the long Byzantine twilight . . . a period of anonymous corruption with none of the heroic about it" (*The Romantic Agony*). "I dream of the Byzantine Emperors," wrote Apollinaire in one of his earliest poems.

In scientific, historical, and sociological writings things were not much more hopeful. Camille Flammarion and the "Baron" de Novaye gave learned recapitulations of the prophecies of world's end, the first (1894) with an added description of the arrival of the comet in the twenty-fifth century after anarchist revolution and world war; the second (1896) with a vivid account of the Apocalypse in the twentieth century. Apollinaire had Flammarion's more benign picture of the end of the world, *Uranie* (1893), in his library; he printed predictions similar to those of the Baron de Norvaye in 1905 and 1912. This is the first great period of science fiction, with J.-H. Rosny in *The Cataclysm* (1896) and Wells in *The Time Machine* (1894) discussing terrestrial finality and dominating a host of minor writers whose works bore titles like *The Crack of Doom, The Yellow Horde,* and *The Violent Flame.* Apollinaire ghosted part of a novel on a scientist-superman in 1900 (*What to Do?*) and made scientists his Antichrists in *The Glory of the Olive, The Assassinated Poet,* and a story "Touch at a Distance." In fin-de-siècle short stories Poe's macabre fantasy merged with Wells's and Verne's scientism to create a tone of learned detachment in violence characteristic of Villiers de l'Isle-Adam, Marcel Schwob, and Alfred Jarry, all influences on Apollinaire. All of them exploited the end-of-the-world theme. "Even now," Wells wrote in 1894, "for all we can tell, the coming terror may be crouching for its spring and the fall of humanity be at hand" ("The Extinction of Man").

In philosophy and sociology the movement upward of the world toward a materialist or idealist heaven was being exhaustively analyzed by anarchist disciples of Max Stirner, Proudhon, Hegel, and Marx, who coupled their utopianism with predictions of bourgeois decadence and extinction. Perhaps no one was listened to more attentively than the Hungarian sociologist Max Nordau, whose monumental *Degenerescence* (1894) ponderously attempted to diagnose the French malady and thus the world's—France's culture being the highest—by citing the Symbolist poets' and painters' esoteric cults for Wagner, Nietzsche, the Mona Lisa, the Virgin Mary, Salome, the Wandering Jew, the Pre-Raphaelites, Mallarmé, hashish, the Cabala, Ludwig of Bavaria, Aretino, Sade and Nerciat, Dostoevski, Ibsen, and suicide as symptoms of "the twilight of nations." The book was an immediate sensation in England and France and remained a topic of discussion in French literary circles up until World War I; Apollinaire reported on Nordau's opposite views in 1904.

The effect all these influences had on an impressionable adoles-

cent who from the beginning was an authority among his school-
mates on current intellectual trends cannot be overestimated.
They explain the pessimism of his earliest poems and their obsession with the finality of death ("Tell me, did you know my soul
was mortal?") with all its ambivalence:

> —For we are afraid of dying—
> We want to die ("Hell")

the crepuscular futility of the universe:

> Our spherical machine turns and lulls me to sleep
> Where life is mortal and lives after death
> In Latin it's terra the German calls it Erde
> A clear echo perhaps has succeeded in answering Merde
> ("The Sky Becomes Cloudy One Morning in May")

> One must not plumb the future
> It is better to live and enjoy the freshness of evening
> Where one falls asleep dreaming hopelessly of the beyond

and the desire for flight:

> And I'd like to flee
> I'd like the unknown of this evening country
> I'd be like an eagle since there wouldn't be any
> Sun to stare at . . . ("There comes to me sometimes . . .")

They also partly explain recurrent returns to a latent pessimism at
unguarded moments of future enthusiasm over the new city to
rise out of the ruins of the old:

> It seems to me that peace
> Will be as monstrous as war

> O time of democratic
>   Tyranny ("Orpheus")

> Take pity on the Gods
> The Gods who will die
> If humanity dies (*Couleur du temps*)

As a subject, the end of the world is found throughout his work. He lost most of the manuscript of his first novel, *The Glory of the Olive*,[6] on a train; a remaining fragment shows Enoch as a bell-boy in a Marseilles hotel denouncing the Antichrist, an Australian agronomist (in prophecy he will come from the East) named Apollonius Zabath who has arrived in Europe in 2107 to prevent the election of *De gloria olivae*, the last pope. As predicted, he defeats Enoch, just as the fragment ends; this scene is later incorporated into *The Assassinated Poet* where Enoch becomes the poet's spokesman Croniamantal, denouncing the mediocrity of world democracy in the same divinely inspired terms.

In another fragment of *The Glory of the Olive*, Apollinaire described Enoch falling from the sky in the company of Elijah, a professional dishwasher, and meeting Isaac Laquedem, the Wandering Jew, doomed to die shortly at the Last Judgment. Isaac's connection with the Antichrist forms the framework for *The Heresiarch and Company* (1910), Apollinaire's first collection of short stories. In the first story, "The Passerby of Prague," he describes his own meeting with the Wandering Jew in Prague in 1902 and again hints that the latter's wandering days may soon be terminated; and in the last story, "Touch at a Distance," he casts himself in the role of an avenging Christ destroying with a revolver a presumptuous former friend who has discovered the scientific secret of ubiquity and the polygamous art of playing the Messiah in all the major cities of the world.

In his second collection of stories grouped about the title novella "The Assassinated Poet," a like outline is followed. Introduced by the anti-intellectual Armageddon denounced by Croniamantal, the book ends on a triumphant picture of the *Poet Resuscitated* at the beginning of World War I, preceded by a story about the return of King Arthur in 2105, an event scheduled for 2108 in *The Glory of the Olive*. Similarly, his major collection of poetry, *Alcools*, is framed by the poet's spiritual death in the poem-preface "Zone" and his poetic ascension in the epilogic "Vendémiaire." In addition, there are several apocalyptic visions in between: "The Synagogue" with its Leviathan and its final citation from the Psalms on God's vengeance over Christian heretics; "The House of the Dead" with its gay resurrection scene; "Cortege" with its revelation of the poet's divine gift of resurrecting others;

"One Evening" with its eagle and archangels; "The Betrothal" with its description of the end of the poet's world and his second coming; "The Brazier" with its celestial beasts; and "Vendémiaire" itself with its death of kings (Revelation 19) and new Eucharist in a Parisian millennium.

In a mysterious prose poem of 1907–8, *Onirocritique* ("Dream-criticism"), there is a marvelous panorama of world's end—much resembling the end of the world in the Apocalypse—with the poet as *the last man* wandering over depopulated lands left full of song, empty cities, and the crowns of kings. And in his last work, the play produced posthumously *Couleur du temps* ("Color of the Weather"), allegorical figures representing the wealth of the past, contemporary science, and prophetic poetry destroy each other for the sake of a beautiful phantom in an Antarctic world of absolute cold. Humanity falls victim to its illusions as a final chorus of the quick and the dead chant "Farewell farewell everything must die."

III   *The First and Second Coming:* *"The Thief," "Merlin and the Old Woman"*

The nihilism of *Couleur du temps* is unusual in Apollinaire's work; more often his idealism and Nietzschean energy led him to revel in the more picturesque aspects of world decadence—the dance on the edge of the abyss—rather than to allow it to become an ultimate destructive force. The Dreyfus affair with its sudden illumination of the depths of bourgeois corruption and its call to action gave the lie to the case for the death wish and latent melancholy; and the socialist newspapers that Apollinaire read from 1898 to 1901[7] lived literally in weekly headlined expectation of the Revolution. "Destinies are dreamers," he wrote in a school notebook, "present-day society is dying of uncertainty; let us spread more confusion: it is good that it die." He and other poets wondered who would be the blond Superman, the new Christ, to lead the fray: "The poets go singing Noël on the ways/ Celebrating Justice and attendant upon tomorrow" ("The Poets").

"Ravochol-Jesus" and Vaillant had been crucified on the guillotine, but new saviors were everywhere coming out of the suburbs. In 1898 Ernest La Jeunesse, a quixotic admirer of Napoleon, wrote a serious introduction to a new gospel by a cousin who believed he was the Messiah; in 1900, Nietzsche, dying insane, wrote to a friend that he was the Christ who had saved the world a second time (Rémy de Gourmont reporting this, remarked that it was probably true); and in 1901, the *avant-garde* play of the year in Paris was Saint-Georges de Bouhélier's *Tragedy of the New Christ*, "the great revolutionary drama" in which Jesus returned to contemporary workers "menacing with his prophetic parables the outworn hierarchies of a dying society" (I am quoting from a sympathetic reviewer). Bouhélier's Messiah ended by giving himself up to a second martyrdom for the crimes of his well-meaning but overzealous anarchist disciples. This poet-playwright, incidentally, had been heralding the rebirth of the Poet-King-God-Christ-Prometheus-Hero-Savior and his attendant pantheon for ten years before *The Tragedy of the New Christ;* Apollinaire listened to his metaphorical lectures in 1901 and may have profited by them in his later eulogies of Picasso and his friends (1905–8).

The solitary, prophetic anarchist-savior, a descendant of Manfred and Julien Sorel and influenced by Kropotkin, Ivan Karamazov, and Zarathustra, became so popular by the end of the century that Alfred Jarry, reviewing Frederic Hauser's *The Resurrected One* in 1901, could act quite bored by the subject (he had already set several burlesque Christs and Supermen in motion himself). It was probably about this time that Apollinaire was putting the finishing touches on two anarchist allegories that became important poems, "The Thief" and "Merlin and the Old Woman" (*Alcools*).

While anticipating a new savior he attempted to destroy the old, turning in "The Thief" to Christ's *first* coming. Christ "comes like a thief" in the Apocalypse. Apollinaire's thief seems at first a mysterious Symbolist figure, strongly resembling—in physical appearance at least—the Christ anticipated in Henri de Régnier's "Vigil of the Beaches" ("La Vigile des grèves," 1890)—until he turns out not to be mysterious or poetic at all. The two poems are similar enough to permit me to think that Apollinaire was intending to make a reference to his predecessor in "The Thief"; just as the introduction of his protagonist into a Mediterranean orchard at the beginning of the poem, "Marauder stranger unfortunate unskilful/ Thief thief," might be a conscious parody of a pagan orchard god's cries in a Parnassian poem by Heredia: "Don't approach! Go away: sail on by, Stranger,/ Insidious Pillager" ("Hortorum Deus"—1893).

In Régnier's poem, exotic virgins waited in exile on pagan isles for the coming of the Beloved, also called the harvester, fisherman, shepherd, sweet knight, and victorious swimmer, his face pale and his brow wounded by thorns, who would be accompanied by a unicorn and a peacock, who would drink from their cups and be their King. This was the Bridegroom for the attendant Virgins. Who arrives in Apollinaire's poem? A weak sneak thief, "unfortunate unskilful," covetous of the exotic-erotic fruits of paganism but too devious to ask for them outright and too impoverished in his own right to be able to offer any symbolic wealth in return.

"The Thief" is the most direct and violent attack Apollinaire ever made on Christ and Christianity's Jewish patrimony; it is a barbarous, clanging poem, full of dissonances and ambiguities, erotic puns, drunken verbalisms, and an extraordinary compendium of the pagan marvelous culled from his already considerable knowledge of ancient lore. For his setting, he chose the ancient world of the Middle East from Italy to Mesopotamia and extending in time from the Exodus to 29 A.D. and including—in the future—Spain under the Moors. In this setting he placed the narrative of Christ, the first Christian ("I am a Christian"), who comes to steal the pagan fruits of the earth without at first revealing His identity to the excited pagans, and without accepting the inherent conditions of their rich inheritance:

> I confess the theft of the sweet ripe fruit
> But it isn't exile I come to feign
> And know that I expect the usual unjust
> Tortures if everything I stole I return

These conditions are primarily those of profane love, the only possible love—which leads them to what is for Him an insulting misconception about His virgin birth, "Since they the maiden and the adult had in the final analysis no/ Pretext [for my birth] but that of nightly love" (stanza 4)—and full possession of the talismans, cults, and rich magic of the past, which even includes much of early Christianity with its pagan roots:

The black bishops ignorantly adoring
By the isosceles triangles open at the morse of their copes
Pallas . . . (stanza 18)

Love means sensuality. The wise men make Socratic (homosexual) gestures at the thief, and a woman finds that he is nobler than "the dolphin the male viper or the bull" and hopefully asks him if his sect worships an obscene sign. Moreover, the thief is not even aware of the erotic implications of his own religious symbolism: when they discover his identity, the pagans scoff, "So be it! the triad is virile and you are virgin and cold" (stanza 31). Although attracted by the fruits of evil, he naïvely discards them ("The birds with their beaks have wounded your grenades/ And almost all your figs were split"). Instead of adoring an obscene sign, his only sign is the sign of the cross (stanza 31).

Complementary to eroticism is exoticism. The ancients at first welcome the thief as a handsome, mysterious member of their own race who obviously has no need for their fruits; but after he spurns them, they nobly pardon him and hospitably offer him food their broth-drinking Spartans and bean-shunning Pythagoreans would not touch. Then as the watchers do in Régnier's poem, they pass in review the great invasions, migrations, and festivals of the past, dazzling the thief with their wealth of spectacle and inviting him to display his own wares. But "the fruit-thief cried I am a Christian"; and the poem pivots to a frontal attack on Christian dogma in a burlesque dialectic Apollinaire uses in another early blasphemous work, the novel *The Putrescent Enchanter* (*L'Enchanteur pourrissant*). The chorus mockingly compares the "thief" to the real thieves, bad and good, Gestas and Dysmas, to be crucified on his left and right:

Ha! Ha! the thief on the left in the fray
Will laugh at you as horses neigh
. . . .
If you're not on the right you're sinister (stanzas 22, 24)

They compare his voice unfavorably with that, semidivine, of Orpheus; they scoff at his ideas of the Trinity and Virgin Birth (stanza 25); they ridicule his two poor symbols, the reed and the cross; they tell him he should have accepted Abgar V's invitation to live with him at the marvelous court of Edessa. In a last stanza, dropped at the time of publication in *Alcools*, they mock the idea of hellfire as they return to the Eleatic school. Truly, everything is theirs ("Tout est à nous"—stanza 26): in the scholarly articles of the 1890's which Apollinaire used for some of the poem's sources, one that seems to have particularly interested him attempted to prove the ascendancy of Babylonian over Hebrew and Christian myth; because of recent archeological findings, Babylon was as much à la mode as Byzantium.[8]

But the most serious charge leveled against a credulous, puritanical Christ is His inhumanity, His inability to allow the flesh to play an equal role with the spirit in determining the whole man. A woman asks Him, "Thief do you know the laws better in spite of mankind"; the equivocal shadow, symbol of magic, and, to the Christian, the evil inherent in things of the flesh ("the sorrow of your flesh") is *human* and accepted by the ancients (stanza 27); it prevails against the fire of God (stanza 22).

I have paraphrased "The Thief" at some length since my interpretation is not that of exegeses to date. Indeed, it is indicative of the poem's ambiguity that in other interpretations the fruit-thief is commonly represented as a fairly sympathetic Symbolist or Parnassian poet, a latter-day Christian greatly resembling his author. "Your father was a sphinx and your mother a night" is a line become famous as a reference to the exiled Pole's mysterious origins. He too was the son of a maiden and an adult, and his Slavic mother had what might be vaguely termed a "Ligurian voice" (stanza 5) since she brought him up in Liguria. In this view the poem would either represent the victory of a new symbolism over the old (the pagan attack being interpreted ironically) or more reasonably an ambivalent, Manichaean statement on the predicament of the modern poet caught between two worlds, two mythic structures, Christianity and paganism, fire and shadow, soul and body.

Although it would have been natural for the young Apollinaire (he must not have been older than seventeen when he began the poem) to draw upon his earlier religious ideas and his own traits for some of the features of a poetic Christian-thief, and although it is undoubtedly true that "the man protesteth too much," his revolt like Baudelaire's or Rimbaud's denoting hidden ambivalence and spiritual torment, I feel reasonably certain that the thief is Jesus and that the poem is an anti-Christian, pro-pagan (primarily, pro-Pythagorean) satire. My thesis is based on the following arguments:

(1) The pagans ask themselves of the thief, "Why didn't he go live at the court of the King of Edessa?" The most remarkable legend in the ancient history of Edessa, a tale which swept Christendom as "the legend of Abgar" in the fourth and fifth centuries and which Apollinaire could have read in the *Journal Asiatique*, a periodical he used for other references in the poem,[9] was that King Abgar the Black (7 B.C.–A.D. 50), suffering from an incurable disease, had heard of Jesus's miracle-working and written Him a letter inviting Him to come live with him at his court and chase out his demons. Jesus wrote back—the texts of both letters were known throughout the Byzantine Empire—that He couldn't come because He was returning to His father, but that after His ascension He would send a disciple. Thaddaeus accordingly arrived, cured the king and converted the town, which thus became the first Christian city in the world—according to the boast of its fourth-century bishops.

(2) The thief has reddish hair (stanza 31) like the Christ of traditional iconography from the fourth century on ("The Portrait of Edessa"). One of Apollinaire's fictional characters is "reddish-haired as a Christ" ("The History of a Virtuous Family, a Basket, and a Gallstone"), and Christ is "a torch with reddish hair" in "Zone." [10]

(3) Apollinaire referred on two occasions to Judas Iscariot as "that sainted Cainite who began in finance, continued in apostasy, and ended as a sycophant." *Sycophant* in its basic Greek context signifies "denouncer of a fig-thief."

(4) Finally, the thief rises from the sea like Régnier's Savior; he has the pale, feminine beauty of the Symbolist and Pre-Raphaelite Christs; [11] he carries the reed and the cross from the Evangels; he will be mocked by the unrepentant thief in his Passion. But, his mother has a Ligurean voice? So have the oriental musicians of stanza 8: Apollinaire defined "Ligurean" in 1914 as a Celtic word meaning "who has a beautiful voice" (letter to Lou, Dec. 25).

If I am right and *the thief* is the orthodox and Symbolist Christ denied in favor of the marvelous pagan, where is Apollinaire's new anarchist Christ ascendant? As I shall indicate in the next section, he proposed several candidates; one of the earliest may have been the son of Love and Memory in "Merlin and the Old Woman" (*Alcools*).

Apollinaire had signed off a letter to school friend Toussaint-Luca in January 1899, just a year after Émile Zola had published his famous vindication of justice in the Dreyfus case "J'accuse," ". . . I leave you, hoping that Souvarine will come, the blond who will destroy cities and men. Let 1899 hear another voice like Zola's and the Revolution is in the fire." [12] Now Souvarine is the solitary, absolutely free Russian terrorist in Zola's *Germinal* who destroys a mine—with the miners in it—and whose ideas ("Anarchy, void, the earth washed by blood, purged by fire") are similar to those in Apollinaire's anarchist poems "The Poets," "The Doukhobors," and "Future." He is blond like Émile Henry, the young anarchist Don Quixote guillotined in 1894 for throwing a bomb into a crowded café, and like the "blond beauty" of Apollinaire's "Future" won by heroes whose torches "make a halo around every brow."

In "Merlin and the Old Woman," the son of the old couple will also be haloed with fire. He will be handsome and unhappy, marching alone looking at the sky with the dawning sun on his back on the road from Rome—one of the two native cities (Babylon is the other) of the Antichrist. Or, he may be walking *toward* Rome with the sun on his brow, as Mme. Durry suggests in her thorough discussion of the poem. His ambiguity is matched by that of his mother "Memory equal to Love" who could be an allegorical recasting of either Morgan la Faye or the hundred-year-old woman whom Merlin loved in the medieval *Prophecies of Merlin*. And Michel Décaudin has pointed out that Merlin and Viviane had a son in Edgar Quinet's *Merlin the Enchanter* (1860) who had reddish-blond hair like his grandfather Satan. In any event, Merlin's son is finally reminiscent of Apollinaire himself, "son of light" (first stanza), with his ashy-blond hair, born illegitimately at Rome. He was early aware of the many destinies which conspired to make him the ideal candidate for the Antichrist—or, better, a second, truly pagan Christ.

IV *Antichrists: Isaac Laquedem, Simon Magus, Merlin the Enchanter, Guillaume the Hermit*

I mentioned above that Apollinaire was acquainted with the opinions of Church Fathers and nineteenth-century anthropologists about the Antichrist; in addition, he knew medieval and sixteenth-century authorities on the subject like Nicéphore Calliste, Malvenda, and John of Hildesheim, and admired the prophetic works of Nostradamus and the false Saint Malachy. Works of more recent adapters of the legend were equally familiar to him, Edgar Quinet and Léon Bloy showed up in his library, and he became personally acquainted with Marcel Schwob and Alfred Jarry. Nietzsche's Antichrist was discussed in the circles he frequented, and he had occasion to refer to Paulus Cassel and M. D. Conway, both of whom had treated the story of the Wandering Jew as a later development of that of the Antichrist and a continuation of the Messianic Dream. From his work with the radical press he knew that Dreyfus, the Jews, Zola, Anatole France, and later, Prime Minister Combes were termed Antichrists by the reaction. So it was not surprising that besides creating his own scientific Antichrists in *What to Do?*, *The Glory of the Olive*, and "Touch at a Distance," he should elaborate on traditional ones, Gestas, Isaac Laquedem, Simon Magus, and Merlin, in other works.

We have already caught a glimpse of Gestas, the bad thief, one of many apocryphal personalities regarded as the Antichrist in the Middle Ages; in a minor poem of 1901, "Terza Rime For Your Soul," this thief represents the amorous poet. In the story "The Heresiarch" of the preceding year, he becomes in the mind of an Italian arch-heretic none other than the Holy Ghost made flesh, who has violated at one time in his nefarious career a sleeping virgin! The epicurean, masochistic heretic is naturally excommunicated (as Tolstoy will be the year following); Apollinaire remarks that he is no different from other men, who are all "both sinners and saints, when they aren't criminals and martyrs."

Isaac Laquedem, who had conducted Apollinaire on a guided tour of Prague in 1902, appearing there as a delightful sensualist who had flouted Christ and was enjoying his *superhuman* immortality,[13] wanders through other works of Apollinaire eternally waiting for the fifteen Sibylline signs of the Last Judgment. In this he inherits the archetypal myth of Cain and Wotan, according to comparative mythologists M. D. Conway and Charles Schoebel (1887), becoming in turn Moses (immortal in folklore), Enoch, Elijah, Tiresias, Laquedem, Arthur, Merlin, Christ, and Antichrist among others. Our poet will add to the list Empedocles, Apollonius of Tyana, Pan, Orpheus, and the ubiquitous poet-wanderer, himself.

Vertical displacement in the legend of the Antichrist often accompanies horizontal and temporal peripatetics, a miraculous ascension having been interpreted as constituting a direct attack upon God by Saint Ambrose, Saint Jerome, and Saint Thomas, all of whom wrote that the Beast would try to rise in the air like Simon Magus. Secular scholars of the 1890's prosaically agreed with them by considering fourth-century legends of the magician's prowess to be variations on the Antichrist stories of the first century: in Simon's flight before Nero and his destruction by Saint Peter, they said, he followed the path of Satan—to be cast down at the end of time by either Saint Michael or Christ—and the Dragon of Revelation. In *The Glory of the Olive*, the Australian Antichrist Apollonius Zabath had "planed above other men like an eagle." In "Simon Magus," a story in *The Heresiarch and Company*, Apollinaire follows the traditional legend for the most part, the Biblical precedents of Luke and Acts and the apocryphal story in the Acts of Saint Peter, while adding the demonic angels of the Cabala to help Simon in his miraculous flight.[14] But after he has the mage shot down by Peter's prayer, Apollinaire adds a modern moral. He has given Peter's name to Simon and made the two figures resemble each other as closely as Castor and Pollux; he ends his story with a final victory of the immortal magician as he attempts to buy or win by gaming the dying body of his Christian rival. Antipeter as well as Antichrist, the father of gnosticism and heresy thereby triumphs over the father of the Church. A curious postscript: the first French histories of aviation included Simon (Peter) Magus along with Icarus as a forerunner of the Wright brothers.[15] Appropriately enough, Apollinaire has him anticipate the flight of the twentieth century in "Zone."

Simon Magus also arrives, horizontally and temporally this time and in the company of Enoch, Elijah, Empedocles, Isaac Laque-

dem, and Apollonius of Tyana, at the tomb of Merlin in *L'Enchanteur pourrissant* ("The Putrescent Enchanter"). More than
any other Apollinaire character Merlin is the antithesis of Christ.
The son of a virgin and a devil, he is nonetheless baptized (like
Jesus, Simon Magus, and Apollinaire) as he retains mastery over
all the diabolical powers of the underworld. He takes after his
father, Satan. He extols suicide and revolution before his six immortal visitors:

When the fruit is ripe, it drops and doesn't wait for the gardener to
come and pick it. Let man, that fruit ripening freely on the tree of
light, do the same. But you who did not die, who are six in the forest
like the fingers of the hand and a dagger in the hand, why don't you
close up, why don't you double up? O fingers that could ransack; O fist
that could stab; O hand that could beat, that could indicate, that could
scratch decay. . . .

He is buried underground by a sterile, ignorant love, in contrast to
Saint Simeon Stylite's pillar "which leaps to the sky." His solitary
nature as a poet leads him to hate crowds, while "God loves those
who meet together." He places man higher than Christ. Yet he
would be an angel were he not baptized, perhaps one of the marvelous host described in "Simon Magus."

As in "The Thief," Apollinaire satirizes divine birth and resurrection in *L'Enchanteur pourrissant*, this time in scenes of a "funereal Christmas" and a "voluntary damnation." In the first of
these, he seems to have taken his lead from a medieval Merlin
prophecy that, at the end of the world, three descendants of the
Magi will arrive in starless darkness at the desert birthplace of the
Dragon with gifts of an olive branch, ashes, and a knife.[16] His
Magi are the relics in the Cologne cathedral; their bodiless heads
come guided by *shadow* and bring alchemical gifts to Merlin's
tomb. In the second scene, that of the damnation, Ariosto's heroine Angelica, who has been converted to Christianity, thereby for-
getting "all that is pagan, magic and even natural," is raped to
death by an assembled company of demons and magicians while
she is praying to the Virgin; a veritable Black Mass is consum-
mated over her body "in an obscene and pious position." Her crucified form is borne aloft by choiring angels, until suddenly she is
inexplicably precipitated from Heaven by Saint Michael. Merlin

explains that she has been damned in his place and remarks that if his body were living it would sweat blood. After the death of Love—*the funereal Christmas*—the diabolical redemption.

What has become of Merlin's savior son "looking at the sky" in "Merlin and the Old Woman"? No mention of him is made in *The Putrescent Enchanter,* and by the time Apollinaire wrote the final section of the book (probably the summer of 1904) the death of love had in fact struck him down. A parallel decline in expectation of the Revolution made the living death of unrequited love that Merlin's entombment principally symbolized especially dark. The hope implicit in the last stanza of "One Evening" and in earlier poems that the beloved would embody the resurrection had not been realized. One of these earlier poems gives witness to the deflation Apollinaire must have felt in his darkest moments: in "The Hermit" (*Alcools*) he carries his revolt from the Church to a summit of burlesque in the caricature of a lecherous old ascetic who, fleeing his self-inflicted sufferings for God, finds minor but satisfactory salvation outside the Lord.

When Enoch had asked Merlin in *The Putrescent Enchanter* if it were certain that a savior had arrived, Merlin had replied, "Why do you ask me, since you know me so well? Patriarch, who isn't a savior? Perhaps you will be the true savior yourself when you come back to die. . . ." The hermit is Apollinaire's most pathetic, bedraggled Antichrist: his problem is that he can be neither spiritual savior nor pagan lover. Like Saint Simeon Stylites in *The Putrescent Enchanter* "assailed by temptations according to the temperature," he suffers a new kind of fleshly Passion-in-reverse by *not* sweating the bloody sweat, the hematidrosis (in French, *hématidroses*); *not* perceiving the comforting angel on his Mount of Olives; *not* having his unleavened bread consecrated (a pun on his enforced sterility).[17] Nor does a transcendent Magdalen, his mysterious *Unknown,* arrive. Half-crucified by his libidinous desires, his sole ascension that of his anxious flesh, he finds nothing but the cruel passion of owls nailed to impure peasants' huts. His salvation is achieved only when he abandons the desert for a counseling job in the city, as he discovers like Saint Jerome a kind of purity in the vicarious sexual activity of the confessor.

If "The Thief" is not Apollinaire as I believe—the poet is rather the thief's pagan interrogators—I think that there can be little doubt that the hermit, like Merlin, is he. In 1915, in a period of mental and physical frustration, he wrote defiantly, "I can occasionally at the beginning of a decision have that confusion, that profound agony of Christ on the Mount of Olives who knew the bloody sweat, the hematidrosis, but I've finished being the hermit (*mais ermite c'est fini*) and I march straight ahead" (letter to Lou, April 29). The first draft of "The Hermit" probably only included stanzas 16, 17, 18, 5, (21, 22, an addition), 19, and 23, in that order, which contain lines based on the poet's Belgian frustrations in 1899.[18] Many of the erotic images in the remainder of the poem reflect adolescent attitudes and humor (one is reminded of Jarry's "The Passion Considered as an Uphill Bicycle Race"). Probably no longer a virgin after the age of fifteen (he wrote Louise de Coligny that he had experienced entirely the joys of love at that age—April 8, 1915), he was subject for the rest of his life to sudden attacks of masochistic, onanistic depression, at which times he hungered after the purity and security of the monastery or the grave. The final stanza of "The Hermit" may well reflect a similar moment of world-weariness:

> For all I desire is to close my eyes
> Exhausted couple in the panting orchard
> Full of the pompous death rattle of the currant bushes
> And the sainted cruelty of the passionflowers

> Great Pan love Jesus Christ
> Are definitely dead The cats wail
> In the courtyard In Paris I weep

he wrote, probably in 1904. But, "who isn't a savior?" And Merlin had prophesied, "For a long time the earth will bear no more enchanters but the time of the enchanters will return. . ." The Behemoth in the same book had told some wyverns, "man is closer to a metamorphosis than you . . ." In the years 1903–5 Apollinaire met André Salmon, Max Jacob, Mécislas Golberg, and Pablo Picasso and set out with them on the tremendous artistic adventure of the twentieth century. On confronting Picasso's harlequin families in 1905 he again cried, "Noel!"—and his own martyred face, along with those of his three new literary friends, in one of

Christ and Antichrist

the best stories of *The Heresiarch and Company,* spread out on the floor of Picasso's studio on the artist's solitary napkin transformed into a new veronica and a Christlike sun ("The Napkin of the Poets"). He was finally beginning to move in a company of saviors.

CHAPTER 2

The Death of the Sun

Le soleil et la forêt ce sont mes père et mère—Poèmes à Lou

I *The Myth*

APOLLINAIRE like Rimbaud was a "fils du Soleil," a son of
the Sun; like Rimbaud and Baudelaire he had a dominant
mother and no father. The physical and mental attitudes that resulted in his case affected, as in the cases of his revolutionary
predecessors, the course of modern poetry.

Here historical coincidence rises—as it usually does in the lives
of myth-shapers—to the level of destiny and myth. Apollinaire
was not responsible for his illegitimacy, his name "Apollinaris," or
his birth in Rome of noble Slavic and Latin blood; nor did he plan
his arrival in the steps of Baudelaire, Rimbaud, and Mallarmé in
the autumnal last days of a Romantic, autumnal century. He
did profit by the concurrence and exploit the breadth of his
myth; but, as it often happens, it is exceedingly difficult to ascer-
tain where the man stops and the myth begins. Suffice it to say
that both he and friends like Picasso and Max Jacob had Rimbaud's precocious awareness of the gifted man arriving at the
privileged moment of history, in addition to their having the example of Rimbaud's Promethean myth in itself before them.

How conscious Apollinaire became of what Freudians would
now term the Oedipal import of his inheritance is evident in several passages in his writings. In *The Putrescent Enchanter,* for
example, the forty-year-old heroine Angelica (Apollinaire's
mother, Angélique de Kostrowitsky, was in her forties at the time
of writing) is raped, murdered, damned, and then freed in a kind
of incestuous episode which redeems the entombed (wombed)
Merlin-Apollinaire; in the pornographic novel *The Eleven Thousand Rods* (*Verges*) (an obscene pun on the eleven thousand
sainted virgins supposedly massacred by the Huns at Cologne and

the phallus—with overtones of the scourging rods of the Old Testament) the most sadistic ghoul-queen of a whole succession of bacchantes is a lovely Polish aristocrat, a "madonna," with a *face angélique.* In "Touch at a Distance," on the other hand, the adventurous Antichrist shot by Apollinaire-Christ has a name which was originally based on that of his erstwhile father. In 1908 he wrote of the originality of modern art, "You can't carry your father around everywhere; you abandon him with the other dead." The problems involved in such an abandon he implied in a 1914 review of *The Playboy of the Western World,* "Poets have always more or less tried to kill their fathers, but it's a very difficult thing to do, witness the Playboy," after discussing in a parallel article Freud, the subconscious, and father-and-son rivalries. In his fiction especially, he never could lose his father; if nothing else, his father's name kept turning up as Constantino, François, and Françoise in stories from *The Assassinated Poet,* and Dormesan and "la Chancesse" (Françoise) in *The Heresiarch and Company.*[1] Incidentally, Synge's play was one of his favorites for its realism, poetry, and tragic laughter; on the contrary, he disliked Renard's *Carrot-Top* (*Poil-de-Carotte*) with its message of father-and-son harmony. He revolted against a father authority when he left first the Church and then bourgeois society; he attempted to become his own father when he began to use the phoenix symbol for himself; and—again like Baudelaire and Rimbaud—he could never really leave his mother either, she whose "door" led to everything and nothing ("The Door"—*Alcools*).

On the archetypal side of his myth, it is significant that he grew up during the golden age of comparative religion, folklore study, and evolutionary anthropology. If he did not know the animistic treatises of Cox, Tylor, Frazer, and Lang, he was acquainted with the ideas of their continental counterparts Angelo de Gubernatis, Mallarmé, Nietzsche, Rémy de Gourmont, Edouard Schuré, Louis Ménard, Paulus Cassel, and Charles Schoebel, and with at least some of their ingenious unravelings of nature myths through history. To them as to him the solar cycle of incestuous creation, death, and regeneration was the universal, primordial myth, the guiding rhythm of life and religion: Mallarmé, for example, wrote in his adaptation of George Cox's *Tales of the Gods and Heroes* that Oedipus' marriage with his mother came out of one of the oldest Indian myths, "from ancient phrases speaking of the sun uniting in the evening with her from whom he had issued that morning." The scholars and poets split the Orphic universe between the masculine and feminine principles, Tammuz and Ishtar, Cybele and Atys, Venus and Adonis, the priests of the sun and the priestesses of the moon; and they traced the evolutionary rise of man toward spirit and the Oversoul from Krishna through Orpheus, Dionysus, and Christ to himself. To Apollinaire as to Gérard de Nerval and Mallarmé, the violent love-death between Sun (Christ, Eros, phallus, phoenix, poet) and Night (Mary, Psyche, womb, siren, beloved) was an accepted poetic truism.

This child of Apollo prided himself on being able to look the sun straight in the eye like an eagle; [2] yet like other poets of his time he was symbolically slain every night—and every autumn. No theme was so popular in Symbolist art and poetry of the 1880's and 1890's: one has only to glance through the works of Laforgue, Mallarmé, Régnier, Catulle Mendès, and Gustave Moreau to be surfeited—as was Ezra Pound, writing against "the crepuscular spirit in modern poetry"—by twilight gardens and bloody sunsets. To cite one well-known example: Rostand's Cyrano de Bergerac was pathetically yet heroically struck down in a convent garden in an autumn of 1898 amid growing darkness and falling leaves.

Night, on the other hand, with her inevitable extension *shadow* and her association with the sea (the three words are feminine in French) was the familiar companion of an adolescent whose pen names were Guillaume Macabre and Nyctor and who watched many sunsets over the Mediterranean.

> Farewell youth white Noël
> When life was but a star
> Reflection I used to watch
> In the Mediterranean sea
> More lustrous than meteors ("The Hills")

I have mentioned the Virgin-Night association in the line describing the fruit-thief, "Your father was a sphinx and your mother a night," and the play of fire and shadow, Christ and the pagan world, in "The Thief." At the end of the poem, Jesus left as the evening came on (in "One Evening" the eagle descended as the beloved's nativity star came into view). In another line of "The Thief" there is a description of pagan frescoes figuring "solar and nocturnal incest in the clouds" which parallels references in an early poem to the sun, "that circular and benevolent god," and to night "his incestuous mother" ("Ignorance"). To evolutionary anthropologists, the Christian equivalent of Indian, Egyptian, and Chaldean creation myths was God's self-engendering through a virgin mother. In the words of the skeptical pagans, "Double becomes triple before having been."

The extent and importance of the Sun-Night relationship in Apollinaire and the extent of his subsequent fall from grace may be observed in a second dualism, the theme of *hyperdulia* or spiritual adoration of the mother-deity as opposed to the sexual idolatry, the *antidulia,* of the underworld mother Lilith.

The Romantic *sylphide,* the feminine ideal, had visited the child Wilhelm de Kostrowitzsky when a dark, unknown woman appeared at the opening of the curtains around his bed, watched him quietly, and then disappeared. He never forgot her (letter to Madeleine, October 20, 1915). One of his first loves, that recorded in Chapter Nine of *The Assassinated Poet* for the peasant girl Mariette, shows an early stage of his quest for the pure ideal, the Rose of the World, the woman he was later to call Rosamond. She was undoubtedly related to the *rosa mystica* of his cult for the Virgin at the Marist school of Saint Charles; and when he lost his faith, she remained for him as for many another Symbolist poet an emotional ideal shining through the anarchism and materialism of his disbelief. In early love poems his loved ones were his "divinities" and his "Madonnas" deprived of corresponding metaphysical belief. In two poems, however, his faith in the divinity of the poet allowed him to deify his creations and to realize a kind of materialistic ladder of love in his imagination, raising "a madonna" to "Our Lady very real and necessary" ("Spring"), the mother of "a marvelous god/ Created by man because man created the gods" ("The Dome of Cologne"). In "One Evening" his cries went out to her as both Madonna and Messiah. When he lost Annie Playden, a loss made immortal through its telling in "La Chanson du mal-aimé" ("The Song of the Poorly Beloved"), he translated the seven swords traditionally placed in Mary's heart to his own (they are sometimes placed in Jesus' heart) and described the death by love of a poor student in Germany for a blonde rose with the features of a Raphael Madonna ("The Rose of Hildesheim"). It was not until he became divine again, his own phoenix-son, and again betrothed to Mary—the artist Marie Laurencin—that he could move back under the sign of the Virgin, "the pure sign of the third month" ("The Betrothal"), and aspire anew:

> Dove, love and spirit
> Who engendered Jesus Christ
> Like you I love a Mary
> May I marry her ("Dove")

He then added an epigraph to "The Song of the Poorly Beloved":

> . . . My love is like the fine
> Phoenix if it die one evening
> Next morning finds it reborn

Throughout this personal death and ascension cycle, incest with his mother, either positive (creative) or negative (masochistic) is a hidden theme. It is usually most overt, as in the case of Angelica, in his fiction: besides *L'Enchanteur pourrissant*, we find it in a story "The History of a Virtuous Family, a Basket, and a Gallstone" and in his first pornographic novel *The Exploits of a Young Don Juan,* in both of which—if we apply a Freudian interpretation—sisters are substituted for the mother. Having been an apprentice Decadent, he well knew the importance of incest in literature: he admired Rousseau's *Confessions* and Rétif de la Bretagne's *Monsieur Nicolas,* campaigned in 1904 for Georges Poltis' play *Cuirs de Boeuf,* a mystery play on a blazing passion between a mother and son, and referred in his own writings to folk traditions of incest from medieval writers to Charles Perrault and the Grimm brothers.[3] In 1915, at the end of his semi-incestuous love affair with Louise de Coligny, he wrote her about his fellow soldiers' incestuous dreams, "It is curious to note how incest becomes dominant in troubled periods. History proves this . . ." (letter of April 15). The age of Anguish is an age of incest!

This incest is most openly found in Apollinaire as part of the sterile misogyny he felt in his poorly loved periods (a good deal of the time). There it becomes a major theme connected with the myth of the impure demon-mother Lilith, antithesis of Mary, goddess of Night in Assyrian myth, bird of night to the Israelites, mother of Sodom and Gomorrah to Rémy de Gourmont, a widely feared incubus with (in Apollinaire) an attendant train of vices including menstruation, Lesbianism, and flagellation.

Lilith in Hebraic belief was Adam's first wife who, chased from Paradise, became the consort of the devil, the leading child-stealing demon. Apollinaire first turned her into a symbol of frustrated motherhood and sterility in *The Putrescent Enchanter*. He evidently knew the legend that she had lost a hundred children a day and had been pursued by angels to the Red Sea, for he made her an ingenious symbol of menstruation who had created the Red Sea "against the desires of men" before turning to deceive Beelzebub with female lovers (*Poem to Lou XLI*). A symbol of the impure roses of women, their *hematidroses,* as against Mary, the *rosa mystica,* she reappeared in three works commemorating the loss of a mistress, *The Putrescent Enchanter, The Assassinated Poet,* and *Poems to Lou.* Menstruation unaccompanied by Lilith, on the other hand, characterized women—"twelve times impure," wrote Vigny—in several poems of *Alcools* from "Merlin and the Old Woman" to "Annie" and "Zone." In *The Exploits of a Young Don Juan,* the protagonist deflowered his sister during her menstruation period.

After the loss of Annie, love became bad, Apollinaire hinted in 1908; besides "The Song of the Poorly Beloved," another poem to commemorate that loss was "The Emigrant of Landor Road," in which Lilith again appeared as the wife of the devil, beating her lover on rainy days and Fridays. In the last chapter of *The Putrescent Enchanter,* Viviane explained that, to the contrary, *he* beat *her* when he caught her with her Lesbian lover, a dragonfly; Viviane felt that he was prejudiced and pointed out that complete male-female accord was impossible. As for herself, she continued, instead of resembling Merlin, she resembled the infernal dragonfly—or else obscenely dancing houseflies consecrated to Beelzebub, to Lesbos (see "a Mytilene flotilla" in *Calligrammes*), and to death. Beelzebub, the lord of the flies, became a beautiful temptress in Cazotte's *The Amorous Devil,* Apollinaire noted in 1915; he often commented on the insect's grim dance at the Western front when he was losing Lou; and when he lost Marie he met millions of them in the company of a Thanatos-Pan piping the good dames of Saint Merry off to their own unmasculine ideal ("The Musician of Saint Merry"). His final comment on women, in the novel published posthumously, *The Seated Woman* (*La Femme assise*), concerned the main character of the novel, the Lesbian Elvire: like a certain Swiss coin of his childhood, he said, and like all women, she was false and didn't pass.

With flagellation and other forms of brutality, Apollinaire's misogyny coupled with incest in his most exacerbated pages. His mother, according to many reports, had the nineteenth-century Polish aristocrat's freedom with the whip; her son's interest in the same can be traced through his poems and letters to Lou and Madeleine and in his erotic novel "The Eleven Thousand Rods" (1907), a work whose bloody, tragicomic episodes are "punctuated by the dead sound of birches on robust or over-ripe flesh" (Robert Desnos).

When he met Lou in 1914, he was immediately attracted to that redhaired aristocrat, a convent-bred *révoltée* like his mother and a narcissistic flagellant to boot; he quickly became her twenty-fourth lover and cruel tyrant-slave, pointing out that hers was "the major vice, that of Eve listening to the serpent whistling like a whip" and that their mythic flagellation was comparable to that of Xerxes on the treacherous sea (letter of March 31, 1915). Another letter in which he imagined trampling her naked breast with his artillery boots seems to parallel a passage in the semiautobiographical short story "Giovanni Moroni" where a similar beating is administered to the protagonist's mother (Miss Davies points out that this was probably Apollinaire's Roman foster mother). It is also similar to the beating of Françoise by Constantino (note the names) in "The Favorite." It is undoubtedly significant that the young Don Juan's first sexual relationship in *The Exploits of a Young Don Juan*, like that of François d'Ygrès in *The Assassinated Poet*, was with a pregnant woman, and that Croniamantal in the latter book caused the death of his mother in a good Romantic tradition stemming from Tristan and Rousseau by the simple method of being born. When Croniamantal came into the world the midwives were conversing on the sterile love of Sodom as his mother died "uttering a howl like the one the eternal first wife of Adam makes when she crosses the Red Sea."

Violence, usually misogynic and masochistic, is the keynote of Apollinaire's fiction. After he lost the English girl Annie in the Rhineland and in London, he had an unfaithful English Peeress shot in "The Sailor From Amsterdam," a Rhenish Countess driven away for the same reason in "The Countess of Eisenberg," and he wiped out a whole English fleet—on Christmas—in "The Mylords' Noël." He had one of his heroes carry off the Slav girl Mary in "The Otmika" and another eat the legs of a dead German mistress, Mary-Sibyl (Marizibill) in "Cox City." His jealous castration impulses toward male lovers were equally severe. One was brutally murdered for the sake of a realistic sequence in "A Fine Film" (the murderer coolly left to win at the gaming table); one suffered a heart attack when he found that his mistress had thrown out his treasured gallstone ("History of a Virtuous Family, a Basket and a Gallstone"); one was shot by a jealous husband after he had learned to camouflage himself like an insect for protection ("The Disappearance of André Subrac"); and two carved themselves up in a knife fight over a blowsy barmaid ("Que Vlove?"). In the last story, one of the brawlers, dying, fell on his *derrière*, "bloody, you would have said, as if by menstruation."

He often associates gambling, his mother's vice, with violent love-deaths. In "The Favorite," a story which begins with a beheaded setting sun bleeding in the west, the passionate former mistress-for-a-night of King Victor Emmanuel of Italy, lying on the dead body of a workman, is trampled on by her latest lover who has just lost at lotto. In "The Departure of the Shadow," the hero —Nyctor in the manuscript—gratuitously wills the death of his mistress amid a pawnbroker's memories of drawing lotto numbers in Rome, an event followed by scenes of suicide and mother transgression. Finally, in a kind of apotheosis of frustration and sterility which he conceived as Marie was leaving him, a Dutch millionaire, a great lover of women and gaming, loses his fortune and is killed by the dying hand of a male transvestite he has picked up at the gambling den ("Rendezvous at the Gambling House"). Apollinaire's gamblers rarely win.

Castration and purity (sublimation) motifs, finally, like those in

"The Hermit" are found everywhere in his work. In 1912 and again in 1916 a world-weary, loveless Apollinaire contemplated retiring to a monastery; in "The Piedmont Pilgrims" (1903) he vicariously did so in a hot southern countryside full of dust and whirlwinds of flies. In *The Glory of the Olive*, young Nyctor was a virgin and prayed to remain so; at the front in 1915 after Lou had departed, Sergeant Kostrowitsky jubilantly kept a vow of "god-like" chastity for at least seven months. The pull and counterpull of Eros and Anteros, desire and the death wish, are beautifully portrayed in Chapter 12 of *The Assassinated Poet*, where Cronia-mantal leaves his love momentarily "to die of thirst by the spring"; in "The Women" where cozy indoor comfort is contrasted with the cold German winter; and in the gay, apocalyptic poem "The House of the Dead" where the poet finds a refuge from love in his glaciers of memory and in the past. The legend of a monk falling asleep for centuries upon hearing the bird of eternity, a pictur-esque symbol of Nirvana desire (or, to M. D. Conway, of the desire to be the Messiah) recurrently turns up in his works. Other variations on this theme are the suicide motif of "One Evening" and *The Putrescent Enchanter* which he returns to in the poems "The Song of the Poorly Beloved," "The Emigrant of Landor Road," and "The Lorelei," (compare Mallarmé's "Victoriously fled the beautiful suicide" and Baudelaire's "The sun has drowned it-self in its coagulating blood"). Romantic madness caused by the death of love, a sort of mental suicide, is ambivalently feared and willed by the author of "The Passerby of Prague" and "The Rose of Hildesheim." Both the suicide and madness themes are related to the theme of the Superman (Apollinaire knew Lombroso's theo-ries on the affinity of madness and genius) who is at the same time master and slave of his destiny. The tormented sun could set heroically: Merlin praised cremation as well as suicide in *The Pu-trescent Enchanter*, and Apollinaire discussed the nobility of be-heading in his first version of "The Dancing Girl" (*"La Danseuse,"* *La Revue Blanche*, 1902).

A glance over the poems of *Alcools* which were conceived be-fore 1908, reveals the importance of the Sun-Night theme. In the Rhenish scene of "The Night Wind" ("Le Vent Nocturne"), for example:

The Death of the Sun

O the pine tops creak as they knock together
You can also hear the south wind cry
In triumphant voice from the nearby river
Elves laugh or trumpet as the blasts go by
Atys Atys charming and half-dressed
It's your name mocked by the elves tonight
For a pine has fallen in the gothic wind
The forest is like an army in flight
Whose lances O pine trees wave at the turn
The villages dark now meditate
Like virgins poets and the old
And will wake to the step of no passerby
When on their pigeons the vultures fall

                                        (cited in entirety)

Here the dramatic emasculation of Atys—son and lover of Cybele, the Mother of the gods—in one of his emblematic pines is mockingly contrasted to the creative meditations of the physically sterile, virgins, old people, and poets, after the sun has set and the lights gone out. The virile armies have fled; and the contrast between creativity and sterility, flight and fall, is pointed up by the Manichaean whiteness and darkness of the last line (the European vulture is a heavy, dark bird, the largest European bird of prey). At the time the poem was written the founder of psychoanalysis was singling out birds (later, airplanes) as important dream symbols of erection and castration (he also wrote that his ideas were scooped by the poets). Apollinaire's last line echoes two lines from "Merlin and the Old Woman": "And their hands rose up like a flight of doves/ Brightness on which night swooped like a vulture."

Some of the same symbols are found with attenuated force in "Sick Autumn" ("Automne malade"), another Rhenish poem about the melancholy, creative enjoyment of sterility. There the descent of the birds of prey is accompanied by that of the year, snow (purity-sterility), and fruit. The meditating old people are absent (Apollinaire wrote in 1905, "old people wait without meditating, for only children meditate"), and the nightlike vultures have been turned into falcons of the day; but the virgins are present as loveless water sprites, and the elves and armies have become mating stags:

Poor autumn
Die in whiteness and in wealth
Of snow and ripe fruit
At the top of the sky
Falcons soar
On [or "above"] naïve little green-haired nixies
Who have never loved

At the distant edge of the forest
The stags have bugled

When he wrote "Sick Autumn" Apollinaire probably knew that the falcon (*épervier*) was the bird of sun gods Ra, Horus, and Apollo, and was associated with undines in European folklore. Elsewhere in *Alcools* the phallic setting sun is more overtly connected with water, in "Lul de Faltenin," for instance, where the solar ship and beheaded Medusa ("jelly fish") play roles, or in "The Emigrant of Landor Road," where the sea swells toward night after the emigrant's suicide by drowning.

Other poems from this first period in which sunsets are associated with the death of love in autumn are "The Song of the Poorly Beloved," "The Emigrant of Landor Road" ("an autumn port"), "The Saffron" ("Les Colchiques"), "The Thief," "Autumn," "Rhenish Autumn," ("Rhénane d'automne"), "Sign," and, in their earlier context, "Adieu" and "The Lady." The contrast between flight and darkness is made in "The Emigrant of Landor Road," "One Evening" (in reverse), "Sign" ("The doves this evening make their last flight"), and "Merlin and the Old Woman." Finally, poems in which some kind of mutilation, castration, or crucifixion accompanies the death of love are "The Song of the Poorly Beloved" ("the scar on her naked neck"), "The Emigrant of Landor Road" (decapitation, flagellation), "Palace" (crucifixion, and, in the manuscript, decapitation), "Lul de Faltenin" (wounds, decapitation), and "The Hermit" (mortification, nose-bleed). I shall examine some of these poems in more detail below; let me close this section with three beautiful lines from a later poem in which the errant poet, searching for himself, comes upon a memory haunted by his main theme:

The Death of the Sun

> Whom do you recognize in these old photographs
> Do you remember the day a bee fell in the fire
> It was you remember at the end of summer ("The Traveler")

II *"The Song of the Poorly Beloved"*

Cain the wanderer, having killed his God and looking for a wife, appeared in London in the fall of 1903 and again in the spring of 1904 in the person of Guillaume Apollinaire, walking through the foggy streets at twilight in the company of a juvenile delinquent who turned out not to be Eros after all—he reported that Eros was dead like Christ and Pan—but Anteros, the bad twin brother of love.[4] This lad was to take him to his beloved:

> One foggy night in London
> A ruffian who resembled
> My love to meet me came
> And the glance he threw me made
> Me lower my eyes for shame

When his love appears, we find that it is she who resembles the ruffian, she is the prostitute to his pimping as she staggers drunk from a pub, a scar on her naked neck. The poet recognizes "the falseness of love it [him]self."

So begins "The Song of the Poorly Beloved," one of literature's most beautiful complaints, a modern elegy to rank with love lyrics of Catullus, Ronsard, and Verlaine, "Rhyming out love's despair/ To flatter beauty's ignorant ear." Yet this terribly twentieth-century poem, chronologically the first in *Alcools* to describe the "heap of broken images" (Apollinaire's "water bad to drink") which the lost contemporary poet meets on his wanderings and the first to set a tone for the most recent poetic cries of distress, owes almost entirely its imagery, prosody, vocabulary, ideas, and references to the medieval and Symbolist literature Apollinaire studied in his adolescence. In thus successfully bringing old themes in an old garb to a modern *ethos* Apollinaire reveals himself for the first time one of the world's great poets.

This miracle he accomplished mainly, I think, by his faith in his myth, his transcendent belief that he was in no way inferior to the tragic poets and heroes of history. Like T. S. Eliot he hungered for

[51]

cultural unity and significance; but unlike Eliot, he felt no personal inadequacy before the great shades of the past lost in the
sterile wasteland of the present. To the contrary! He was one of
the enchanters foretold by Merlin; he literally knew

> . . . lays for queens
> Slave hymns to Muraena eels
> The romance of the poorly beloved
> And for the sirens songs

Although he found himself at the moment powerless to win his
own siren-queen or to create a new kingdom of love on earth, he
was able to turn a doomed quest into a courtly romance and himself into a knight-errant doing battle with the demons of destiny
by the immortal power of the word; for this knight-errant was also
a troubadour with an astonishing repertory of lays, hymns, complaints, and curses at his command. He was ready and eager to
transport his listeners from London to the Red Sea and from cosmopolitan, twentieth-century Paris to fourth-century Asia Minor
and Kalidasa's India.

As in "The Thief" and *The Putrescent Enchanter* the past in
"The Song of the Poorly Beloved" is contemporary: a seventeenth-
century Cossacks' curse against the Turkish Sultan becomes the
frustrated lover's imprecation; the goal of Columbus becomes the
beloved; and the mythology of the ancient world mixes with medieval demons and unicorns to bring another fabulous cortege to
life. But no longer is this literary framework a symbolic, enchanted world of its own, replacing a pale, lifeless Christianity;
rather, it is determined by a powerful psychological line running
through the poem, the poet's chaotic yet logical emotions of hope,
despair, desire, madness, melancholy, jealousy, and hatred caused
by the death of love.

Mr. L. C. Breunig in his excellent critical study of the poem[5]
points out how closely Apollinaire keeps to the timetable of his
love, from his stay in Munich with Annie in the spring of 1902
("Aubade," stanzas 15–17), the first visit to London in November
1903 (beginning), the Paris winter and spring of 1903–4 (stanzas
10, 38–40), to June 1904 (stanza 55) when he is back in Paris after
the disastrous second visit to London in May. All of this chronol-

ogy transmits a consistent pattern of life to the work. On and
through this pattern, he weaves a series of shorter narratives taken
from the lives and legends of kings in which his life theme is supported or contrasted for associational depth; such are the narratives with the Pharoah of Egypt, Ulysses, King Dushyanta (lover
of Shakuntala), the Turkish Sultan, and mad King Ludwig of Bavaria. Finally, an imagined interlude describing seven swords in
his heart proves his vaunted ability to create his own legend and
make it a psychological truth—part of the whole psychological
truth of the poem.

Two examples will serve to illustrate Apollinaire's skill in com-
bining personal narrative with associational imagery. Following in
the footsteps of his cockney cupid at the beginning, he relates

> We seemed between the houses
> The Red Sea's open wave
> He the Hebrews I Pharoah

seizing upon the metaphor from a purely visual scene of fog and
red brick walls. On further examination, however, the image falls
apart: the Promised Land of the beloved is not sought by the
ruffian but by the poet; the boy is not being pursued but followed;
and Jehovah would punish the wrong party should He follow His
Biblical precedent. But the fallacy of the image is used by its author to establish the truth of the next one: in the following stanza,
knowing that the waves will not tumble, he invokes Jehovah to
attest to the sincerity of his love: "Let these brick walls fall down/
If you were not well loved."

Then exaggerating the false analogy between himself and Pharoah, he demonstrates his point in a magnificent hyperbole:

> I am the King of Egypt
> His sister-spouse his men
> If you're not my only love

A sardonic, disconsolate attitude has broken through the fancy,
shattering it in its own terms and transmitting depth and power to
the underlying emotion; and the later image of love aspiring toward "the white streams of Canaan" is given added meaning.

In a contrasting example, the image is remarkably precise:

I have hibernated in my past
Let the Easter sun return
To warm a heart more iced
Than the forty of Sebastus
Less martyred than my life

These are forty Roman soldiers convicted of Christian belief in
the Roman garrison at Sebastus in Asia Minor during the fourth
century, who, forced to spend the night on a frozen lake, were
burned to death in the morning. Their saints' day comes during
Lent (March 9). Apollinaire brings the mystery surrounding the
little event from an obscure place and age outside of the great
lines of history into the ageless yet individual soul of the poem.

The narrative and images thus ebb and flow with the rhythms
of the poet's torment. The ballad-like beginning in a London autumn with its exoticism, hope, and doubt is brought to a sudden
conclusion by the realization that Love is as false as the beloved.
The poet's doleful state is immediately contrasted with the joyful
returns of Ulysses and Dushyanta to their loves, and the principal
conflict in his mind begins; the desire for forgetfulness with its
accompanying aspiration after new love ("Milky Way O luminous
sister . . .") as against the impossibility of forgetfulness because
of the beloved's desirability. Having hibernated through the cold
winter's loss in the past—in his memory—he aspires to life in
spring and calls upon the Easter sun to compensate for a loveless
present—which reminds him of another spring and a holy Lenten
Sunday when he sang his pagan happiness, at dawn, to his beloved. Back to an empty reality in Paris, a reality in which both
sacred and profane love are dead, he ironically considers his
powers as an enchanter ("I who know lays for queens . . .") subject to painful memory; he is faithful as the womenless Zaporogian Cossacks to their steppes and Decalogue. In a sudden burst
of liberty, he momentarily regains dominance by phrasing his despair in the Cossacks' brutal invective. Then reality again with its
pattern of future hope dissolved in the torment of desire alternat-
ing with recollections of beauty, until again his frustration centers
on his grief's holocaust, which moves from a martyr's pyre to the
sacrificial altar of the god of evil to the empty shadow of death—
the only god remaining. Meanwhile, spring has returned to Paris,

again in ironic contrast to the poet's unhappiness, a contrast first summarized by a humorous image announcing the coming dislocation of insanity:

> And I my heart is as heavy (*gros*)
> As a Damascan derrière (*cul d'une dame damascène*)

and then bursting forth in the semi-incoherency of confused erotic memories with the seven phallic swords. His madness next is metamorphosed into the ill-fated life of Ludwig II of Bavaria and the haunted Starnberger See where the Wagnerian king was said to have committed suicide:

> By a mistressless chateau
> The bark with singing gondoliers
> On a white lake under breath
> Of trembling winds in spring
> Sailed siren dying swan
>
> One day the king in the silver water
> Drowned himself then openmouthed
> Returned floating on the wave
> To sleep inertly on the bank
> Face turned to the changing sky

With this final metamorphosis, his last and gravest crisis of despair has spent itself, and a passive melancholy takes its place, precluding the possibility of his own suicide: "I wander through my lovely Paris/ Without the heart (courage) to die in it."
The modern days and nights of Paris take over his life with their Barbary-organs, their trolley cars, their cafés crying out to the beloved, "Towards thee thee I so dearly loved." He is left singing sadly to himself, "I who know lays for queens . . ."

Even after the varied experience in poetic creation revealed by the large body of Apollinaire's earlier work, it is easy to wonder where such a rich tapestry found its tight synthesis of form and matter. In regard to subject matter, I have already mentioned its debt to the past: in fact, Symbolist and Parnassian poetry and art (Apollinaire, like Picasso, was an admirer of English and French Pre-Raphaelites Walter Crane, Moreau, Redon, Carrière, Puvis de

Chavannes, etc.) were teeming with swans, sirens, unicorns, Rhenish scenes, cypresses, weeping willows, will-o'-the-wisps, aegypans, Argyraspides, aubades, and *danses macabres* of men led by destiny through shadowy lands.

Verlaine and Rimbaud before Apollinaire evoked the god Misfortune (*Malheur*) while Alfred Jarry, Marcel Schwob, and Rémy de Gourmont were experts in hagiography, often inventing their own saints like Apollinaire's Saint Fabeau; the sainted forty of Sebastus were discussed at length in many of their common source books.[6] The seven swords in Mary's heart were cited by Baudelaire, Laforgue, Lecomte de Lisle, Rémy de Gourmont, André Suarès, Édouard Fazy, and Henri de Régnier among others;[7] and *Shakuntala,* translated by Théophile Gautier, was a popular play among Romantic orientalists. Men danced to the violins of Destiny in Albert Samain, were led by Evil Chance in Saint-Georges de Bouhélier's *The Heroic Life of Adventurers, Poets, Kings, and Artisans* (1895)—which also celebrated the death of the gods and the birth of heroes—and sailed through sidereal zones toward the ideal in Henri de Régnier's poems. Rodin's famous statue of the Bourgeois of Calais had brought the inevitable alliteration "corde au cou (neck) à Calais" to literature (Rémy de Gourmont also used it); and Ludwig of Bavaria as a Decadent myth-in-the-flesh of esthetic madness driven to suicide was idealized by Wagner lovers. The slaves fed to Muraena eels by the Roman gourmet Vedius Pollon were poetized by Victor Hugo and painted by Gustave Moreau; and the old legend of the Cossacks reviling the Sultan became popular among Turk-hating Slavs and Armenians at the end of the century.

The English woman was the vampirish *femme fatale* par excellence in many a bloody tale ("The exotic perversions which were the vogue of the fin-de-siècle were *sadisme à l'anglaise* and the Slav soul," writes Mario Praz), and all readers of popular novels of the time were well acquainted with the foggy, vice-ridden streets of London. Perhaps the erotic seven-swords sequence is the most original section of the poem in terms of subject matter; but there, too, we find the Mount Gibel ("gibeline"), Carabosse, Rhenish landscape, and the antipopess Joan (in the first, 1909 version of the poem) of fin-de-siècle poetry.

As for form and theme, Villon and—surprisingly—Shakespeare

could lead the list of influences. The critic Henri Ghéon in 1913 called attention to the similarity between the *Song* and Villon's *Testament* with the latter's profoundly personal yet narrative form interspersed with ballad interludes illustrating the author's thought—including the "Ballad of the Lords of Yesteryear." Like Villon, Apollinaire wove poem fragments written at various times and places into his basic narrative fabric; in the first, punctuated version of 1909, which he had been assembling over a period of six or seven years, he employed no less than eight ellipses to compensate for its fragmentary appearance. His aristocratic origins and Nietzschean philosophy (discussed in Chapter 3) made royal names and titles come naturally to him as symbols, especially since, as a republican anarchist, he believed that he had arrived at the period of the end of kings. A few kings had been assassinated by anarchists during his youth, and he had seen and even met some living ones in his travels with the Viscountess de Milhau in Germany. This interest, constantly nourished by reading in history and legend, plus his admiration for Shakespeare—partly inspired like that for Villon by Léon Cahun, the librarian at the Mazarine Library—had caused him to see *Richard II* in London and buy a copy of the play, which, Mr. Breunig suggests, may have given him the inspiration for his identification of himself with the royalty of "The Song of the Poorly Beloved" ("For God's sake, let us sit upon the ground/ And tell sad stories of the death of kings . . ."; "Thus play I, in one person, many people . . ."). I only add to Mr. Breunig's remarks that the scene from the play that Apollinaire liked the most ("the greatest in the theater") was the tragic Act IV in which the betrayed Richard compares his fate to that of Jesus fallen from glory into *shadow* among Judases and Pilates.

But all the popular sources and the most careful construction cannot account for the poem's rich self-sufficiency and personal music. Apollinaire's vaulting egoism combined all that he had learned poetically with the acuity of his feelings—whether remembered in tranquillity or not—to place him not only at the summit of contemporary French lyricism but in the ranks of the kings and heroes of the past. The main myth of "The Song of the Poorly Beloved"—and of all the body of poetry of which it forms a part, in the final analysis—is his own.

III   "The Emigrant of Landor Road,"
      "Lul de Faltenin," "Palace"

Unlike "The Song of the Poorly Beloved," "The Emigrant of
Landor Road" begins on a fairly cheerful note, even though decapitation is involved: again a tourist in London, the traveler this
time is preparing to emigrate to America like Annie, former resi-
dent of Landor Road, and is getting dressed up for the occasion:

> Hat in hand he entered right foot forward
> The chic shop of a tailor caterer to the king
> This merchant had just cut off a few heads
> Of dummies decked out very comme il faut

Is this tailor Thanatos? The dummies (*mannequins*) were corpses
in "The House of the Dead." In any case, the headless forms dress
our emigrant up like a millionaire in the suit of a dead lord, and
he sails away for good:

> For returning is fine for a soldier of the Indies
> The brokers have sold all my medals (pun: spit) of gold
> But dressed in new clothes I want finally to sleep
> Under trees full of monkeys and mute birds

Believe it or not, the "soldier of the Indies" is probably Tommy
Atkins back from Mandalay[8] (the "flying fishes" later become
dolphins), whereas the "medals" may be the poet's unappreciated
poems. As he boards the ship in a port of autumn and it sails away
into the future and the unknown, in two beautiful images the past
seems to disappear: "For a long time he watched the coastline
die/ Only children's boats were trembling on the horizon," and
beauty to be born: "A tiny little bouquet floating at random/ Covered the ocean with an immense bloom."
But creative desires awakened by this vision are crowded out by
his past, now inescapable and interior, weaving a tapestry in his
brain. As a last escape, he finally unites with the sea, to the cries of
a familiar siren (*sirène* can also mean "boat whistle" and "prostitute"):

[58]

> To drown changed into lice
> Those stubborn weavers questioning endlessly
> He married like a doge [the sea]
> To the cries of a modern siren without a spouse

Like the Rimbaud of "The Drunken Boat" ("Le Bateau ivre") he
has cried, "May I go to the sea!"—but he does not return to Europe and "the puddle/ Dark and cold" of childhood. He has
chosen instead the death by drowning of the sun: in the final
stanza, after his suicide, the Western sea swells into ravenous
night.

"Lul de Faltenin" was the most priapic of the seven swords
planted in the poet's heart of "The Song of the Poorly Beloved"; it
would appear indeed that the name means bluntly "phallus,"
"Lul" being a Flemish word for the same and "Faltenin" deriving
from *phallum tenens*.[9] The name might have been one of Apollinaire's pseudonyms (he signed a postcard "Lul" in 1915, and was
amazed upon being notified of the death of a certain Guillaume
Faltenin during the war). The manuscript of the poem leaves no
doubt that it was intended among other things to describe a sunset in the sea,[10] so we can divide it into three levels: the narrative
description of some sailor, perhaps Ulysses, descending into the
sirens' grottoes; the self-defeating solar *liebestod;* and the poet's
abandon of self to onanism, prostitution, and sterility. Two symbols
of aspiration are present: the stars, used to represent the amorous
ideal in "The Song of the Poorly Beloved," here found at the pole
opposite the erotic grottoes; and the swimmer, a favorite symbol
of Apollinaire, with implications that are literary (he sometimes
resembles Baudelaire's sidereal swimmer in "Elevation"), biographical (Apollinaire was a good solitary swimmer), mythologi-
cal (Rémy de Gourmont pointed out that the aspiring swimmer
was one of the most common folk archetypes), and, naturally,
Freudian. In "The Song of the Poorly Beloved" the two symbols
were united:

> Milky way O luminous sister
> Of the milk-white Canaan streams
> And our white lovers' forms
> Dead swimmers shall we struggle on
> Your path towards other nebulae

Here, too, the poet at one point finds himself among the stars, this
time with a godlike self-sufficiency we shall meet again:

> . . . my wisdom
> Equals that of the constellations
> For I alone night give you stars

But the spasm is short-lived; he sinks back mutilated to the sirens'
nest at the end of the poem as the sun and the stars go their
opposite ways:

> Birds you stuck out your tongues at the seas
> Yesterday's sun has rejoined me
> The otelles cover us with blood
> In the nests of the Sirens far
> From the flock of oblong stars

"Palace" is an erotic allegory like "Lul de Faltenin." Where the
latter describes a physical decline and fall, however, the former
reveals more of a mental one, the failure of the mind's spiritual
quest for the *rosa mystica*. To Apollinaire as to English Pre-Raphaelites, Rosamond Clifford, the *rose of the world*, beloved of
Henry II and mistress of a fabulous palace and labyrinth at
Woodstock, was a favorite symbol of a kind of labyrinthine pursuit
of love reminiscent of the one in Guillaume de Lorris' *Romance of
the Rose*—or, in a negative way, Boccaccio's *Laberinto d'amore*.
In his notes for *The Bestiary* (1911) he translated a verse from a
celebrated sixteenth-century ballad about Miss Clifford's ri-
valry with Henry's jealous Queen, Eleanor of Aquitaine:

> The king therefore, for her defence,
> Against the furious queene,
> At Woodstocke builded such a bower
> The like was never seene.[11]

He also made her the main object of his quest for beauty in a
delightful little occasional poem of *Alcools* called "Rosemonde."
In "Palace," however, she is far from the courtly ideal: she is
"Madame Rosemonde," mysteriously rolling her little eyes as she
sits on her royal lover's pointed knees. In short, she has joined the

ranks of Helen, Angelica, Vivian, and Salome, *femmes fatales* who have fallen low from their Romantic idolization by nineteenth-century writers and painters under our poet's scabrous pen. Her fall is accompanied by a corresponding cynicism in language.

The poem is constructed on four main puns. The title also means "palet" in French; the pilgrim thoughts (*pensées*) are also flowers, "pansies"; the *tongues of fire* of the poet's Pentecost are nothing but tough meat (a play on words that Apollinaire inherited from Aesop and used in 1904 for the title of his first review *Le Festin d'Ésope*—"Aesop's Feast"); and the *orient* is both the region where all religions were born and the orient of a pearl, a word perhaps taken from the line "Her sparkling eyes, like Orient pearls" in the old ballad (it is here applied to another, more exotic region of the anatomy). Lesser puns, many of them erotic, are rampant, and the palace already becomes phallus in the first stanza, raised, significantly enough, out of the flagellated roses of a crucified sun.

All this wordplay has naturally led critics to regard "Palace" as a Jarry- or Jacob-like satire directed against Symbolist preoccupations. André Salmon has written that he and Max Jacob used to tease Apollinaire on his poetic tastes ("Still too Symbolist!" they would cry after he had read his latest creations aloud to them), and the poem in *Alcools* is dedicated to Max Jacob. It is true that crepuscular dream-gardens and haunted palaces abounded in the works of the older generation Apollinaire admired. For three examples close to "Palace," in a novel of Rémy de Gourmont a phantom woman lover discovered that eternal beauty was found only in an invisible "palace of symbols" surrounded by sterile ponds with dead *pensées* the only flowers (*The Phantom*); a nude English vampire sat on her lover's knees in an Oriental garden in Octave Mirbeau's *The Garden of Tortures*; and roses "whipped by the brutal wind" nostagically shed their petals toward the Orient in Pierre Quillard's *The Grieving and Heroic Lyre* (1897).

But if Apollinaire is satirizing his former masters in "Palace," he is also satirizing his own obsessions. Among other signs of love's demise, he finds that Cypress wine (from *Cypri botus,* a medieval symbol for Christ?) is bitter to him when he tastes it at agapes of the white lamb; and he waits in vain for the Pentecostal ascension of his thoughts en route to the Orient. Stillborn, his brain turns into

prehistoric meat; he can only rage when no Holy Ghost descends
at his own agapes:

> Ah! God damn it what did those cutlets cry
> Those great patés those marrow bones and stews
> Tongues of fire where are they my pentecosts
> For my thoughts of all the lands of all the years

Thus "Palace" is as frustrated as "Lul de Faltenin"; it is a Rabelaisian orgy of mental chaos in which the mystic rose palace becomes
another dead-end grotto. One noted critic considered the poem to
be primarily an erotic dream in which the *palace-palet* was that of
a woman's nether mouth.[12] The wide range of Apollinaire's fancy
plus his use of similar erotic sybolism in other works makes this
interpretation plausible (see Appendix B).

In a part of the manuscript of *The Assassinated Poet* probably
dating from 1907, Apollinaire wrote of his main character,
"Claude Auray who had loved and was no longer in love believed
that he could love no more." [13] The previous year he had announced publicly, after praising the thought of Pascal, Racine,
Goethe, Baudelaire, and Rimbaud, "I possess no significant composition, and I regret it." [14] He published nothing new besides his
pornographic works from January 1906 to August 1907. This was
the time of a sort of Passion for him: an important manuscript of
"Betrothal" (1908) gives us an insight into it.

[I have dreamed] poems so grandiose that I have had to leave them
    unfinished . . .
Because my desire for perfection
Surpassed [my taste] my very taste and the powers of one man
[Then I realized that each moment carries in it its own perfection]
But I had that ability that taste that science
And I fell asleep
An angel exterminated during my slumber (*sommeil*)
The lambs the shepherds (*pasteurs*) and sad sheepfolds
False centurions were removing the vinegar
Beggars badly wounded by spurge were dancing
Then after the flight and death of my poetic truths
I awoke after five years [and followed] one city night

· · ·

The Death of the Sun

The city seemed an archipelago with its nocturnal lights
Women were asking for love and dulia
And dark awakening so feeble I remember
The passing women that evening were never pretty[15]

The version published in 1908 has this cry:

Forgive me my ignorance;
Forgive me for not knowing any more the ancient game of verse.
I know nothing any longer and I love uniquely.
But flowers, in my eyes, turn back to flames.
I meditate divinely. . . .[16]

It was not a coincidence that his spiritual death and resurrection
paralleled the great crisis in modern poetry and art, during which
the moribund Symbolist sun finally set, leaving room for a host of
new stars in the esthetic Empyrean. In the next chapter, I shall
describe Apollinaire's transfiguration in the period of 1908–10 and
the long and winding road that led him to his Mount Tabor.

CHAPTER 3

The Phoenix

*Je suffis pour l'éternité à entretenir le feu de mes
délices—Le Brasier*

I *The Death of God*

IN the second issue of his little magazine *Le Festin d'Ésope*
Apollinaire printed an article by his friend Jean de Gourmont
which began, "The death of God which Zarathustra proclaims signifies the divinization of man and perhaps the culminating point
of our civilization" (December 1903). Another close acquaintance, the Polish anarchist Mécislas Golberg, wrote a few months
later, "the whole work of Renan can be summed up in a few
words: the divinization of man and the hope of human perfection"; he also cited Nietzsche's phrase, "We have killed God, we
must become gods ourselves" (*Europe Artiste*). Apollinaire wrote
admiringly of Rémy de Gourmont, "[If he] did not adore any god
[the god he adored was Nietzsche] he would be our Renan" (August 1904). His own godhead was in eclipse at this time, but when
he finally began to realize his divine potential three years later it
was toward the artist-Christ of Renan, Nietzsche, and Gourmont
that he moved rather than toward the socialist-Christ of Kropotkin, Souvarine, and Sébastien Faure.

Five admirable long poems and a *Bestiary* of short ones embody Apollinaire's angelism of 1908–10, "The Brazier," "The Betrothal," "Cortege," "Vendémiaire," a prose poem *Onirocritique*,
and the quatrains illustrated by Raoul Dufy in *The Bestiary*. Apollinaire called the first two of these his profoundest works. They
are certainly among his most hermetic. I shall attempt their exege-
sis below; but first, I must trace their author's political and critical
thought through the period covered in Chapters 1 and 2 in order
to show how ideas prepared the way for a poet-god's rise out of
his own ashes.

II *Influences: Rimbaud and Picasso, 1890–1905*

If an English or American reader should get the impression that the theme of man trying to play Prometheus and replace God is uniquely a Continental literary phenomenon exemplified in writers from Sade through Rimbaud and Nietzsche to Sartre, let him meditate on his own classics: Percy Shelley, Walt Whitman, Captain Ahab, the Connecticut Yankee, Mister Kurtz, and Willie Stark were equally caught up in the Romantic "spiritual hunt" (*la chasse spirituelle*) for secular resolutions of irrational problems. Walt Whitman particularly was close to French Symbolist thought in his remarkable "Song of Myself," a mid-century epic that infiltrated into the French poetic scene at the end of the century and very likely influenced Apollinaire's "Cortege" and "Vendémiaire." Whitman's discovery of Christ and the Superman in himself was American literature's main contribution to the potent intellectual energy released to Europeans by Rimbaud, Nietzsche, Gide, and Bergson.

Arthur Rimbaud (1854–91), the *adolescent satan* (Hugo's term) who reoriented the course of French literature before leaving it in his twenties for the sterility of the African desert, had already become a legend before his death at the age of thirty-seven. Charles Maurras wrote that for young poets of 1890 the *man with the soles of wind* (Verlaine's term) was "a magnificent navigator and sea-adventurer, perhaps a prisoner like Ulysses and like Merlin in the pearly grottoes of an Oriental fairy. We imagined him as another Orpheus devoured by black bacchantes. And he was the symbol of modern poetry itself, vagabond, exiled, far from laws, customs, civilizations." [1] By 1901, the year of Apollinaire's first published reference to Rimbaud, lines 93–94 from "The Drunken Boat" in his dance manual *French Grace and Manners,* Rimbaud's young tastes had become canons, a whole program of study for the budding writer:

I loved idiotic paintings, tops of doors, décors, saltimbanque canvases, signboards, popular engravings; obsolete literature, church Latin, badly-spelled pornographic works, novels by our grandmothers, fairy tales, little children's books, old operas, folk refrains, popular rhythms. (*A Season in Hell*).

Apollinaire later proved himself to be an authority on all these items. He was probably first attracted to them by their picturesque side, the background of the poet-wanderer; as he matured, however, he more and more comprehended their Promethean import, until he showed by 1910 that he considered them essential steps in the artist's return to godlike primitivism and mystic illumination. The same could be said of Picasso. Both poet and painter, born within a year of each other and grown up under the same signs of the Symbolists' materialistic mysticism and semireligious anarchism, admired the poet of Charleville. Like him, they lived "on the frontiers of the illimitable and the future" and sought "the limit of life at the confines of art." [2]

Apollinaire's 1905 essay on Picasso, the first major critical study of the painter, is astonishing for its prophetic delineation of the paths along which the Catalan's demiurge was subsequently to lead him; and it even anticipates in a precise way Jung's article of the 1920's on his archetypal descent into the Egyptian blue. The essay may indeed be in large part responsible for Picasso's own search for occult powers in his vision when he went from the rose period to cubism in the years from 1906 to 1908, as Maurice Raynal, a French critic who knew both men at the time, has hinted (*Picasso*, 1922). In it there is the important idea of the artist as *voyant* or seer, an idea found everywhere in nineteenth-century literature and expressed dramatically by Rimbaud in two famous letters (not published until 1912, however), and in *A Season in Hell* and *Illuminations*.

Formerly, Apollinaire had written that man created the gods in his imagination; now he would modify "create" to "find": he has met an artist who has only to *see*, to let himself be penetrated by his past and the past of others, to discover human divinity:

If we knew, all the gods would wake. Born of the profound knowledge humanity had of itself, the idolized pantheisms resembling it have slumbered. But in spite of eternal sleeps (*sommeils*) there are eyes reflecting humanities like divine and joyous phantoms.

Picasso has watched human images floating in the azure of our memories and which participate in divinity to damn metaphysicians. How pious are his skies . . . (*La Plume*, 1905—in *Chroniques*).

Picasso's externalized, naturalistic vessels for this divinity are subjects always loved by Apollinaire and by artists: the saltimbanques. Embellishing the theme of the passionate clown with its analogies to life—the clown as isolated traveler, masked illusionist, serious player of absurdity, tragic mime of human idiocy—he like Rimbaud and many a Symbolist and Romantic back to the Shakespeare of Hamlet and the Ronsard of "The world is the theater and the men actors" had capitalized on a classic symbol of the romantic personality; but now with Picasso, the saltimbanques no longer imitate life but create great religious art: "You can't compare these saltimbanques with buffoons (*histrions*). Their spectator must be pious, for they celebrate mute rites . . ." They are the first-born of immaculate women in strange stables ("Noël! they gave birth to future acrobats among familiar monkeys, white horses and bear-like dogs") and at last become demi-gods, artist-creators ("The adolescent sisters . . . order spheres into the radiating movement of the worlds . . ."). Innocent, hypersensitive, and rootless, the adolescents have infinite inner depths and distances which bring them close to the primitive springs of being and to animals (". . . animals teach them religious mystery . . .") until they become inseparable from the spiritual animality of nature:

. . . Placed on the limit of life, animals are humans and the sexes indecisive.

Hybrid beasts are conscious of Egyptian demi-gods; the cheeks and foreheads of taciturn harlequins are blighted by morbid sensitivity.

The saltimbanques are also associated with the poor and downtrodden of the world, Picasso's principal subject matter of his previous style, that of the blue period. In another article, Apollinaire compares the saltimbanque boys to the young men of the people and their mothers to the young mothers of the working class (*Revue Immoraliste,* April 1905), while he says here of the children of the latter, "They can leap and the tricks they complete are like mental evolutions." Among these lonely ones, the old women are atheists, devoted to memories, innocent and good; the old men are animated by distant lands; the children are wise and wander without having learned the catechism; the youth is old; and the crippled beggars, mad as kings with too many elephants bearing little pavilions, encompass the universe in their gaze: "There are travelers who confuse flowers with stars" (*Chroniques,* May 1905).

Thus the whole of humanity participates in a primitivistic reversal of evolution, from civilized man to his pariahs, to his Christ-like saltimbanques on the limit of life, to animals, to the demi-gods, to the gods themselves, to, finally, the humid bottom of the abyss—with the parallel movement from old age to youth to the recollections of immortality of children. This is the traditional voyage of the seer who usually descends into "the dark night of the soul" (Saint John of the Cross) before he ascends, an *illuminatus,* to the stars.[3] Rimbaud had traced out the same voyage in "The Drunken Boat" and in his mythic life, recorded in advance in *A Season in Hell,* passing beyond pariah and saltimbanque down through the history of Western man to the religious East to finally a godlike—or bestial—end in the desert and on the beach. Gauguin had pursued his demi-gods and madonnas as far as the South Seas. And Picasso, the *voyant* whose eyes passively reflected the rhythms of the universe ("Those eyes are attentive as flowers always trying to gaze on the sun") was very soon to take five more occidental pariahs and turn them into the primitive fetishes and bitch-goddesses of his celebrated *Demoiselles d'Avignon,* the *opus initians* of modern art.

III *From the People-Christ to the Divine Poet, 1899–1908*

Even as an adolescent Apollinaire was caught in the typical intellectual dilemma of his time between positivism and idealism. In politics, this dilemma was translated into his admiraton of the working masses and their strong leaders and his realistic awareness of potential mediocrity and demagoguery in both. He was an artistic individualist like Rimbaud, appalled by human misery and obsessed with the desire to change the world; he must have been disillusioned by the failure of the revolutionaries to take power after the Dreyfus affair as Rimbaud had been disillusioned by the fall of the Commune, and agreed with the poet of *A Season in Hell* that scientific progress, while essentially desirable, was too slow. Like the other poetic revolutionaries about him, cursed with

what the Marxists used to call the crime of anarchistic individual-
ism, and believing in a pseudo-Christian blood-sacrifice to redeem
the world, he distrusted political pragmatism. "I hold that politics
is detestable, deceitful, sterile and injurious," he wrote an editor
of the socialist *Plume,* refusing at the same time to comment on
the detested Franco-Russian alliance and mentioning that the
Russian people would need religious props for some time to come.
He wrote in an early manuscript (incorporated into Chapter 12 of
The Assassinated Poet) that human equality was impossible, and
pointed out to the royalist Charles Maurras in one of his notebooks that "the tyranny of unity [under a king] would not do
away with unity of number, it would merely make two tyrannies
instead of one . . ."

The anarchist newspaper, *Le Journal du Peuple,* which he read
for at least two years, from 1899 to 1901, and which was edited by
a former Jesuit seminarian, Sébastien Faure, was also averse to
political solutions. In its first issue Faure spelled out his credo:
"*The Journal of the People* will scrupulously avoid that horrible
and repulsive thing which always and fatally soils and sterilizes:
Politics" (February 6, 1899). Faure went on to list his paper's
other main enemies, nationalism, anti-Semitism, clericalism, militarism, and capitalism; a front-page article by Laurent Tailhade
in the same issue stigmatized the "old agonizing society" with its
throne of excrement raised to Fear by Religion, Patriotism, Family, and Property. In a later number, Faure, in a typical burst of
rhetoric, predicted that a New City, "animated by the wind of liberty, full of songs of life after the complaints of death," would rise
out of "the ruins of cities sterilized by the pestilential wind of
repression" (April 1, 1899).

Apollinaire's anarchist poems included some of these ideas (as
did his later *Onirocritique*), and he published one of them as late
as 1903. But by that time he was writing for the serious and intelligent *Européen,* a pacifist, socialist weekly with a cosmopolitan
outlook, and echoing in pleasantly detached little articles its anticlericalism and antipathy to Russian and Turkish tyranny. He had
even gone so far as to support two socialist politicians himself,
Francis Michaux in 1902 and Pierre Baudin in 1903. His old aristocratic anarchism was never very far below the surface, however,
and his would-be internationalism gradually succumbed both to a

latent germanophobia and anglophobia and to the French intellectual's prejudice—shared by many other nationals, however, including H. G. Wells—that French ideas and particularly the French language were destined to save the world for civilization. It was ever difficult for him to take a moderate position: his Catholic-nurtured anticlericalism was restrained for the *Européen* but burst forth in the stories of *The Heresiarch and Company*. There he ridiculed the practices of baptism, communion, and canonization ("The Sacrilege," "The Latin Jew"), the doctrine of the holy trinity ("The Heresiarch"), salvation through repentance ("The Latin Jew"), papal infallibility ("Infallibility"), divine retribution ("Three Stories of Divine Punishment"), relics ("History of a Virtuous Family, a Basket and a Gallstone," "The Napkin of the Poets"), and Christ's kingdom ("The Passerby of Prague," "Simon Magus," "Touch at a Distance"). "There is not a branch of science which does not contradict by irrefutable facts the so-called truths of religion," one of his spokesmen told the pope ("Infallibility"). He later said that he was one of the few writers to grasp the profound implications of the division of Church and State in France in 1905.

In spite of his dogmatic stand for "the tree of science where revolution ripens" ("The Poets"), however, the demands of idealism were never absent. As an amateur anthropologist and a neo-Freudian before the letter, he could transfer his early love for the Christian trinity into a belief in the cyclical myth of incestuous creation and sublimation with its symbolic death of the Father; in one of his notebooks he did the same for science, conceiving it as a trinity of History, the Father (science of the past); Mathematics and "other exact sciences," the Holy Ghost (science of the present); and Philosophy, the Son (science of the future). Mathematics with its "indisputable facts" he saw as the most important of the three, as it represented Love and was the unifying force between past, present, and future. As he came to expend more of his energies on artistic creation, he passed through stages in which first the Father (the past—sometimes the feminine "Memory") and then the Son (the revolutionary, prophetic vision) came to dominate, stages reflected in poems like "Merlin and the Old Woman," "The House of the Dead," "The Song of the Poorly Beloved," and "The Betrothal." By 1908 he realized that a dialectical process was at work in his philosophy: he saw the Poet-Father historically uniting with an inner reality the Mother-Muse in an act of love to produce the Son-Future, the work of art. The work of art in turn became a new historical reality, the masculine *prototype,* which, acting upon the female, the author's brain, produced a new creation, and so on.[4] In short, he came to believe that facts could produce nothing but facts, and that an intervening artist was essential to activate the upward cycle or spiral toward the New City of the future.

In 1908 he saw scientific truth as no less true than artistic truth but important only as an adjunct to it; in an article of 1905 he had systematically composed his *vale* to positivistic doctrines of humanistic anarchism as possible social patterns for progress. As the one analytical, inductive excursion into his basic philosophy of life, this article, "Government" from his little magazine, *La Revue Immoraliste* of April 1905, deserves our close attention here. The following is the way I interpret its main arguments:

Egoism, the basic human instinct, seeks its own fulfillment in power and pleasure, which, for the individual, constitute happiness: "Man to follow his instinct must only seek his happiness." Virtue, then, is passion accompanied by action (Spinoza) that creates collective and individual happiness, as when the individual helps himself or others; any other action is vice, a sin against the species. This includes vegetarianism (only Apollinaire could mix gastronomy and higher thought!). The supreme pleasure of the ego in which both power and pleasure are joined is *voluptuousness* (*volupté*), found in the generative act, which is also the greatest sign of love the individual can make to the species. This act creates unity between individuals, the vicarious sympathy for fellow members of the same species, which can in turn cause the pain of commiseration when another individual suffers. As this pain will naturally seek relief in virtuous (egoistical) action, individual charity which carries love to the level of the species is born. But certain actions are individually virtuous and collectively sinful such as charity itself (since it collectively and impersonally salves the conscience of the rich and thus opposes the happiness of the poor) and, especially, politics (since collective laws cannot include the happiness of all). And because *power* is the other main drive of the ego for its own fulfillment, human society is built on inevitable conflicts: a social solution to the opposing drives of individual egos is impossible.

If the laws of politicians are sins their conduct is reasonable and virtuous. They obey natural instincts which cry to every man the words of Macbeth's witches, "Thou shalt be king." They obey natural egotism which invites every man to take the first place on earth among his fellow men.

If Spinoza with his views on the pleasure principle, charity, compassion, and relative organic virtue is at the source of this thought, an attitude emerges which is surprisingly close to Freud (as is Spinoza) with his two instincts of sex and power (death); and closest of all to Nietzsche and Rémy de Gourmont. The latter, indeed, wrote in the *Européen* of November 1, 1902, that Nietzsche did away with doctrines of rationalized Christianity like Kant's categorical imperative and replaced them by a principle of liberty and individual royalty. Nietzsche's egoistic power drive, distrust of the Hegelian belief in government, and, above all, his faith in the privileged individual, are all near Apollinaire's thought. Only does Apollinaire omit the Nietzschean idea that some egos *should* exist at the expense of others. That is to say, he omits it here; but the doctrine of the Superman is implicit in the essay, as well as occult belief in the microcosm-macrocosm embodied in every man, his potential to become a king and a god—and an animal and a devil. Apollinaire points out that a *social* utopia is impossible but makes no mention of an *esthetic* utopia at this time; yet it is significant that his key article on Picasso will appear the next month. The direct opposite of "Government" in style, discursive, impressionistic, and poetic, the latter article rather than its predecessor sets the pattern for Apollinaire's future critical writing, as it describes a powerful *esthetic* ego's ability to give the gods back to mankind.

Thus did the artistic side of Apollinaire's anarchism gradually assume dominance over the political. Much nostalgia for the old militarism remained to him of course, and traces of proletariate sympathies can be discovered in the last works of his life; but more and more did he find himself on the side of the poetic kings and heroes he had identified himself with in "The Song of the

Poorly Beloved." He still attended anarchist meetings after 1911 [5] and wrote for the socialist press as late as 1910 (in *La Démocratie Sociale*); but his change of outlook (and his nostalgia for his former ideas) had been recorded in two poems of 1909, "1909" and "Poem Read at the Marriage of André Salmon." The first of these, "1909" (*Alcools*), is an updating of his old revolutionary poem "To the Proletariat," a view of his adopted country France as seen from the side of the "divine alcoves" instead of from the bottom of the mines. From a rough beauty fashioned by the hands of workers she has become a very chic Marianne indeed with her elegant Ottoman gown and her "blue eyes white teeth and very red lips." But she makes the poet uneasy; he remembers his love for "the atrocious women of the enormous suburbs" and wonders when the midnight hour (perhaps the *novissima hora* of medieval millenarians) will strike. "Poem Read at the Marriage of André Salmon July 13 1909" (*Alcools*) is a brilliantly conceived résumé of the changes that have taken place since the two anarchist poets first met at the revolutionary sessions of *La Plume* at the café *Le Départ* in 1903. They were deceived at that time, he says; no one is going to take the Bastille again and renew the world in this timid democracy; he knows now that only "those founded in poetry" can renew it. It may not have been long after this that Apollinaire changed "the courageous, thrice-powerful anarchists" in the manuscript of "Vendémiaire" to their victims the "courageous, thrice-powerful kings" who appear in the final version of the poem in *Alcools*.

Literary influences played a large role in this evolution. A survey of his reading before 1908 shows that from a solid background in literary classics and an eclectic interest in all the fin-de-siècle tastes (including Rimbaud's), he became increasingly aware of a special significance in the works of Baudelaire, Rimbaud, and Mallarmé, and their idealogical ancestors.

Besides the literature of Rimbaud's canons, we know from letters and internal evidence in his writings that his early reading covered much of the same material that was given to Croniamantal in *The Assassinated Poet*: Virgil's *Eclogues*, Theocritus, Villon, Ronsard, Racine, La Fontaine, Shakespeare, Goethe, and Cervantes. He wrote in answer to a Spanish inquiry in 1915 that he had read *Don Quixote* several times in his childhood and that it "gave me the curiosity to read the Chivalraic Romances which I devoured later at 20, so Cervantes' goal was not attained"; he even read with "inexpressible pleasure" Avellenda's plagiarizing continuation of the novel.[6] He knew Dante, Petrarch, and Boccaccio, and used characters from Ariosto, Tasso, and Ovid in *The Putrescent Enchanter* along with the fairies and enchantresses out of Don Quixote's library. He liked dime novels, Nick Carter and Buffalo Bill, *Robinson Crusoe,* popular serials, detective stories, novels of Paul Féval, Pierre Prudent Legay, Émile Gaboriau, and many others. In his late adolescence and early twenties, he read widely in scholarly reviews, medical journals, books of natural history, encyclopedias like Migne's, Bayle's, Larousse's, Moreri's, and the Dictionary of Trévoux, ancient grammars, dictionaries of Old French, books on blasonry and gastronomy, dance manuals, medieval travel books, the Golden Legend, and saints' lives. His first education in sex may well have been out of books like those read by his young Don Juan, books also found in the Heresiarch's library (and in the library of his ecclesiastical uncle?) by Oribasius, Galenus, Fracastor, and Bandello.

His first writing is full of imitations of Symbolists, Parnassians, and Naturists with a few conscientious copies of Shakespeare and Ronsard. The great fervor for life that swept through the literary chapels at the beginning of the century and which coincided with a period of travel in the Rhineland and love for Annie shook him free from a fin-de-siècle muse, and his wind-blown Rhineland poems, some of the most beautiful of the genre in French, brought German Romantics like Brentano and Heine into a Latin view of the Rhenish landscape (touristic travel poetry was beginning to be popular at the time). He returned to Paris in 1902 full of everyone else's ideas about the "healthy, vigorous, true, cosmopolitan," and *humanistic* literature that was rising out of the defunct little Symbolist and Parnassian circles of the 1890's and creating a new harmonious and classical age of reason in the new century.[7] He praised in his articles Decadents and Romantics, Moréas and Verhaeren, Verlaine and Raoul Ponchon, Robert Randau and the *vers libristes,* René Ghil, and the Neo-Naturalists. He translated a long article from the German for the *Grande France* on Rimbaud, Mallarmé, Baudelaire, and the Parnassians,

and slanted it along the lines of his admiration for the humanistic
verse of Fernand Gregh.[8] As always, he celebrated French classi-
cists Racine, La Fontaine, and Molière. He liked proletariate
songs, "the pure gold of Mallarmé," the prophecies of Ezekiel, the
classicism of Ernest Raynaud, and the fantasy of his special
friends Alfred Jarry, Charles-Henry Hirsch, Félix Fénéon, and
André Salmon—which resembled his own. He began to take his
manuscripts to Rémy de Gourmont for criticism.

By 1905 he was admiring with Picasso the mystic thinkers Saint
Teresa, Pascal, and Goethe, and he began referring to the latter's *Conversations with Eckermann* as if it were his bedside book.
In his essay on Picasso he sketched out a visionary's way, and in a
tribute to Mécislas Golberg he praised that poet's lynx eyes, casting their own light ("more intelligent when the obscurity is greater"), and placed himself and his friends under the sign of Golberg's martyred *Prometheus repentent*. This was the year he had
the most scorn for metaphysicians, "mellifluous liars." In 1906, he
said he was for an art of "fantasy, feeling, and thought," the art of
Racine, Baudelaire, and Rimbaud. In 1907, silence. Finally, by
1908, the time of his Promethean resurrection had arrived, he was
traveling with Jean Royère in Mallarmé's Symbolist wake, and the
revolutionary end of the world he had foreseen had become his
end, the one suffered by seers:

Formerly the dead came back to adore me
For my life had the power to cause the whole universe to be re-
born
And I was hoping for the end of the world
But mine [arrives] [is advancing]
      arrives [like] whistling
      like an icy hurricane (manuscript of "The Betrothal")

Like Picasso, he was one of those travelers confusing flowers and
stars: "Flowers, in my eyes, turn back to flames" ("The Betrothal").
He was the prophet of an esthetic new order:

We know that our breath has had no commencement and will not
cease, but we conceive before everything else the creation and the end
of the world. (*Chroniques*, June 1908).

. . . each work becomes a new universe with its particular laws. (*Chroniques,* November 1908).

Every day, perhaps, a powerful will changes the order of things . . . and wipes out the memory and even the truth of what existed the evening before. (*La Phalange,* August 15, 1908).

IV *Orpheus and Ixion: Ideas of 1908–1909*

Apollinaire in 1908 and 1909 suddenly found himself in the forefront of *avant-garde* literary and art movements. A friend of the Mallarméan Jean Royère, he became the novel critic for the latter's review *La Phalange* ("The Phalanx") from March 1908 to April 1909; he was chosen for the delicate office of presenting poems by young contemporary poets in a lecture on Symbolism in April 1908; he published an article in June 1908 on the Fauvists that was to become the first chapter of *The Cubist Painters* (1913); and he wrote important essays on painters and poets Matisse, Royère, Salmon, Braque, Théo Varlet (a disciple of Rimbaud), Paul Fort, Jarry, and a galaxy of women writers including Colette and Mme. Catulle Mendès. In most of these writings he expressed ideas that related to a new Symbolist crusade on the part of *La Phalange,* a magazine which he called "that young review which, almost alone in France, defends the cause of lyricism" (*Symbolist Poetry*). These ideas expressed in essence the philosophy he was to advocate during the remainder of his life for both poetry and painting.

A parenthesis here. Apollinaire, who became after 1908 a leading apologist for the modern art movements Fauvism, Cubism, Orphism, abstract art, Dadaism, and Surrealism, has been considered ignorant and incompetent in matters of painting by no lesser authorities than Picasso, Braque, Duchamp, Villon, and Vlaminck, as well as by his first publisher, art dealer Henri Kahnweiler, and art historians Gustave Pimenta, Adolph Basler, and Pierre Cabanne. His influence on modern painting has been ignored by critics Jacques Rivière, Herbert Read, André Richard, Pierre Marois, and François de Herain.[9] On the other hand, artists Derain and Delaunay, poets Rock Grey and André Salmon, and critics Maurice Raynal, Georges Lemaître, Stanislas Fumet, Jean Cassou, Robert Motherwell, Christopher Gray, Michel Ragon,

Lionello Venturi, and John Golding have praised his perceptiveness, universality, critical acumen, and prophetic influence on the painters.[10]

Yet in all this difference of opinion, no artist or critic on either side has pointed out in a systematic way what seems obvious enough when a close look is taken at Apollinaire's art criticism: (1) the criticism was based on the same philosophy of revolutionary estheticism that his 1908–10 poetry embodied; (2) this philosophy, instead of deriving from the painters' ideas as has been claimed, was a logical development out of the ideas of Symbolist poets Gérard de Nerval, Baudelaire, Rimbaud, Mallarmé, and their followers; (3) Apollinaire thus brought to his critical articles a philosophy which, as Mr. Breunig writes, "although it existed in poetry after Baudelaire, was revolutionary in painting," [11] and which Apollinaire also applied in his criticism of poets André Salmon, Jean Royère, Théo Varlet, and—himself; (4) he devoted the last ten years of his life to an extraordinary effort to impose this philosophy on the world in a synthesis of literature and art that would include and transcend the principal new movements, Cubism, Futurism, Imagism, Surrealism, Dramatism, Simultaneism, etc., in a kind of "popular front" of art he called "the new spirit," which, he claimed, would revolutionize twentieth-century society from top to bottom and bring forth a new golden age; and (5) such a synthesis required a good deal of rationalization of what he thought to be impure and imperfect works of art, and was sometimes based more on promise than actual production. He wrote the Futurist Ardengo Soffici in 1912, for example,

. . . don't you think that, for a new artistic conception to impose itself, second-rate things must appear at the same time as those which are sublime? In this way one can judge the extent of the new beauty. It is for this reason and for the sake of great artists such as Picasso, for example, that I support Braque and the Cubists in my writings, for to subscribe to the general condemnation of some would entail personal criticism of a talent which deserves only encouragement.[12]

"It is time to become the masters," he wrote at the same period.

What, then, were his main critical ideas? Ideas which, since they were at the very basis of modern art, assume an extraordinary importance for the study of the development of twentieth-century esthetics. Inevitably, they were the result of the revolutionary rise of his thought into a new dimension of his Promethean conception of the universe. His new vision fell into a new trinity, roughly equivalent to his early one of Science, History, and Philosophy. This trinity contained three realities: the external reality of nature, science, and the picturesque; the inherited inner reality of imagination, instinct, and intuition; and the final reality of art. The last reality, created out of the union of the other two, reacted upon them in the upward cyclical movement already described.

He never denies the truths of science in this period, science "[which] makes and unmakes that which exists"; [13] he merely considers scientific questions analogous to questions of religion, philosophy, and psychology, that is, questions dealing with the minor, incomplete realities of nature, which become dull and commonplace when used by their greatest exponents the Naturalists, writers like Zola, Maupassant, and Huysmans.[14] Art based on them must necessarily be relatively transient, this side of eternity, impure, and imperfect, and subject to the laws of cause and effect and relative truth.[15] Only when these realities are infused with the modern picturesque or marvelous—for example, in twentieth-century Paris with its dazzling electrical illumination (recently installed), its smoke-filled cafés, its prostitutes, its bohemians—will they become the subject matter for the writer, into which he may dip as a painter dips into his colors. "The marvelous should be the first care of the novelist," he counsels, adding that he should be conscious of reality.[16]

The greatest reality beyond the work of art itself, however, is in the artist. In the poet's inner night "divine cadavers float in the brightnesses," and Psyche, the only living being, sings her eternal song. André Salmon's memory contains the mysterious folk songs, "the most ancient monuments of poetic thought." All of civilization's great cultural achievements of the past, although forgotten or disregarded by the artist at work, are contained in him. Pursuit of knowledge, discovery of instinct and intuition, are the ways here toward shaping the artistic self, in which the ageless popular instinct will play a great role.[17] In one of his book reviews Apollinaire praises Mécislas Golberg's book, *The Morality of Lines,* in which that curious philosopher reduces all art and life to "a point" which he then demonstrates to be the beginning and end of art:

The soul of life is the personality, individualization, the search for a constant, immutable form across varieties and clumsily experimental multiple divergences . . . The individual: a point.[18]

Matisse having told Apollinaire that he had found a personality constant for himself, the writer comments, "Instinct was rediscovered. You [Matisse] finally submitted your human consciousness to the natural unconscious . . . What an image for an artist: the omniscient gods, all-powerful, but submitted to destiny!"

The artist, therefore, becomes the absolute creator, the supreme master of the universe. The most common term Apollinaire uses at this time in speaking of the artist is *divinité:* the painter "must, before all, give himself the spectacle of his own divinity, and the canvases he offers up to man's admiration confer upon them the glory of likewise exercising momentarily their own divinity"; "the poet is analogous to divinity. He knows that in his creation truth is infallible. He admires his work." Their creations will not be limited to the false appearances of the past, to the unknown future, or to the temporary fashions of the present; rather, they will incorporate past, present, and future in one essential, ecstatic unity, a higher reality of truth constantly renewed which belongs only to eternity.[19]

The truth of this final work of art will naturally seem *false* at first (he will later say *surprising*) in regard to the more readily apprehensible truths of nature and science; the poet "knows the error which animates his creation, false to our visions but presenting to momentary powers an eternal truth." [20] This is the doctrine of the willful lie, advocated by Nietzsche ("a man must be a liar in his heart, but he must above all be an artist" [21]) and summed up in Picasso's statement that art is a lie the artist makes into truth. The artist's individual vision can only be true to him alone until he succeeds in imposing it upon humanity—or until humanity succeeds in acquiring it. The end of a world is thus implicit in each masterpiece: the poet's discoveries "give the lie to former truth.

Such is the poetic work: the falseness of an obliterated reality. And even the memory of it has disappeared. Comparison is impossible. Life and truth are undeniable." In art, the famous "painting-object," so sought-after by the Cubists, is born: "The painting will exist inescapably. The vision will be entire, complete, and its infinity instead of denoting an imperfection, will only bring out the relationship between a new creator and a new creation and nothing else." [22] And for this false, yet divine creation out of self which gives birth to a new reality, Apollinaire finds a striking new celestial trinity, another solar myth, that of King Ixion who had intercourse with a cloud believing it to be Hera, from which union the centaurs were born.[23] The vision of the goddess is in the creator; whether Hera, Psyche, Muse, or the illusory nude sister of Narcissus pursued by her twin brother in the fountain, she is the breeder of art. "Every divinity creates in his own image; thus the painters. And only photographers fabricate the reproduction of nature." [24]

Nevertheless, external, scientific nature at the base of the pyramid of art still must be considered as a verifying factor. Apollinaire's pragmatic knowledge of art techniques led him to concede a certain amount of relativity to absolute creation. "Reality verifies what the writer imagines . . . It animates a work which without it would only have the impersonal existence of cadavers." In painting, works of Derain are "samples of that noble discipline which purifies reality 'and grants authenticity to nature' (Mallarmé)." [25] But for the most part, a great work of art actually *transforms the external reality of nature into its own reality.* Picasso by lending us his eyes has enabled us to find the gods again and use them to change the world. The poet re-creates the old world into the new image he has of it: "Founded in poetry we have rights over words which create and destroy the universe." The rule of Merlin the Enchanter is over; in Apollinaire's new Classicism, two Greek enchanters who hold all nature in the power of their song, take his place. He cries out, "New Amphions, new Orpheuses, young poets . . . will soon . . . make wild animals and the stones themselves susceptible to their accents" (*Symbolist Poetry*). Later, in 1912, in perhaps his supreme statement of Orphic anthropomorphism, he will write:

Without poets, without artists, man would quickly weary of the monotony of nature. The sublime conception he has of the universe would come crashing down with dizzying rapidity. Order, which appears in nature and which is only an effect of art, would vanish. Everything would return to chaos. No more seasons, no more civilization, no more thought, no more humanity—indeed, no more life; sterile semi-obscurity would reign forever. (*The Cubist Painters*).

He then gives a striking example of this anthropomorphism in a demonstration of how Renoir's creation of a *type*, a social illusion out of his vision, actually caused society to model itself upon it and thus resemble it for future ages. Considered false and even ridiculous at the moment of its conception, Renoir's vision is now regarded as the true expression of his time.

Other terminology of Apollinarian criticism becomes clear when placed against this idealogical backdrop, *obscurity* and *simplicity, inhumanity* and *humanism,* and harmonious *order* as opposed to adventurous *chance.*

In the eyes of the profane, artistic truth in its pure simplicity is as obscure as it is inhuman—like a lily, for example. Jean Royère's tongue is as clear (pun: "bright") as the flames of Pentecost; Gérard de Nerval knows another purity which dazzles neither mathematicians nor grammarians who are continually asking what it *proves;* Max Jacob is a simple poet and appears a strange one.[26] One is reminded of Saint Paul's famous statement that "The wisdom of this world is foolishness with God."

What about Apollinaire's prophecy of a new humanism to arise out of twentieth-century art? How can this be reconciled with the essential *inhumanity* of the work of art? In reality, he says, this inhumanity is "the highest manifestation of the human spirit," the highest sublimation of our animal nature; it is "beyond all natures which try to keep us back in the fatal order where we are nothing but animals." It is actually the ultimate humanism: "To consider purity is to baptize instinct, humanize art and divinize personality." [27]

Being an absolute, moreover, the poem or the painting is a perfect unity like its creator, at the same time a complete organism and a chance product of nature's chaos. Both order and chance are essential to the creative process. Adventurous chance without order leads to the "hazardous ingenuousness" of Henri Rousseau's canvases (an opinion Apollinaire will soon change); to the "ignorant frenzy" of impressionism, an art ruled by chance; or to the unrestrained cult of the personality of Expressionism.[28] Order without adventure leads to the dull realism and psychology of the contemporary novel (Apollinaire campaigned for three years in *La Phalange* and *Les Marges* for the *realistic* novel of fantasy). Adventure and order are reconciled by the talent of a Jean de Gourmont with his restrained audacity; by an André Salmon with his necessary, concrete, and marvelous vision; by the poems of a Jean Royère with their harmonious and joyful mystery; and by the reasonable, ordered explorations into personality of a Matisse or a Braque.[29]

Perhaps the best symbol Apollinaire finds to represent his duality into unity of life and art is one always favored by Symbolists and illuminists, the flame. In one image he summarizes the three plastic virtues of the new (Fauvist!) painting, virtues we have seen him apply also to poetry:

The flame has purity which tolerates nothing foreign to its nature and cruelly transforms into itself whatever it attains.

It has that magical unity, whereby each little flame when it is divided is like the single one.

Finally it has the sublime and undeniable truth of its light. (*Chroniques*, 1908).

It seems clear from this synopsis why Apollinaire's art criticism has created so much difference of opinion among painters and critics: many of the paintings do not jibe with his theories. These ideas of 1908–9 are in essence the same as those of 1910–12 which he published along with them in *The Cubist Painters*. There, Picasso is the supreme example of the divine creator; he is the leader of the "scientific Cubists" (the term "analytical Cubists" is used today) who rearrange subjects taken from chaotic nature along the lines of science (geometry) and intuition until the new construction—of a violin, say—has its own new order, grandeur, harmonies of light, and truth. The "Orphic Cubists" (Orphists) on the other hand, take mainly color forms from external reality and arrange them more instinctively and with less external reference into plastic harmonies than the analytical artists. Both groups have as their common denominator light, the origin of fire's truth and the greatest gift of external nature. Futurists, finally, although basically instinctive artists like the Orphists, are too impressionistic, too involved in painting subjects outside themselves like "the speed and the dynamism of the machine age" to arrive at perfection.

If any modern artist or art critic formulated these ideas in a coherent, universal way before Apollinaire's articles of 1908–9, the evidence has not been forthcoming. Poets and literary critics, on the other hand, the disciples of Rimbaud and Mallarmé that Apollinaire frequented, had long been applying them to literature.[30] Although Picasso, another admirer of Rimbaud and Mallarmé, did not usually communicate his ideas other than through his painting, André Derain, whom Apollinaire believed to be the main influence both on Matisse's Fauvism and on Picasso's epoch-making move to Cubism,[31] was a vocal source of Symbolist ideas, having been a former intellectual anarchist turned esthetic revolutionary with as much interest in Nietzsche's ideas as in Cézanne's cones, cubes, and spheres.[32] Apollinaire's great role was to put these poetic ideas into action, first by living them in his life and writings, and secondly, by convincing others of their relevance. Being enthusiastically convinced himself, he played this role with great success; yet he could not but be disappointed by art works which, he thought, did not come up to his standards of perfection. Any one reading closely *The Cubist Painters* and *Art Chronicles* can sense immediately an aberration between theorizing and reviewing, the reserve Apollinaire must have felt before many of the Cubists' tangible productions. How could it have been otherwise when Braque and Picasso—to name only the best—chose dull monochromatic subject matter from nature rather than the poetic marvelous he advocated (and which they had formerly used) and then decomposed and reordered it by the lesser truths of mathematics?

It is obvious that he more highly esteemed the more *truthful* and instinctive works of Matisse, Derain, Dufy, Marie Laurencin, Rousseau, Chirico, and Chagall, the "divinely drunken" color poems of Picabia and Delaunay, the archetypal, mystical sculpture of Archipenko, the Fauvist works of Braque, and the blue and rose paintings of Picasso; and he often maintained that Renoir was the greatest living painter. The semiabstract paintings of the Orphists particularly, which he considered as deriving from Fauvism (*Chroniques,* February 1913), more precisely fitted his theories of autonomous, poetic art, and he was rarely reserved in his enthusiastic admiration of them. On the other hand, he repeatedly referred to works of the analytical Cubists as "enumerations" and "experiments." Those artists were going through a stage, he said, and not even, originally, an essential one, with "less grace than crudity," toward ultimate masterpieces. He had waxed enthusiastic over Michelangelo's beliefs that religious art was the greatest art and that great art was essentially a religion, and he wrote an essay in 1912 on Picasso as a continuator of Michelangelo's tradition in which again he used the blue and rose paintings as examples. Thus when he writes in *The Cubist Painters* that the great religious painter of the future has not yet arrived ("May he come one day . . . may God command him, force him, order him . . . he will be here, perhaps he is here already, near us all, I know his name, but I dare not say it . . ."), it is plausible to think that he is referring to Picasso's failure to fulfill as yet his early promise. He often uses the future tense in the work: the drama *will* break forth, the painters "created in the image of God" *will* rest one day and "admire their work." But in the meantime—while waiting for the new Michelangelo to reveal himself—"what fatigue, imperfections, grotesqueness."

Thus did Apollinaire set as the highest goal for life its divine creation through art, and join the "life for art's sake" writers of the nineteenth century—Baudelaire, Flaubert, Rimbaud, and Mallarmé—to say nothing of Yeats, Rilke, and Proust, with whose writings he was not acquainted. Like many of the works of those other authors, his two complementary Orphic poems "The Brazier" and "The Betrothal" prove that the subject matter of the poem-object —that microcosm of the universe—can only be itself, its description of its own voyage to itself, its own creation of itself. It is thus an absolute, an eternal unity of form and matter, constantly renewed with each new reading, the most significant absolute the poet-explorer can discover. He creates Byzantium by sailing poetically to it.

V *"The Brazier"*

Apollinaire's joyful voyage to the godhead of pure poetry in "The Brazier" is at the same time mobile and immobile, horizontal and vertical, like the voyages of Dante and Mallarmé's Igitur: he travels both upward toward the Empyrean and outward toward Désirade—while remaining firmly pinned to a bank of the Seine. Dividing the poem into the symbolic three parts, which I shall characterize generally as representing renunciation, renewal, and elevation, he relates both the poem's and the poet's voluntary martyrdom and final ascension. In the analysis that follows, the parenthetical references are to the critical works I have just discussed.

In the first section, renunciation, we find two principal images of his criticism: the flame and King Ixion. In the pyre of his lyrical personality Apollinaire heroically—with the same leap in the dark toward purity he took in other traumatic periods of his life—sacrifices his past, consecrating it to the flames ("The flame which transforms cruelly into itself what it attains"). This past consists primarily of his beheaded past loves, sacred and profane. Divine love has become as bad as any other, "Our hearts hang on the lemon trees" (lemons, Mary's fruit, are symbols of the golden hearts, expiational ex-votos that Apollinaire had once seen in a chapel dedicated to the Virgin[33]).

From the excessively human past, the poet turns to the divine future and evokes the vegetable cries and whinnying centaurs (born of Ixion's false embrace of a "phantom of clouds") of a world of demi-gods proper to artistic creation. Back in the present he becomes immobile, pinned to Paris and ready, like the building stones in the Amphion legend, to undergo passively the lyrical experience. He will build the city of art out of his own transcendency.

In the second section, renewal, the phoenix theme becomes overt as the martyred poet joyfully accepts the pain of losing Love for the fire of his delight ("Théo Varlet knows the anguish of delight"). In a burst of self-sufficiency, he boasts that he who had stripped off his soul to the sun in the first section ("[Picasso's] meditations strip bare in silence") now requires the sun to need protection from his brilliant face—luminous, incidentally, like the legendary faces of Moses, Pan, and Christ. The past was a degeneration from the Tyndarides to these flames; but now the ancient swan-gods (Zeus was the swan-father of the Tyndarides) die singing in them (in Théo Varlet's psyche, "One would say that all the swans are going to die"). The poet's life is renewed out of them. Flaming in his own pyre, he cries that he has nothing in common with those who are afraid of burns (in the last, suppressed stanza of "The Thief," the pagans scoff at Christians' fear of hellfire). He flames, *emigrates,* and ascends all at once.

To describe the ultimate in experience, Apollinaire has chosen to portray visually physical elevation and horizontal extension at the same time in a heavenly theater and a marine city, brought together by a pun on *places* (theater seats—city squares). The third section thus opens with a close-up of the world of outer space glimpsed in the first section, a world where light thinks ("The flame has the sublime and undeniable truth of its light"), the future flames, and a city is built, Thebes-fashion, out of art. A favorite gnostic beast, Shamir, Solomon's traditional stone-cutting worm, has constructed the celestial theater of the city ("The worm Shamir who could build the temple of Jerusalem without tools, what a striking image of the poet!"). Into this city, Apollinaire introduces two other symbols popular with French occultists of the turn of the century, Pan, the central figure of the zodiac, and the medieval astral pentacle. Again immobile, seated in one of the *places* before the divine spectacle ("the artist must above all give himself the spectacle of his own divinity"), he becomes a star, a human pentacle (cabalistically, the five-sided figure is the symbol of Pan and the microcosm-macrocosm). He is devoured by flames ("André Salmon will lyrically create the stars by his own transfiguration"). His pentacle is "vain" because it does not prevent his ardent consummation; but it does not keep him from watching the *bright, inhuman* actors—"new beasts" like the centaurs—of this apocalypse of art triumph over lesser mankind. Pan as a shepherd-god with a flock of sphinxes, symbols of art and knowledge,[34] has just passed through the poem. As the poet watches the tamed men on earth with his stellar eyes ("men will be astonished

by the miracle of his stellar eyes admiring the world"), he ends
the poem by musing that he would prefer to their lot his own of
being eternally devoured by knowledge in the "sphinxeries"—
where he will hear Pan's song for the rest of his life.

Thus does he reverse his old Sun-Night theme in "The Brazier."
Beheaded and burned alive like the setting sun, no more does he
dive into the Western water like the emigrant or sink into the
twilight sterility of "Palace" or "Lul de Faltenin"; rather he replaces the gods Zeus, father of the Tyndarides, and Hera, the
phantom of clouds, to rise transfigured as his own solar myth, out-
dazzling the sun. His final flamelike unity is that of his creation,
the poem. And in his apotheosis there is just a suggestion that a
new love will appear in the heavens, a physical incarnation of the
second member of the trinity:

> We await your good pleasure O my beloved
>
> . . . .
> When will Désirade [Columbus' island] become blue on the horizon

Night is no longer a murderess. She may indeed rise from the sea
like Aphrodite to be illuminated by a new Sun.[35]

VI   *"The Betrothal"*

Apollinaire took similar trips to the stars in other poems of this
period. In "Pipe" the ascension is again immobile and again in-
volves wisdom (the owl). *Onirocritique* begins close to the coals
of heaven and ends, after a dreamlike spectacle of inhuman new
beasts being shown off by a shape-shifting poet-enchanter, with
the end of the human world. In "Cortege" (*Alcools*), the poet
becomes a kind of comet as he goes off into space illuminating
himself in an "oblong fire whose intensity will go increasing/Until
it will become one day the only light." In "The Betrothal," finally,
"An Icarus tries to rise up to each of my eyes/And sun-bearer I
burn between two nebulae."

"The Betrothal" is more biographical than "The Brazier" and
recounts Apollinaire's Passion in more detail; but it is the same
journey to the same divinely phallic pyre of creation. It picks up
the search for a new love just touched upon in the last section of
its complementary poem, and carries a betrothal theme to its con-

summation on three levels: profane love, sacred love, and divine poetry. A similar ladder of love to that of "Spring" is realized (the first section is taken from that poem), but here the Christian progression of innocence-sin-renunciation-confession-hope-salvation is followed in the symbolical nine parts. Apollinaire's new madonna, *Marie* Laurencin, to whom he was newly "betrothed" at the time of writing, is found throughout, but, as he later truthfully told his fiancée Madeleine Pagès, "no woman is the object of the poem"; it treats rather of all women—and all poetic creation. More of an *ars poetica* than "The Brazier," it is also less unified, its fragmentary appearance (it was put together in at least four versions, with extracts from earlier poems attached to it) being justified, as in "The Song of the Poorly Beloved," by a psychological, biographical logic reflecting a typically diffuse modern psyche.

It is less original in subject matter than "The Brazier." Saint-Georges de Bouhélier and the Naturists often celebrated the Poet-God's betrothal to the Virgin and Nature and the subsequent rebirth of the gods; and in his little magazine of the 1890's, *L'Annonciation,* Bouhélier had announced among other things that the Poet-King was coming, that he would be Adam, Orpheus, Pan, and Jesus, that the theater would replace the cathedral, that the poet would sacrifice himself as the Lamb in a love-mass to the Maternal Virgin Fiancée, and that he would renew himself and mankind, re-create the universe, resuscitate the gods, etc. Jean Royère in 1908 called works of Verlaine, Mallarmé, Valéry, and Régnier, as well as the new poems of Apollinaire, "Transfigurating Poetry." The *Alcools* version of the poem is dedicated to Picasso whose blue madonnas especially appealed to the poet; and Maurice Denis' "Easters," "Betrothals," and "Annunciations" were favorite paintings of his.

He had compared Picasso's mysticism to that of Saint Teresa; that earlier Spanish visionary had described in *The Mansions* spiritual betrothal and marriage with God, while her master Saint John of the Cross had shown that the three steps leading to such a betrothal were the Purgative, the Illuminative, and the Unitive— the same steps that were taken in "The Brazier." The Spanish mystic had also pointed out that a joyful death in the flames of the spirit was the only way to life ("The Flame") and that spiritual death was preceded by the voyage into the depths, into "the dark

night of the soul" (Apollinaire's "sleep"). Yet both "The Brazier"
and "The Betrothal," closely related as they are (their fragments
unite on the manuscript), incorporate these old symbols so sub-
jectively that they become highly original. They justify the poet's
claim that they are the profoundest poems in *Alcools*.

The dedication of "The Betrothal" to Picasso may have more
significance than many of the other dedications in *Alcools*, made
often just for friendship, to pay back a favor, or for minor
relevancy.[36] The seer-painter's example was probably an inspiration to the poet; it is likely that the reference of the 1913 version
of the poem,

> Let us prophesy together O grand master ["masters" in 1908] I
> am
> The desirable fire consecrating itself for you

was made more specific in order to refer to him.

By 1908 the Spanish painter had overthrown his esthetic goals
of the blue and rose periods, and, after living for a time with
classical and primitive gods, was undertaking experiments based
on more conceptual formalizations of the universe: he was applying Cézanne's plastic techniques to his art, attempting to make it
as self-sufficient, nonanecdotic, and *inhuman* as possible. How did
this affect his admiring poet-friend? Mutual acquaintances report
that when first confronted by "The Demoiselles of Avignon" he
found the painting excessively audacious[37] (my guess is that he
found it disappointing). But after the rose period, Apollinaire
probably did not cull many ideas from Picasso himself anyway:
the artist was notoriously stingy of theoretical ideas, and André
Derain who wasn't, and whom Apollinaire considered to be the
mentor of both Picasso and Matisse anyway, was a good enough
influence in his own right. We have seen that Apollinaire applied
Symbolist ideas of autonomous art to both Fauvist and Cubist
painting.

His fictional account of his first meeting with Picasso leaves no
doubt that Symbolist paintings of the blue period were sufficient
to inspire the same ideas:

> He knocked on the door and cried out:
> "It is I, Croniamantal."

And behind the door the heavy steps of a weary man, or one who carries a very heavy burden [!], arrived slowly and when the door opened there was in the sharp light the creation of two beings and their immediate marriage. . . .

. . . Croniamantal . . . looked silently at the new painting on the easel. Clothed in blue and barefoot, the painter was also looking at the canvas where in a glacial mist two women were remembering.[38]

There was also in the garret a fatal thing, that great piece of broken mirror . . . It was a fathomless, vertical dead sea at the bottom of which a false life was animating what doesn't exist. Thus, opposite Art, there is its appearance, into which men put their trust and which lowers them when Art has elevated them. . . .

(*The Assassinated Poet,* Chapter 10).

Nevertheless, the later example of Picasso's extraordinary change from passive Dyonisian reflector of the gods to active Apollonian explorer into himself, seeking "traces of inhumanity found nowhere in nature," must have been an additional shattering experience. At least, here is his 1912 account of the Picasso revolution:

Then, severely, [Picasso] questioned the universe. He became accustomed to the immense light of the depths . . .

There is the poet whose muse dictates his works, there is the artist whose hand is guided by an unknown being who uses him as an instrument. . . . Other poets, other artists, on the other hand, force themselves and turn toward nature, they have no direct contact with it, they must draw everything out of themselves, and no demon, no muse inspires them. . . . Men created in the image of God, they will rest one day and find their work good. But what fatigue, imperfections, grotesqueness!

Picasso was the first kind of artist. Never has there been so fantastic a spectacle as the metamorphosis he underwent when he became the second kind.

Picasso resolved to die . . . (*The Cubist Painters*).

"The Betrothal" celebrates *Apollinaire's* death and rebirth, new-found ignorance, and gropings toward himself and nature. Part I presents his old poetic truths, a tender, Symbolist dawn of love with its King Charming, Madonna, and ex-voto hearts hanging among the lemons. Suddenly (Part II) the sun sets on his hopes; Love dies as in "The Brazier"; and an avenging angel strikes. He is crucified by his "friends" (there are several biographical indications that he had persecution feelings at this time and good reasons for them) and sleeps for a time. He wakes to find women decanonized and beauty fled, as it had formerly fallen in *The Putrescent Enchanter;* the manuscript fragment quoted at the end of Chapter 2 also mentions the death of his "poetic truths" and a five-year sleep! Part III describes an ascension like that of "The Brazier" and a different kind of martyrdom, a torment of silence (Théo Varlet, silent for two years, "could not speak and was grieved to be silent"). His end of the world has arrived. In Part IV, sorrow and nostalgia for his lost past, including Italian churches and the lemon groves of Part I, sweep over him; and in Part V, he has advanced to a stage where he can say, "I love divinely," and hope for powers of objective creation in a magnificent image taken from Genesis and from his creative flame:

> But if the time came when the finally solid shadow
> Should multiply and realize the formal diversity of my love
> I should admire my work

After his six days of creation, in Part VI he rests. There he finds himself facing the greatest martyrdom of all for a sensualist like himself, the sacrifice of his six senses. In "Cortege" he will boast that he knows "The five senses and several others" (the first one here seems to be "love"). In "Lul de Faltenin" he had abandoned himself to his senses in erotic grottoes. His new austere esthetic, however, demands a godlike detachment from things of the flesh; and he will later rebuke Futurists and Expressionists for their slavishness to sensation. In Part VI, therefore, he casts off love, hearing, touch, sight, smell, and taste, in that order; and he especially regrets having to transcend the taste of Marie (a pun on *laurel-Laurencin*[39]). I add as a postscript that he happily never fully succeeded in this purification process; usually, he took his sensual nature to the stars with him!

In Part VII, torment has turned to joy. No longer afraid of lies, he proceeds to tell a couple—thereby telling the truth—offers his divinely erotic passionflowers in ex-voto—with *two* crowns of thorns!—and is off: the storm is over, angels are working *for* him, and the day is holy. In Part VIII, as in the second section of "The

Brazier," he sets sail, after having stripped to the sun, and moves
under the constellation of the Virgin, the third sign of the summer
solstice.

The important final section, that of the martyrdom, is one of the
most obscure passages in Apollinaire. Here is the punctuated version of it (1908):

> Flaming Templars, I burn among you.
> Let us prophesy together, O grand masters, I am
> The desirable fire consecrating itself for you,
> And the fireworks turn, O lovely, lovely night.
>
> Bonds loosed by a free flame, ardor
> My breath will extinguish, O dead, at forty (*à quarantaine*)
> I aim at (mirror) the glory and misfortune of my death
> [or, I aim at glory and misfortune *with* my death,]
> As if I were aiming (*viser*) the bird of the quintain.
>
>   . . .
> Uncertainty, feigned, painted bird, when you were falling,
> The sun and love were dancing in the village.
> And your gallant children, well or badly dressed,
> Have built this stake, the nest of my courage.

Some already-charted points of reference may help us to orient
ourselves. In the last two stanzas of "Lul de Faltenin" the poet
was flaming in defeat in the bird-sirens' nest; here the image is
one of triumph, the sirens are gone, and the poet-phoenix is alone
in the nest of his courage. That he will rise out of the nest is
suggested by the second stanza (he often uses "breath" for prophetic poetry) and by the image of the dancing sun in the last
stanza, which replaces the setting sun of "Lul" and the other crepuscular poems. A sunlike bird does set or fall, but its name is
"uncertainty"; it is feigned and artificial; and it is, perhaps, replaced by the courageous bird of the last line.

Since the poem is about a betrothal, I assume that some sort of
flaming marriage ceremony is taking place. In "The Brazier" Apollinaire used the builder of the Temple of Jerusalem, Shamir, to
build the temple of art for his New Jerusalem; here the poet is a
guardian of that temple, another Knight Templar, martyred like
the Grand Masters of the Templars Jacques de Molay and

Geoffroi de Charnai who were burned at the stake in 1314. Apollinaire knew many of the works of the occultists, Gnostics, Pythagoreans, Rosicrucians, Freemasons, etc., which abounded at the end of the century, and he used some of their symbols, the main ones of which were fire and light. In the manuscript version of "The Betrothal" his five-year *sleep* had perhaps the Freemasons' connotation of "spiritual death" or "suspended animation"—which he referred to in 1915 in a letter to Lou ("our loves are *en sommeil* as the Freemasons say"—March 29). To the occultists, the Templars represented purity and masculine abnegation and devotion, especially since the knights swore to serve only one mistress, the Virgin Mary, Queen of Heaven. This may be the *betrothal* here. Believers also credited the medieval legend of Jacques de Molay having correctly prophesied with his last breath the death of the pope in forty days. In any case, the Knights Templars make apt symbols for the small band of crusaders who set out with Royère, Matisse, and Picasso to defend the *temple of art* (an expression Mallarmé used), to serve Beauty, and to purify the world with their ardor.

The second stanza is particularly ambiguous. *Quarantaine* means "Lent" in French as well as "quarantine" and "forty," so that the phrase *à quarantaine*—an unusual one by the way—could mean "at Lent," "at the age of forty," "in forty days," "in a group (or in groups) of forty," and "in quarantine." Lent, of course, is the time of the Passion, and the two Grand Masters (as well as the forty of Sebastus) were burned during Lent. Dancing around bonfires at this time (the last stanza), was an ancient European custom. And the sun was believed to dance on Easter Day. But the expression still remains extremely equivocal, to say the least. And who or what is the "bird of the quintain"?

The 1908 punctuated version, unlike the one in *Alcools*, separates the last stanza from the rest of the poem, thus separating the two birds, that of the quintain from that of "uncertainy." I have translated *viser* by its uncommon meaning "to aim" rather than the usual "to aim at," for Apollinaire's erotic writings make it quite clear that if the *quintain*, the iron ring of the medieval jousting game, is one of his symbols for a female sexual organ, the bird, besides being a phoenix, is a phallus. "To aim at" could still be used in its common meaning of "to emulate." The separation of the two stanzas, then, would suggest that the poet is *summarizing* in the last stanza what has preceded it. The second bird, that of uncertainty, may have been the first to fall, that is, the aged, artificial phoenix; and the *quintain* may be the true pyre-phoenix nest for the triumphant new phoenix, the "bird of the quintain," to fly out of. From jousting knight, the poet would then become flaming Knight Templar, *rising* from his former fall.

Whatever the obscurities, I believe I can affirm with a reasonable amount of certainty that the last section of "The Betrothal" is one more example of the erotic solar cycle. In it Apollinaire brings together Christian and pagan symbols of death and resurrection to form another unified poem-star; his flame again represents purity, unity, and truth. With "The Brazier" at the summit of his symbolism and at the most penetrating depth of his inner voyages, it reveals that he has been able, even more than Picasso, to place order in his universe. He has found it good.

CHAPTER 4

The Traveler

Écoutez mes chants d'universelle ivrognerie—"Vendémiaire"

I Myths of 1909–1913

EACH work of fiction and poetry that Apollinaire published established a different myth for the poet. In *The Putrescent Enchanter* he was the Antichrist Merlin, buried by love but still creating a marvelous world of enchantment. In *The Bestiary, or Cortege of Orpheus,* a "divine" masterpiece like "The Brazier" of the 1908–9 period, he was Orpheus, in command of nature, turning bird and beast into symbols of his poetic aspirations. In *The Heresiarch and Company,* that "Cortege of Orfei," he was Benedetto Orfei himself, the epicurean Italian heresiarch of the title story with his mystical eroticism and his sainted vision of what true religion really is, that is, marvelous science fiction. He was also the heresiarch's company, the picturesque band of wanderers and Antichrists he knew so well from his travels through literature and Europe.

The public reception of *The Heresiarch and Company*—which barely missed winning the Goncourt Prize for 1910—helped to orient the creation of the composite myth of *Alcools,* his greatest achievement. He was enchanted by Thadée Nathanson's review of his short stories: the former editor of *La Revue Blanche* wrote of him, "He speaks with precision of the sites and inhabitants of so many countries in the world that no one knows exactly where he comes from, and everyone wonders where he *hasn't* been." [1] After the appearance of *Alcools,* Apollinaire compared himself to a traveling spectator of the world, a sailor, adding on one occasion, "Each of my poems commemorates an event in my life." [2] In composing the book he had broken up the chronological order of his poems to extend to his "song of himself" the widest—and highest —range possible.

After the summits of the 1908 poems, it was inevitable that he would turn to the more horizontal aspects of life, not only to play Saint Paul to his own messiahship, but to bring more of the modern marvelous into art. The publication of "The Betrothal" and the article on Théo Varlet in November and December 1908 marked the upper limit of his search for "purely poetic thought." It is difficult for anyone to remain in the rarefied atmosphere of absolute art for longer than privileged moments, and Apollinaire, now completely dependent upon his pen for a living (he had formerly scratched out a livelihood in finance), was too busy with his rapidly ascending literary career and his journalistic labors to continue toward perfection and its ultimate condition of ecstatic silence. Thus he became linked with the Unanimists for a time, searching like them for the place of poetry in the collective world soul, and extending the experience of "The Brazier" back to the beginning of time and to the ends of space. In "Cortege" he brought the second coming of himself—he who could "resurrect others"—up from the depths of the past:

> All those arriving who weren't myself
> Were bringing one by one the pieces of myself
> They built me little by little like a tower
> The people piled up and I myself appeared
> Formed by all bodies and all things human

In "Vendémiaire" (discussed below) he hymned his New Jerusalem, Paris, as the center of the universe.

Simultanéisme became the order of the day to him as it did to Unanimists and to the poets of dozens of little artistic movements with names ending in *-isme* that were flourishing all over France (André Salmon counted as many as fifty in Paris alone). Many of them felt the need to impose art—especially French art—upon a rapidly moving twentieth century by a universal synthesis of all the arts and all the genres, with historical and legendary perspectives, and geographical and scientific cosmopolitanism. Science fiction, the literature of travel through space and time, fantasies on the machine, travels in the Orient and in America, poems by Valéry Larbaud and Marinetti, and novels of Gide, Claude Farrère, John-Antoine Nau, and Paul Adam provided readers in the new century with a new world outlook. Apollinaire found himself somewhat ahead of the game. His first published prose had been the science-fiction account of a brain surgeon who played God and the travel stories of *The Heresiarch and Company. The Putrescent Enchanter* was a simultaneous play-novel-poem uniting druids, prophets, heroes, and princesses in an anachronistic vision of one night; and "Salome" (*Alcools*), like a Flemish painting, leaped frontiers and centuries to bring Saint John's decollation up to seventeenth-century Europe. Lesser travel poems like "1904" and "The Door" accompanied "The Song of the Poorly Beloved" and "The Emigrant of Landor Road." After 1908, he became even more of a world citizen.

The Heresiarch and Company had terminated with a series of five short stories which included a linguistic misapprehension in Tuscany and cannibalism in Canada along with the rise and fall of the cosmopolitan Antichrist Dormesan. New short stories treated of a Dutch millionaire who gained his wealth in South America ("Rendezvous at the Gambling House"), a lonely ventriloquist in a London rooming house ("Loquacious Memories"), and a phantom fiancée in Cannes ("The Posthumous Fiancée"). And in *The Assassinated Poet,* the hero, Croniamantal, traveled from Belgium to Paris, Rome, Munich, Monaco, and Aix-en-Provence before embarking at Paris upon a literary career.

André Billy, in the summer of 1910, directed a symposium to which some leading young novelists of the day, including Aurel, Montfort, C.-F. Ramuz, and Lucien Rolmer, contributed their views on contemporary trends in the novel. Summarizing their opinions, Billy wrote, perhaps referring to Apollinaire's three-year crusade for novels of fantasy, "A resurgence of the novel of imagination or adventure has been predicted. None of my correspondents refers to it . . . The novel will thus continue to be realistic." [3] Apollinaire was writing at this time *The Assassinated Poet*, one of the most Rabelaisian and least naturalistic novels since the death of Alfred Jarry.

In Chapter 14 of this work, the triviality of realistic novels is humorously attacked, and the alienation of the humble people of the crowd—those constant subjects of realistic novels—from poetry is proposed as a major theme. New imagined worlds are united with a symbolic plot and autobiography, until the whole

becomes an exotic world in which the fantasy has an edge of satire. The following is a piece of pure poetry, free of all chains:

MAHÉVIDANOMI
RENANOCALIPNODITOC
EXTARTINAP + v.s.
A. Z.
Tél.: 33–122   Pan : Pan
OeaoiiiiioKTin
iiiiiiiiiii

(The last line is plagiarized from Francis Jammes's "The Poet and
the Birds").

In a few passages, the self-sufficient worlds of poetic imagination of the 1908 period are represented. Croniamantal, having become a poet at Paris, has only to close and to open his eyelids like
jaws to swallow and renew the universe, and to imagine the least
details of enormous worlds. When he finds refuge from external
reality in his memory, truth, outside of time, appears to him. In a
book which satirically describes the people of the world following
Lycurgus' and Plato's lead and banishing poets from the Republic,
he turns Plato's cave inside-out and reveals that the poet's imitations of reality have the highest reality ("opposite Art there is its
appearance into which men put their trust and which lowers
them when Art has elevated them"). At another point, he "dies of
thirst by the spring," presumably one of the springs of creation:

CRONIAMANTAL
O spring! You who gush forth like endless blood. You who are cold
as marble, but living, transparent, and fluid. You always new, always
the same. I adore you, you who animate your verdant banks. You are
my peerless divinity. You will quench my thirst. You will purify me.
You will murmur your eternal song to me and lull me to sleep in the
evening.

The mood is a passing one in *The Assassinated Poet*, however;
Croniamantal soon turns back to the literary world of Paris with
its realistic fiction ("A woman stepped on his toes. She was an
authoress and didn't fail to assert that the meeting or collision

would provide her with the subject of a delicate story") and to his
pursuit of love in the person of Tristouse (Marie) Ballerinette
across Germany, Czechoslovakia, and France.

In poetry as well as fiction the traveler continued to move,
sometimes, as in "The Emigrant of Landor Road," into places he
had never been in actuality, sometimes, as in "Rosemonde" (*Alcools*) into familiar foreign lands. In this last poem, which is a
variation on the theme of Baudelaire's "To a Passerby," he
glimpses *en passant* a Dutch rose in his eternal quest for the *rosa
mystica:*

> I nicknamed her Rosemonde
> Desiring to recall
> Her flowered mouth in Holland
> Then slowly I passed on
> To quest the Rose of the World

In "Annie" (*Alcools*), the roses are in America, with the rose-
palace of "Palace" becoming an occidental villa surrounded by
another garden full of roses (and equally sterile[4]) "between Mobile and Galveston." In "Ispahan," more realistically in the Orient
this time, he poetically transposes a chapter of a 1908 travel book
by the Princess Bibesco into beautiful symbols of Pan, his Madonna Marie, and the phoenix sun:

> For your roses
> I would have taken
> An even longer trip
>
> Your sun is not the one
> Shining
> Everywhere else
> And your music accorded with dawn
> Is for me henceforth
> The measure of art
> After their recollection
> I shall judge
> My poems the plastic
> Arts and yourself
> Beloved face . . .

> I have perfumed my soul
> In rose
> For my entire life . . .[5]

The voyages into his own past of "The Song of the Poorly Beloved" and "The Betrothal" continued also, with, however, an un-
expected and frightening new dimension. In his symbolic use of
Orpheus and Ixion in 1908 he had pridefully forgotten the ultimate fate of those heroes, the legends that Ixion was pinned to a
wheel in Hell for his presumption and that Orpheus was killed by
women. Now *hubris* struck with such violence that he assumed
that it had been God-inspired (". . . O God who knows my sor-
row/ You who gave it to me" [6]). Lilith again took revenge on him,
this time through the person of the Mona Lisa: he was imprisoned
—although innocent—for the theft of Leonardo's fatal lady from
the Louvre on September 7, 1911. The shock was so great he momentarily regained his lost faith. Moreover, the slow or rapid passing of time, the major concern of the prisoner, entered his poetry
and became one of his major themes. A latent melancholy was
again released ("I've lived like a madman and wasted my time,"
he wrote the following year) which made his search for himself
through the events of his past in new poems "The Traveler" and
"Zone" intensely poignant. Yet even as a chained and repentant
Prometheus in the Santé prison, he never completely lost his poetic omniscience:

> I have just recovered my faith
> As in the lovely days of my childhood
> Lord accept my hommage
> I believe in thee I believe I believe
>
> World suffering by my pride
> You have a life only in me (manuscript of "At the Santé")

The myth of the Wanderer is never better expressed than in
"The Traveler" (*Alcools*). Like the protagonist of Walter de la
Mare's famous poem "The Listeners," Apollinaire, too, knocks on
a moonlit door as he seeks the key of closed eyes: "Open this
door on which I knock weeping." Thus he touches on the more
Germanic side of the Symbolist current, a side which often sur-

faces in modern French poetry, wherein life is regarded as a marvelous, enigmatic dream, made significant only by art.

As in "The Betrothal" the search in "The Traveler" is the only discovery, but here the search is not so much for the self's creative transcendency as it is for a meaning of self outside the artistic experience. Poetic technique is accordingly reversed: instead of following a fairly exact chronological and dialectical progression which turned images from experience into trinitarian symbols of the creative process, here the poet takes memories out of his past and *disorders* them—or, better, brings them to the poem in their natural disorder—thumbing through old travel photographs out of sequence in order to discover their secret significance. "Whom do you recognize in these old photographs?" he asks; the question is reminiscent of André Breton's Surrealist query, "You say that this photograph doesn't look like me; then *who is it?*" [7]

Taken separately, most of the images came out of the real life of the poet, his childhood in Monaco, his travels in Belgium and Germany, his loss of sacred and profane love, his admiration for masculine friendship;[8] pieced together with one imagined image, a shadowy Homeric scene, they become a view of life with reverberations far beyond him—just as two stones, washed together and shaped into a symmetric whole by a river, may include the vast, silent perspectives of two different geological ages. And the poet, the enigmatic image-shaper, can only marvel at what has been created *through* him. All that he really knows is that he is blown by the winds of change: "Life is as variable as the Euripos."

II *The Poet of the Twentieth Century*

"Finally you are weary of this ancient world" ("Zone") *Alcools* begins, on a line that has become a rallying cry for twentieth-century poets: founders of Surrealism Philippe Soupault, Louis Aragon, and André Breton, for example, repeated the line like a slogan in 1917. One must be modern; and what is most modern? Aviation, of course, flight! Christ who holds the world's altitude record, Christianity, Icarus, Simon Magus, and the immortal phoenix, the latter accompanied as in Tacitus, Lactantius, and Claudian, by all the birds of the world. Not to forget those other immortals, Elijah, Enoch, and Apollonius of Tyana. Even you, Pope Pius

X, you the professed foe of modernism, you who nevertheless blessed our French aviator Beaumont last year in Rome,[9] you are the most modern European! But the supreme flyer of all, the most wondrous, the new Messiah, the "first airplane," is the twentieth century itself:

> . . . changed into a bird this century like Jesus rises in the air
> The devils in the abyss lift their heads to watch it
> They say it's imitating Simon Magus of Judea
> They cry if it knows how to fly (*voler*) let it be named thief (*voleur*)
> Angels hover over the pretty acrobat
> Icarus Enoch Elijah Apollonius of Tyana
> Are floating about the first airplane . . .[10]

It is tragic irony that down below Night has turned into the old enemy again and has cut off the poet's flight:

> You mock yourself and your laughter crackles like hell-fire
> The sparks of your laughter gild the depths of your life
> And sometimes you go look at it close up . . .
>
> Farewell farewell
> Beheaded sun

III   Alcools

Once again in "Zone" the poet-Christ is crucified: Marie Laurencin, who is present as the Virgin, a possessive image, and a beautiful mulatto equivalent to Night,[11] has finally left him for good. But if *Alcools* begins with a love-death, the work is so arranged that it embodies as a whole a new birth: it rises finally like the twentieth century and takes our poet along with it.

In *Alcools* Apollinaire assembles the principal poetic achievements of his life, introduces them by "Zone," and summarizes them by the triumphant "Vendémiaire" in the frame of the present. He breaks away from chronology to establish a *simultaneous unity* of poetic personality and theme as consistent as that of "The Song of the Poorly Beloved," "The Betrothal," or "The Traveler." Except for a section of Rhenish poems and one of prison poems, he has placed after each poem one of a different period (usually) and of a different type (always). Throughout he has spaced the long poems, outnumbered by the short ones, in such a way that two never come together, which he has also done for the majority of the poems written in or about Germany, a group that constitutes a little less than half of the collection. The variety of subject matter, theme, and style is thereby so well balanced that never does one section have ascendancy over another, and the work gives the appearance of containing much more variety than it actually does; how much more limiting a chronological arrangement would have been can be seen by the list on page 18.

It is evident what he is about. With the assiduity of a town planner rather than the overliterary "junk dealer" he was accused of being by unfriendly (and even friendly) critics in 1913, he desires to lend his constructions the greatest horizontal and vertical relief possible within the unity of his enthusiastic—yet ordered— vision of himself, life, and art. Marcel Raymond was seeing the trees for the forest when he remarked that each poem seemed to be written by a different poet and that some of the poems were unfinished (*From Baudelaire to Surrealism*); he should have added that the sum of the poems was the organic myth of a poet.

An examination of the main themes and symbols takes us closer into the heart of that myth. The negative Sun-Night theme of the crepuscular poems before 1908 is now completed and brought to a full cycle by the positive phoenix theme of "The Betrothal," the epigraph of "The Song of the Poorly Beloved," the last stanza of "Twilight," and the dawn of "Vendémiaire." In a countercycle, the beloved's ascension at sunset in "One Evening" is transcended in "The Betrothal" and "The Brazier" and ended in "Zone." The theme of the death of love in autumn remains a strong one, with, however, a new emphasis: in new poems "Marie" and "Hunting Horns," images of reluctant acceptance, of the melancholy enjoyment of dying sounds and passing waves, replace those of sterility and suicide. "Zone" is an exception, of course; but it in turn is balanced by the autumnal victory of "Vendémiaire." Particularly does the eternal, cyclical river become an important symbol of the passing of time and love, replacing the murderous sea in "The Traveler," "Clotilde," "Mirabeau Bridge," "Marie," and "Zone." The poet has become more of a pathetic, fated hero—in spite of what he says in "Hunting Horns"—than a tragic victim. Only in

"Zone" does he sorrowfully set when a bloody sun rises; but this poem with its admiration for its wounded hero and its description of the counterrise of the century serves as an excellent introduction to all the rising and falling themes in *Alcools*, day and night, light and shadow, the joys and grief of a poet-errant: "Joy always came after sorrow" ("Mirabeau Bridge").

Light and shadow form one of the four principal categories of symbols in *Alcools*; the others are liquids, plants and animals, and the human body. All are interdependent and part of the poet's psyche; he writes about shadows, "The sun which makes them somber/With them will disappear" ("Clotilde"), what he writes about himself: "I have given all to the sun/All except my shadow" ("The Betrothal"). Above everything else, fire is primary: Apollinaire, a poet of growth and movement like Shelley, makes the flame the source of all things. In this, he reflects the philosophy of Heraclitus "who saw in fire the symbol of general life, the emblem of the organizing and dissolving force." [12]

After light and fire, liquids are most frequently alluded to in *Alcools*. The poems are enclosed between two generalizations:

And you drink this alcohol burning like your life

I am drunk from having drunk the whole universe

just as they begin and end on the edge of the Seine. The external world of nature is everywhere, with about fifty species of animals taken primarily from literary references,[13] and forty plants and trees, mainly from the poet's own personal observation, knowledge, and love. But there is scarcely a natural phenomenon or object, plant, stone, or animal that is not personified, just as in the animistic view of his philosophy, nature is made up of slumbering gods and demons to be aroused by the poet. The stars, the sun, the sea, and currant bushes bleed; petals are fingernails or eyelids; leaves are hands, prayers, or tears. Hair is flowing water or foaming sea; eyes are oceans, stars, fire, saffron, or gems; hands are sunsets, rivers, leaves, doves, or white birds. And invariably all the symbols of the external universe enter the poet's body and mind, both by his direct relationship with them and by his personal use of them: "Flowers in my eyes turn back to flames/I meditate divinely."

Thus the symbolism of *Alcools* forms itself inevitably into the pantheistic triad, the creation myth, of Apollinaire's esthetics: marvelous external reality unites with inner vision to form a new universe of art. External reality for him is a world of multiple relationships, or, to use Baudelaire's term, *correspondances,* between the symbols of other worlds in this one (the sea, shadow, masks, destiny, dreams, magic, mirrors, legendary plants and animals, legendary and historical characters) and symbols of contemporary reality (rivers, light, houses, streets, cities, countries, clothes, games, the body, the dance, seasons, animate and inanimate nature, contemporary personages). The inner vision is that of the poet as Eros and Christ and Anteros and Antichrist, a wandering god betrothed to Psyche and the Virgin, undergoing the death-birth cycle of love and life in melancholy and joy. Both visions, the inner and the outer, combine like Ixion mating with his vision of reality, and the result is *Alcools,* a balanced, clear-obscure, mysterious-realistic, bittersweet, Dyonisian-Apollonian dance of life, represented by its three major symbols, fire, shadow, and *alcools.* Of all the important verbs in the work, the following six occur with the greatest relative frequency: *sing, dance, look, love, weep,* and *die.*[14] All the imagery ultimately combines in one superior view:

> Actions beautiful days terrible sleeps
> Vegetations Couplings eternal music
> Movements Adorations divine sorrow
> Worlds which resemble each other and us
> I drank you and was not satisfied
>
> But I knew thereafter the taste of the universe
> ("Vendémiaire")

IV *Vintage*

The concluding poem of *Alcools,* "Vendémiaire," serves as epilogue for the collection. A hymn to Paris as the central star in the galaxy of Europe, it raises the Parisian poet to heights from which he can command the panorama of his poetic experience. This experience is first incorporated into the cities and regions of Europe he has known, and then assembled into a summary of his absorption of the universe. "Vendémiaire" is a simultaneous synopsis of his past like "Zone"; unlike the latter, it is a poem of triumph, in which, in one lyrical vision, Apollinaire makes his bid for immortality in semimystical fervor and joy.

As in "The Traveler" and "Zone," he disorders his geographical past to bring it up to the plane of the present. From the ancient cities of Brittany, symbolizing one of his earliest enthusiasms, the mysterious medieval Romances, he leaps to the modern industrial cities with their proletariate vigor, also celebrated in the first poetry. Lyons, which he used to visit periodically as a boy, now enters with its history of religious wars, revolutions, and bloody suppression of the anarchists; it then cedes the spotlight to the cities of Provence with their symbols of sacred and profane love. A lament for his beloved Sicily, which has severely suffered from the earthquake of December 28, 1908, next follows, with a beautiful description of the subsequent flight of the sirens from the Strait of Messina into the unknown. Rome represents another event that profoundly influenced him, the 1905 separation of Church and State; and the songs of the cities end with Coblenz speaking for the Rhineland.

It is significant that most of these regions of Europe describe themselves partly or wholly in religious terms. The church steeples in Brittany and the meeting of the Rhine and the Moselle are pictured as praying hands; the Rhone and the Saône are Lyons' lips uttering divine words; the cities of the Mediterranean are broken Hosts; even the northern manufacturing towns speak of the metallic saints of their sainted factories. Prayers alternate with songs on the September night.

At the end of "Vendémiaire," in a joy reminiscent of that of Whitman or Nietzsche, Apollinaire sums up his main themes, symbols, and ideas. Turning his back on Rome, a spokesman for the anarchist's heroic world of the future, he becomes the prophet of the New City—Paris—in which "God can become" (the phrase is Nietzsche's). This God will be the marvelous god created by man—by the poet. Yet humble religious experiences of other men ("men on their knees on the shore of the sky") form part of his

song on the calm autumn night. The theme of "Vendémiaire"
—the theme of *Alcools*—is the poet's superhuman acceptance of
and transcendency over everything in the universe, from "good
immortal worms" (pun: *vers* = also "verses") to fire "which you
must love as you love yourself." He sings some of his main symbols,
seas, animals, plants, cities, destinies, stars, fire; his main themes:
the past living within him ("All the proud dead united in my
head"); the poet's swim to the stars ("He smiled young swimmer . . ."); and lyrical beauty ("Flowers out of mouths"). He
sings even of the lands on the limits of life ("terrible sleeps") and
those beyond his ken ("All I shall never know"). On the top of
existence, containing all mankind in him, he is a cosmos drunk on
the *alcools* of all contained in himself; he cries,

> Listen to me I am the throat of Paris
> And I'll drink the universe again if I like
>
> Listen to my songs of universal drunkenness

Another world has been added to the universe of art as he finally
turns away:

> And the September night was gradually ending
> The red fires on the bridges were putting
>   themselves out in the Seine
> The stars were dying the day was barely breaking

CHAPTER 5

The New City

Je suis dans le ciel de la cité—La Victoire

I Back to the Crowd, 1913–14

APOLLINAIRE'S word was absolutely committed when he was a young poet in the service of the revolution; it became equally committed when he devoted the last years of his life to serving a revolution in twentieth-century art. *Alcools* began with the ascension; *Calligrammes* ("Calligrams"), its successor, which he published in the last year of his life and in which he included poems written from 1913 to 1918, begins and ends with authoritative plans for the building of the New City viewed from his exalted position.

He had striven toward the City all his life; only, he had changed in the years between 1904 and 1910 from a political revolutionary to an esthetic one. In this sense, "Vendémiaire," which was first conceived in 1909 as part of a Revolutionary calendar,[1] can be viewed as one of his most apocalyptic works. In that year he was a regular contributor to the strongly antiroyalist and anticlerical *Démocratie Sociale* and became even more aware than before that he had arrived at the historical moment of "the death of kings"—announced by the Book of Revelation. In the stanza of "Vendémiaire" in which he calls for the death of Rome's traditional emblems, the she-wolf, eagle, lamb, and dove, he prophesies the arrival of a new crowd of "enemy and cruel kings"—perhaps socialists—to take their place at the Eucharistic table and drink Paris' "twice-millenary wine." [2]

Nevertheless, he retained his mistrust of mass demagoguery which he had seen so dramatically demonstrated by the rampaging anti-Semitic mobs at the time of the Dreyfus affair. As an anarchist he had joyfully anticipated the people's coming; but he had not, for all that, made sympathetic the world-wide lynching of Catholics at the end of *The Glory of the Olive,* and he had even had the massacre denounced by Enoch the bellboy. In 1911 he wrote Gide that the latter's Nietzschean parable in *Pretexts,* that inferior flowers in flower gardens crowd out the superior ones, was "unfortunately true," [3] and he published a story in which a tailor attacked the public for its idolatry of science and its destructive hatred of beauty ("The Former Tailor"—reprinted in *La Table Ronde* of September 1952). "The Former Tailor" reminds one of Baudelaire's parable in which a dog is shown to like excrement and shun fine perfume just like the vulgar crowd; similarly, the end of *The Assassinated Poet,* where Enoch has turned into the divine poet Croniamantal excoriating the crowd for its lynching of *poets,* is reminiscent of Baudelaire's dire predictions of a bourgeois end of the world in *Fusées.*

Apollinaire had reasons for his distrust. After 1908, he had campaigned loudly for esoteric poetry, the novel of fantasy, the philosophy of the Marquis de Sade, and the art of his friends the Fauvists and Cubists. In return, he was attacked for the poetry by the Naturalists; the novel would remain realistic, wrote Billy; the apologies for Sade and others put him in jeopardy with certain authorities; and the new paintings were the laughing-stock of the town. Remarkably, he was only the more convinced of the soundness of his ideas before a growing number of enemies and the public scorn; but one can assume that the anarchistic violence of his Futurist manifesto of 1913, singing *merde* to

> . . . Academisms
> The Siamese twins D'Annunzio and Rostand
> Dante Shakespeare Tolstoy Goethe
> *Merdoyant* dilletantism
> Aeschylus and the theater of Orange
> India Egypt Fiesole and theosophy
> Scientism
> Montaigne Wagner Beethoven Edgar Poe
>   Walt Whitman and Baudelaire

and *rose* to

> Marinetti Picasso Boccioni Apollinaire Paul Fort Mer-
> cereau Max Jacob Carra Delaunay Henri-Matisse Braque, etc.
>   (*L'Antitradition Futuriste*)

was hardly the joke some of his friends took it to be. In *The Assassinated Poet* there is a passage where all the she-wolves of distress are described as waiting outside Picasso's door ready to devour the two friends "in order to prepare in the same place the foundation of the New City" (Chapter 10). It was not his nature to take devouring lying down: he intended to do as much of the tearing down of the old world and the building up of the new as he could himself:

> In short O scoffers you haven't gotten much out of mankind
> And barely have you extracted a bit of fat from its misery
> But we who die from living far from each other
> Let us stretch out our arms and on these rails rolls a long
>   train of merchandise ("The Musician of Saint Merry")

In 1913 he found some new tools for the new construction. He turned his review, the *Soirées de Paris* ("Evenings of Paris"), into a crusading journal in favor of "that motor with every tendency impressionism fauvism pathetism dramatism orphism paroxysme DYNAMISM PLASTICITY WORDS IN LIBERTY INVENTON OF WORDS" which he celebrated in his Futurist manifesto. In it he published the political writings of his anarchist friends René Dalize and Charles Perrès along with articles on science fiction, the American Imagists, Henri Rousseau, Marinetti, Claudel, Dramatism, Futurism, and calligraphic poetry in a valiant attempt to rally the dozens of feuding groups of *avant-garde* artists in Europe around a united front. He began joining organizations for the defense of art and for aid to indigent writers; he gave lectures; he wrote prefaces to catalogues; he brought his articles on modern art up to date in *The Cubist Painters;* and he continued writing apologies in the press for the new painting. As could be expected, his poetry became one of his main weapons, as he stepped up his lifetime trend toward *simultanéisme* and broke up his form and prosody to fit a more dynamic, more popular muse.

His new prosody contrasted markedly with that of *Alcools.* The latter had been primarily traditional, with approximately three-fourths of the lines in regular meter, mostly twelve-syllable Alexandrines (with a certain amount of play in the mute e's however) and octosyllabic lines. Masculine and feminine rhymes alternated regularly for the most part as in the most classical verse of Malherbe, while traditional four- or five-line stanzas with alternate or enclosing rhymes predominated. Rhyming was usually conservative except in some of the regular narrative poems in which striking rhymes were used for comic and exotic effects: in "Palace," "Rosemonde," "The Thief," "The Hermit," "Lul de Faltenin," and the beginning of "The Song of the Poorly Beloved." Chronologically speaking, the freest prosody was in the omniscient and occasional lines of 1908–9 ("The Brazier," "The Betrothal," "Poem Read at the Marriage of André Salmon," and "1909"), written at a time when Apollinaire was celebrating the Symbolists' discovery of free verse (in *Symbolist Poetry*); whereas the musical love lyrics of 1910–12 ("Mirabeau Bridge," "Marie," "Hunting Horns," and, perhaps, "Clotilde") and the prison poems of 1911 returned to the primarily regular prosody of the Rhenish lyrics. This last period, however, did see the beginnings of a new style in which the relaxed prosaic qualities of 1908–9 were magnified horizontally to include the long, undisciplined couplets, the free verse, and the emphasis on content over form of "Cortege," "Vendémiaire," "The Traveler," and "Zone."

Alcools' changes in prosody, then, were rather evolutionary than revolutionary, with one major exception: the Futuristic deletion of punctuation on the eve of publication in 1913. As Apollinaire realized clearly, such a seemingly radical innovation for French poetry actually continued Symbolist syntheticism, bringing the lines closer to each other and to the marvelous that lay between them. Except for minor occasional verses like "Hotels" and "Hyde Park," all his poetry, based as it was on pantheistic ambiguity rising into ultimate unity, profited by the change. Subsequent Dadaist and Surrealist visions of the marvelous profited likewise.

The prosody of the new poems (collected in the first section of *Calligrammes*) was strikingly freer, the freest in Apollinaire's poetry since his first adolescent experiments. Perceiving the need of bringing even more of the twentieth century into his simultaneous vision of it in order better to influence it in return, he adopted a synthetic style, incorporating various techniques of European art and poetry around him: Futurism's telegraphic leaps and shocks and its "SUPPRESSION of the elegy syntax adjectives

punctuation classical prosody plot music typographical harmony . . ." (*The Futurist Antitradition*); the advertising hand-
bills, billboards, and signs that he and Fernand Léger admired,
with their diversity of typography, their calligrammatic forms,
and directness of appeal (see the beginning of "Zone"); Dramatism's antidescriptive, simultaneous choral poetry; Cubism's *col-
lages* and its reconstruction of shattered reality; Orphism's use of
complementary colors to create association by contrast; and his
own old stream-of-consciousness techniques bringing "Ideas, old
gossip, oddments of all things/ Strange spars of knowledge and
dimmed wares of price" to a modern idiom. Meter and rhyme, for
the most part, fell by the wayside.

The subject matter of the modern world became correspondingly more important; the early trolleys, gas lamps, and "roses of
electricity" joined with busses, airplanes, telephones, trains, tele-
graph poles, and the Eiffel Tower, and alternated with distant
legends and historical events. With his friend Blaise Cendrars, for
whose famous poem "Easter in New York" he had provided major
influences,[4] he shattered the Romantic, anecdotic "I"—already ob-
jectified by the "you" (referring to himself) of "The Traveler" and
"Zone"—as he made great leaps between his memories, his immediate experiences, and his imagined experiences of others. Like
the sensuous Futurists (the opposite of the conceptual Cubists),
he made poems in the shape of external subject matter, pleasant
little *calligrammes* of watches, mirrors, flowers, etc., much less
profound, however, than the abstract calligrams of his poem-
conversations. All in all, as he later pointed out to Madeleine, his
new esthetic was a kind of new, simultaneous *impressionism* (letter of July 1, 1915). It constituted a new *realism* for the future to
build upon:

And to renew inspiration, to make it fresher and more orphic, I
think that the poet will have to refer back to nature, to life. If he should
limit himself even to noting undidactically the mystery he sees and
hears, he would become habituated to life itself like nineteenth-century
realists who thus raised their art very high, and the decadence of the
novel came at the very moment when the writers ceased observing external reality which is the very orphism of art (*Soirées de Paris*, 1914).

His favorite illustration of his new esthetic was "The Windows"
(*Calligrammes*). In this poem, apparently unrelated elements of
reality are brought together like *papiers collés* and deftly shaped
into a new reality, a new unity. A basic structure of lyrical evocation of Robert Delaunay's orphic paintings "Windows" (the poem
served as a catalogue to a Delaunay exposition)

> From red to green all yellow dies
>
> . . . .
> You will lift up the curtain
> And now the window is opening
> Spiders when hands were weaving light
> Beauty pallor unfathomable violets
>
> . . . .
> The window opens like an orange
> The beautiful fruit of light

looking out upon his famous Eiffel Towers ("Tours/Towers are
streets") and the rest of the world ("sparkling diamond
Vancouver"), serves as a framework for snatches of real or imagined conversation in a café, a sun setting in the Mediterranean, an
enumeration of objects in a room, and some arbitrary associations
culled among friends. As in Delaunay's Pointillist-inspired spec-
trum-smashing, he proceeds by a technique of association by
opposites to encompass as much as possible in his airy view. His
old fatal rhythm of art moving between the individual and the
world, adventure and order, surprise and inevitability, and creation and death, becomes extremely overt as he takes leaps in time
and space from the jungle to the telephone and from the Antilles
to Vancouver in a cosmopolitan, very simplified stream of consciousness. Red and green, night and day, ancient and modern,
tower, street, and well, "Paris Vancouver Hyères Maintenon and
the Antilles" find their unity in their variety when shaped by art.

What has happened to Apollinaire's myth of himself? This poetry's extreme externalization, tending away from chronological
and narrative progression, inevitably weakens the role of the poet-
creator, while it makes the ubiquitous poet-wanderer all the more
omnipresent. Yet even though Apollinaire became for the moment
more of an observer and a builder than a flaming demiurge, he

could still find a prototype for Christ and Ixion in a dancing harlequin child on a sidewalk of Paris ("A Phantom of Clouds"). He was still the superior artist:

> Rails lashing nations together
> We are only two or three men
> Free of all ties
> Let us hold hands ("Ties")

He could still ascend: "We are going higher now and are not touching any more the ground" ("The Musician of Saint Merry"). But he suggested that the artist could transmit his Ixion-like vision to the crowd:

> . . . every spectator was seeking in himself the miraculous child
> Century O century of clouds ("A Phantom of Clouds")[5]

II *The New Painters, 1908–1918*

We have seen that Apollinaire's general theories of painting were essentially the same Symbolist ones that he applied to poetry; yet his close acquaintance with the actual creations of the young painters resulted in a large body of impressionistic criticism concerning more individual efforts. Largely reportorial and sometimes distorted by overconceptual considerations, this criticism was also often extremely perceptive, revealing an acute sensitivity to anything esthetic and an amazing range of taste on the part of the observer. Not surprisingly, he used the word "poetic" to describe aspects of painting not covered by the Cubist experiments, Matisse's colors, Metzinger's subject matter, Willette's gay caricatures, Roussel's myths, the minutiae of the primitives, and the painting of José-Maria Sert, the painter who did not "keep himself from having a poetic imagination" (he added, almost wistfully, "that's rare in our time".[6] Throughout his life his own drawings and doodles owed much to Gustave Moreau, and his taste for literary art combined with his interest in everything from artificial flowers and nudes to Chinese watercolors and religious subjects to produce an eclectic, sometimes irresponsible, and often satirical body of jottings which sometimes sound like Baudelaire's art criticism:

At the Library circle "The Salon of Mountain Painters" has opened. This exhibition shows that mountain climbing is a sport and not an art. (*Chroniques,* March 14, 1910).

M. Cachoud loves night and proves it by exhibiting a great number of nocturnal paintings at the Georges Petit gallery. "They make you dream," says the catalogue. Pleasant locution for "they put you to sleep." (*Chroniques,* May 7, 1910).

. . . The lunar nights of M. Cachoud take on importance as soon as one discovers that the painter is, like Henri Matisse, a student of Gustave Moreau. (*Chroniques,* April 29, 1913).

Indeed, one of the main tenets of his credo was the artist's freedom from systems, a fact which above all else explains his ambivalent attitude toward Cubist paintings; in the catalogue of the first all-Cubist exhibition at Brussels in June 1911, in which he accepted the designation *Cubism* on behalf of his friends, he summed up, "I think I have given in a few words the true sense of Cubism: a new and very elevated manifestation of art but not at all a system constraining talents." (*Chroniques*).

The following panorama of Apollinaire's opinions on individual Cubists, Orphists, Fauvists, and Independents, therefore, requires a certain relativity of judgment on the part of the reader. One must bear in mind that at the time of the criticism, Apollinaire was attempting to preserve his esthetic integrity while at the same time further the (French) cause of the new art, inculcate more poetry and higher standards upon it, keep his Philistine readers informed and unsuspicious (he was often writing for the Enemy, particularly in the *Intransigeant,* where grudging praise was a better weapon than unqualified enthusiasm), and walk the tightrope of support for certain talents over the savage jungle of *avant-garde* partisanship.

Pablo Picasso.—It is significant that after the lyrical article of May 1905 about the blue and rose periods (see above, Chapter 3) Apollinaire only rarely referred to specific later works of Picasso; and he never mentioned "The Demoiselles of Avignon." In his summaries of the painter's output after that date, the most notable of which is the 1912 continuation of the first article in *The Cubist Painters,* there is a noticeable diminution of enthusiasm. The

tone is one of full confidence in Picasso's genius, in his absorption
with reason, art, symmetry, and proportion, and in his ability to
produce divine masterpieces in the future; but Apollinaire finds
no single works to wax enthusiastic over other than the sculpture
"Head of a Woman" and the décor for Cocteau's *Parade* in 1917.
The curtain of *Parade* is mentioned in the calligram "Pablo Picasso" (*Il y a*); but almost the entirety of that mystical word-
painting on Picasso's work is based on the blue and rose periods!
In "From Michelangelo to Picasso" (1912), *The Assassinated Poet*
(1916), and *The Seated Woman* (1918), Picasso is always evoked
as the author of the pre-Cubist canvases, "the painter with the celestial blue hands." The great influence he exerted on Apollinaire
after 1906 and before 1917—when his temporary return to a classical conception of the human figure coincided with the classicism
of the *new spirit*[7]—must be measured in terms of his personality,
his methods, and his goals rather than in terms of concrete realiza-
tions of those things. As Apollinaire's world was at once materialistic, religious, and anarchistic, both ordered and hazardous, he
felt a close spiritual kinship with an art he believed to have derived from the Hellenic purity and truth, the Spanish realism, and
the mysterious, angelic violence characteristic of the art of El
Greco, the Greek painter of Toledo (*The Seated Woman*). He
also believed that Picasso was attuned to the erotic mysticism of
Saint Teresa de Avila (*Chroniques*, April 1905). From "The Betrothal" to "The Hills" the impact of an elementary, omniscient,
constantly renewed and renewing art can be felt in Apollinaire's
works; but the greatest manifestations of that art were always
those lonely phantom figures on the confines of humanity of the
early paintings.

Picasso undoubtedly also influenced a negative aspect of Apollinaire's writings: his erotic misogyny. When in 1912 the poet said
of an anonymous pornographic work, the *Zoppino*, "These almost
macabre details, these nauseating descriptions, . . . these bi-
zarre, appalling, even apocalyptic metaphors, indicate, in my
opinion, a Spanish author" (*The Amorous Devils*, "Delicado"),
he not only indirectly described certain passages of his own
Eleven Thousand Rods, but suggested the psychology which lay
behind many of Picasso's ideas. Picasso was portrayed in *The
Seated Woman* as a lecherous faun "who with women only knew

violence and who despised them" (Chapter 8); and according to several of his friends, he considered *The Eleven Thousand Rods* Apollinaire's greatest work. The evolution of his life and work since the poet's death bears out this portrait. His one published play is remarkable for its nihilistic scatology; and perhaps no major artist since Bosch and the medieval painters of the seven deadly sins has been so obsessed with virility symbols, cruelty, and the masochistic destruction of the female form. If Apollinaire had lived, he would probably have been dismayed at Picasso's failure (with some notable exceptions, like "The Mirror" and "Guernica") to impose on the world the creative side of his vision, and at the extraordinary success of his destructive side; and he would still have regarded the Symbolist works that he held up for thirteen years as masterpieces of world painting as his best ones.

Georges Braque.—The lyrical and exact summary of Braque's art in the catalogue to his exhibition of early Cubist paintings of 1908, in which Apollinaire spoke of his natural purity, civilized innocence, harmony, and angelic qualities—while regretting the rarity of his more colored Fauvist canvases—was followed by no major criticism concerning this painter until 1913 and *The Cubist Painters.* In a letter to Soffici of December 8, 1911, he omitted Braque from his list of those whom he considered to be the five leading young painters of the time: Derain, Dufy, Laurencin, Matisse, and Picasso (in alphabetical order).[8] In *The Cubist Painters* he commended the former sign painter's use of elements taken from his trade and from his age, his good sense, and his ability to verify all the novelties—and trivialities—of modern art. After 1913 he came increasingly to regard the man he had introduced to Picasso in 1907 as one of the first revolutionists, along with Derain and Picasso, of Cubism. Yet his praise remained faint and general until 1916, when he wrote that Braque and Picasso knew more what they were doing than other Cubists. In 1917, he sang his praises as a war hero.

Juan Gris.—The approximation of Gris' work in *The Cubist Painters* is blurred by a quarrel the author had with the Spanish painter while the work was in preparation—at least according to art-seller Henri Kahnweiler.[9] It is true the section on Gris is not remarkable for its enthusiasm. Veiling his words with metaphor and some praise, he criticizes him for his symbolic use of color, lack of unity and newness, materialistic purity, and above all his preoccupation with logic and knowledge rather than beauty. One of Gris' best-known works, a portrait of Picasso ("Homage to Picasso") he had praised earlier for its effort and disinterestedness (March 25, 1912). The poet was sincerely hurt in 1917 when Gris joined Metzinger in a manifesto against *The Breasts of Tiresias,* and he wrote to Pierre Reverdy that he would remain with the great painters of Cubism (among whom he included Braque) and leave the others.[10]

Jean Metzinger.—The sterile intellectualism he found in Gris cast a shadow on Metzinger's work for Apollinaire, although he undoubtedly owed some of his ideas about Cubism to this gifted theorist of the movement. The overexperimentation, rigorous logic, discipline, and conceptual problem-solving of his painting, however, did not exclude the lyricism of his subject matter which Apollinaire found to be its most attractive aspect and which caused him to compare him to Ingres for his grace and poetry. Of all Metzinger's works—which included a 1910 portrait of Apollinaire, the first Cubist portrait—he was most enthusiastic about "Sea Port" ("in which one sees nothing from our new painters"), the fairy-like "Blue Bird" (1913), and "Woman With a Parasol" (1913). Of the latter he wrote:

If one appreciates the beauty of the matter, the variety of the forms, the suppleness of the lines, and the fantasy of the composition, one cannot consider this delicious canvas with indifference. (*Il y a*).

Albert Gleizes.—Gleizes was the only major Cubist about whose works Apollinaire's enthusiasm was unqualified. More interested in color and subject matter (like Metzinger) than Braque and Picasso, he created pictures with "that somewhat clumsy side of great works" (in contrast to Metzinger's perfect logic) and raised his subject matter to brutal, vigorous, and *dramatic* heights of esthetic emotion (Gleizes, like Apollinaire, belonged for a time to Jean Barzun's movement Dramatism). In his works, the greatest individuality was united with the greatest generalization (*The Cubist Painters*). Regarding individual paintings, Apollinaire remarked that his "Portrait of Jacques Nayral" (1911) was a perfect likeness, even though all the forms and colors were invented by the artist; he said of his "Soccer Players" (1913) that it was constructed by a master (he added, "subject has come back into painting and I am not a little proud of having foreseen the return of what constitutes the very basis of pictorial art"); and he called the "insolent fantasy" in the "Portrait of Figuière (1913) "a marvelous manifestation of robust and healthy joy" (*Chroniques*).

Marie Laurencin.—Apollinaire's classification of Marie Laurencin among the scientific Cubists in *The Cubist Painters* indicates to what extent his ideas on Cubism actually applied to all art. In theory, Marie rearranged nature according to inner reality and conceptual knowledge, her art was not imitative and did not descend to "the baseness of perspective," her arabesques were pure music, and she had the French Renaissance qualities of grace, order, harmony, Hellenism, and delicacy, which her lover had praised in the Cubists as part of the French tradition. All of these qualities except the first, however, were also found in the decorative arts. He named a few (lacework, embroidery, etc.); and in the discussion of the personal qualities of her art, he demonstrated that, although it owed much to the Cubists and Picasso (simplification toward the abstract, esthetic reconstruction of nature), it constituted a kind of arboreal, serpentine dance closer to Orphism in its spontaneity, poetry, and movement. He could have added that two of her favorite colors were Picasso's blue and rose. She was both Salome, he said, dancing between Saint John Picasso and Herod Rousseau, and Our Lady of Cubism ("Hail Marie full of grace"). Her paintings explored the second, all-feminine eternity of the universe.

Fernand Léger.—Discussing Léger's entries at the Independents Salon in 1911, Apollinaire called the painting inhuman and difficult, but heralded its increasing discipline and originality (April 21). At the Independents a year later, discussing "Composition with Personages," which he called a work of pure art without any subject, he cited the artist's talent but added, "We can fear . . . that the vein of this artist if it is not nourished by a thought, may soon dry up" (March 20). By the time of the publication of *The Cubist Painters* his friendship with Léger and his interest in the colored, rhythmed canvases of Picabia, Duchamp, and Delaunay and the rhythms of the machine age caused him to devote one of the most poetic essays of the work to this artist in whom he discerned the instincts of modern civilization. He imaginatively described several of Léger's paintings in this essay, including "Nudes in the Forest" (the one he had found difficult in 1910), "Smokers," "Smoke," "The Roofs of Paris," and "The Party." [11] Yet Léger's suspicion that "Apollinaire never liked my painting no matter what he wrote" [12] is borne out by a letter to Soffici from the same period in which Apollinaire called his work feeble, mushy, and transitory, and compared it unfavorably to that of Picabia and Duchamp. [13] Nevertheless, he was entirely in accord with Léger's thoughts on the esthetic value of billboards and poster art and the necessity for a new realism; and much later, in the summer of 1918, he included him with Matisse, Picasso, Marquet, Derain, and Vlaminck in a list of the most remarkable representatives of the new painting (*Chroniques*).

Francis Picabia.—The essay on Picabia in *The Cubist Painters* reveals both the fruit of Apollinaire's long discussions with the artist in the summer of 1912 and a certain confusion about what constitutes subject and form in his paintings. Color and form are equated by the Orphists, says Apollinaire; but Picabia gives a symbolic connotation to his form-color without granting it a personal existence. In other words, the painter is searching for an art like music that would be dehumanized beyond even its subject matter—detached even from the artist—with no other aim than sensuous pleasure. Yet he states categorically, "It is not a question of abstraction" (he later described Picabia's works as becoming more concrete!—*Il y a*). Without mentioning decorative art but with a premonition of some of the more sterile byways of abstract art, he warns, "as a painter of pictures I advise him to take up frankly subject (poetry) which is the essence of the plastic arts." Elsewhere he praised several of Picabia's paintings, including "Edtaonisl," "Udnie," and "Dance" (March 1914), and saw him as a major influence on Marcel Duchamp and Jacques Villon.

Marcel Duchamp.—In an astonishing preview of the goals of Dada and Surrealism, Apollinaire suggests in his discussion of the art of his chess-playing friend that an artist might reproduce irrational elements in nature that do not require esthetic arrangement for their moving qualities; these elements would pass beyond beauty into regions of pure force, power, and energy. An art containing them could depart from the esthetic, higher domain of the artist for the domain of society, thus reconciling art and the people; and Apollinaire (or Duchamp speaking through him) already describes the "ready-made":

Just as a work of Cimabue was paraded about, our century has seen Blériot's airplane, laden with humanity, millenary efforts, and necessary art, escorted in triumph to the Arts and Crafts Museum.

These conjectures only found a place in Apollinaire's esthetic through his discussion of Duchamp's painting, however; it was not until 1917 that he suggested the possibility of important Surrealist worlds through and beyond art for himself.

Robert Delaunay.—In 1910, Apollinaire was unimpressed by the prismatic works of the leader of the movement he was later to christen and elevate higher than the others; at that time he referred to "extravagances . . . solidly painted canvases which unfortunately look as if they were beginning an earthquake" (March 17). At the time of the Independents two years later, however, he had no hesitation in selecting Delaunay's quaking work "The City of Paris" over all the others, which included entries by Gleizes, Metzinger, Léger, Laurencin, Duchamp, Gris, and Chagall; he termed it the most important of the exhibition, a work that transcended archaism and Cubism by being a summary of all painting since the Italians (March 20, 1912). After omitting Delaunay from *The Cubist Painters* in order to devote a special work to him later, by the end of 1912 he had become his principal apologist, describing his discoveries and printing his Orphist theories, some of which reflected his own, in *Les Soirées de Paris* and *Der Sturm*. He traveled to Berlin with him to lecture at the opening of his exhibition there in January 1913. The effect of Delaunay's paintings upon him is illustrated by the two poems "Windows" and "Tower" in *Calligrammes*. The two men quarreled in 1914 (Apollinaire in a typical attempt at synthesis incautiously called one of Delaunay's paintings Futuristic), and they were subsequently parted by the war; they did not see each other again.[14]

Henri Matisse.—Following the article of December 1907 in the *Phalange* in which he discussed Matisse's reasoned disciplining of instinct and his individual pursuit of beauty within himself, Apollinaire had nothing but praise the rest of his life for "the beautiful painter" whom he had been one of the first to defend against the attacks of the Philistines. In his paintings he could find the genius for design, order, and composition that he admired in Cubism, plus the bold color, sensuousness, charm, sureness of instinct, and moral health (lack of mysticism) which attracted him in Orphism. He thus regretted that Matisse's influence on young painters was not as great as Picasso's (*Chroniques,* March 20, 1912). Here was an artist who by careful reconstruction of nature into a higher reality actually created works agreeable to the eyes; and Apollinaire was especially enthusiastic over two brilliantly colored portraits, "Woman With a Hat" and "Madame Matisse" (*Il y a*).

André Derain.—Apollinaire worked with Derain in 1909 when the painter illustrated *The Putrescent Enchanter* with woodcuts, illustrations which, as Apollinaire correctly remarked later, contributed greatly to a twentieth-century renaissance of that difficult medium. It is quite possible that Apollinaire got the idea for the woodcuts from the famous *Dream of Poliphilus* of the sixteenth century. During the period of the flowering of Cubism Derain was involved with mysterious solitary experimentation, so that Apollinaire, although he like André Salmon placed him with Matisse and Picasso as one of the three masters of modern art, felt that he could not include him in *The Cubist Painters.* He said that he would come back to him some day: "It would be too difficult to write well concerning a man who voluntarily keeps himself apart from everything and everyone" The opportunity for this return did not present itself until four years later—after his war service—when he wrote the catalogue preface for Derain's first one-man show (October 1916). In this preface he spoke of qualities in Derain's painting which were also characteristic of his own esthetic at the time: audacity balanced by order, measure, simplicity, realism, and almost religious sublimity. Only was Derain's "disinterestedness" absent from his *new spirit* (*Chroniques*).

Maurice Vlaminck.—Apollinaire consistently praised the work of this Fauvist for its force, blazing azures, and joy. Historically, he saw him as the man who had introduced Derain to African sculpture, a step momentous in consequence for modern art, since Derain in turn brought a taste for fetishes to Matisse and Picasso and thus helped give the new movement its bent toward religious primitivism (see *Chroniques,* October 14, 1912).

[122]

Kees Van Dongen.—Before and during his adherence to the Cubist movement, Apollinaire disliked the work of few artists more than that of the Flemish Fauvist and society painter, Kees Van Dongen. At the Independents in 1910 he saw in his canvases "a vulgarity that the artist is trying to transform into brutality" (March 17); at the time of the Autumn Salon of the same year he wrote, "M. Van Dongen is making progress in banality" (October 1); and by 1913 he was remarking that there were signs on Paris walls that were better than his paintings (February 6). Occasionally he found Van Dongen's sensual art superficially agreeable, however; and in a review for Paul Guillaume's commercial art magazine, *Les Arts à Paris,* in 1918, he deliberately turned his back on "the austere ardor of the contemporary arts" to praise Van Dongen's colors, orientalism, and his Baudelairean "luxury, calm, and voluptuousness" (*Il y a*).

Raoul Dufy.—Apollinaire referred to some paintings by Dufy as well-constructed in 1910 (March 17) and described his woodcuts for *The Bestiary* the same year (December 28). He always considered him an important, if unappreciated artist, and in notes of 1914 placed him in a position midway between the charming but unimportant primitives and Cézanne (*Il y a*). Yet he deplored the influence of his illustrative tendencies on Cubism (May 3, May 5, 1914).

Henri Rousseau.—Apollinaire first began to consider the master of Plaisance as a serious painter in the spring of 1908 at the Independents—and found him wanting. While appreciating his innocent, natural qualities, he damned his lack of culture, his tranquillity, his lack of direction, and the arbitrary and even ridiculous side of his painting (May). Shortly thereafter he became a close friend of the artist, attended his parties, wrote him a recommendation for a prospective father-in-law, posed for two remarkable portraits, exchanged letters with him, and finally, after his death in 1910, became one of the principal disseminators of his legend in the pages of the *Intransigeant,* the *Mercure de France,* and the *Soirées de Paris.* He thus came to realize that the very qualities which destroyed an extremely individual art on a plane of esthetic theory were those in which its greatness lay, and he transformed all the general vices into personal virtues. Still lamenting the fact that Rousseau lacked an education in esthetics and still considering him excessively sentimental and childish, he praised his work for its poetic elements, the charm, purity, and exoticism of its imagination, the systematic variety and delicacy of its detail. Through his association with painters, moreover, he discovered that Rousseau's art contained more of the master's techniques than he had originally thought. Citing Gauguin's statement about his inimitable blacks, he also found that the paintings had a definite science and style and were ordered into finished, harmonious compositions. He finally did not hesitate to place the humble Douanier among the great figures of French art, Poussin, Delacroix, Manet, Seurat, Cézanne, and Renoir. The paintings which seem to have pleased him most were "The Dream," "The Snake Charmer," and—after an initial negative reaction—the portraits of himself. He composed the epitaph for Rousseau's tombstone (engraved by Brancusi and Ortis de Zarate), put him in his poem "Tree," and wrote a tender elegy in memory of his friend:

> A tiny bird
> On an angel they go
> Singing the praise
> Of the gentle Rousseau
> ("In Memory of the Douanier")

Marc Chagall.—It is not known precisely when Chagall invited Apollinaire to his room at *La Ruche* where the scene took place described by Chagall in his autobiography during which the poet pronounced the word "supernaturalism" (*surnaturalisme*) and praised the colors of the mysterious paintings. Apollinaire said later that he encouraged the Russian painter in 1912; and he introduced him to Walden, the editor of *Sturm,* who arranged the first exhibition of his works in Berlin in the spring of 1914. The catalogue was prefaced by Apollinaire's poem "Rotsoge" ("Crossing Europe" in *Calligrammes*) which includes *La Ruche* (the "round house" of line 2) as well as the herring, calf, and aerial view typical of the paintings. About this time Apollinaire wrote: "Chagall is a talented colorist who lets himself go to everything his mystic, pagan imagination suggests; his art is very sensual" (*Il y a*). He also liked the popular side of his imagination, full of fantasy, folklore, and Jewish culture. He most admired his "Paris Seen From a Window" (1914).

Giorgio de Chirico.—Apollinaire rarely spoke at length of the Italian precursor of the Surrealists who frequented his apartment in 1912 and who painted the prophetic "target-portrait" in 1914 (a circle marked the place where he would be wounded [15]), but he never understimated the force and poetry of his strange plastic enigmas. He believed he was the only modern painter of stature not to be influenced by the French school. It is possible that he influenced him himself, as Chirico's Ariadnes and faceless dummies of 1913–14 may have been inspired by the faceless piper and his train of Ariadnes in "The Musician of Saint Merry."

Wassily Kandinsky.—Apollinaire disapproved of Kandinsky's abstraction and lack of order and measure at the Independents of 1912:

Kandinsky is exhibiting some improvisations which are not without interest, for they are almost the only paintings to represent the influence of Matisse. But Kandinsky carries to an extreme Matisse's theory on obedience to instinct and now obeys only chance (March 25).

He began to admire his paintings a year later (after getting to know Delaunay) and came to his defense when he was viciously attacked by a German critic (March 1913).

Max Ernst.—In 1914, Apollinaire mentioned Ernst, "a Rhenish expressionist," in passing (*Paris Journal,* May 20).

III *The New Woman, 1898–1918*

1 And there appeared a great wonder in heaven; a woman clothed with the sun, and the moon under her feet, and upon her head a crown of twelve stars:
2 And she being with child cried, travailing in birth, and pained to be delivered . . .
5 And she brought forth a man child, who was to rule all nations with a rod of iron: and her child was caught up unto God, and to his throne . . .
7 And there was war in heaven: Michael and his angels fought against the dragon; and the dragon fought and his angels . . .
13 And when the dragon saw that he was cast unto the earth, he persecuted the woman which brought forth the man child.
14 And to the woman were given two wings of a great eagle, that she might fly into the wilderness, into her place . . . (Revelation 12)

The Marquis de Sade, the freest spirit that has lived until now, had special ideas on woman, wanting her to be as free as man. These ideas, which will be brought out one day produced a double novel: *Justine* and *Juliette*. It was not by chance that the marquis chose heroines instead of heroes. Justine represents woman of the past, subservient, miserable, and less than human; Juliette, on the contrary, represents his perception of the new woman, a being of whom we have as yet no idea, who is detaching herself from humanity, who will have wings, and who will renew the universe.

(*The Amorous Devils*, "The Marquis de Sade")

Who or what was Apollinaire's New Woman? And what role would she play in the creation of the millennium of art? The answers to these questions lead to the core of the poet's thought, his hopes for an externalization of Psyche and Hera, Cybele and Isis, Aphrodite and the Madonna, Lilith, Eve, Helen, Salome, and Rosamond, in a female spirit of the universe, the panther to his Pan (see his "Second Secret Poem" to Madeleine), the essential second member of his erotic trinity.

In "Tree" (1913) he noted "the Mole-Ariadne," a curious expression possibly derived from the Ariadnes in Symbolist literature and from Rémy de Gourmont's well-known description (translated by Ezra Pound) of the female mole's annual labyrinthine flight through a subterranean palace to elude the amorous male. In 1913, Ariadne was no Juliette: Apollinaire, suffering from the flight of love, pictured her in another poem following a Pan-like flutist into the stars as a member of a new flock of sphinxes ("The Musician of Saint Merry"). But at this point the symbols become jumbled. *Dionysos* was the god who led Ariadne astray according to legend; Apollinaire followed Pan's flute himself in "The Brazier"; and he wrote the flute music himself in "The Musician." In the latter poem, moreover, the flutist was also a sort of Thanatos, a "passer of the dead," amid millions of flies and stinging females; this image reminds us of a line, "I am awaiting the passage of Thanatos and his flock," from an early poem about the death of love, "The Beggar." To unravel this tangled skein of symbols, let us embark on our own labyrinthine pursuit, following Eros and his twin brother in turn through the sunlit or twilight streets of a few of Apollinaire's prose works and plays, in a search for *Her*, the Unknown, the goddess he pursued all his life.

These works are *The Putrescent Enchanter* (1904–11), *The Breasts of Tiresias* (1903–17), *Onirocritique* (1908), prefaces to erotic classics (1909–13), *The Seated Woman* (1918), and *The Color of the Weather* (*Couleur du temps*, 1918). Two things can be affirmed at the outset: Apollinaire's mother, as Mary, Eve, and Lilith, profoundly influenced his pursuit of a feminine ideal; and this ideal varied with the varying stages of the birth-death cycles of his loves for Annie (1901–4), Marie (1907–13), Lou (1914–15), Madeleine (1915–16), and Jacqueline (1917–18).

Before Annie Playden's departure to America and Apollinaire's first entombment as Merlin in 1904, he had recorded his earliest ideas on eroticism in a number of poems of would-be seduction and involuntary frustration. Obviously counting on profiting by his materialistic anarchism and ideas of free love, he had oscillated between the classical "Don't you know we are dying?" and the "I'll make you immortal!" themes, both tempered by a poetic, fin-de-siècle pleasure in watching his rosebuds wither and his princesses sail away. In a good adolescent tradition, onanism and masochism were everywhere, with, however, suprisingly little guilt; his revolutionary beliefs in feminism, sexual freedom, the sainted working girl, anti-malthusianism, and Helen, the fecund muse of liberty, having been enough to justify his erotic desires:

In the century to come strong men and women
We shall fight without masters far from the dead cities ("The Poets")

When a hero calls you by name all men stand up
Helen O liberty O revolutions ("Helen")

By 1904 the revolution was stale, love was dead, and the sexes, said Rémy de Gourmont in a book that was Apollinaire's bible, were never farther apart—an inevitable condition, he added, of a superior civilization ("Let us dream, if it is permitted to dream, of multiplicity rather than unity"—*Épilogues*). Gourmont had elaborated on this idea in his *Physiology of Love* of the year before, a book that was one of the first comparative studies of animal sexuality, and was another work admired by Apollinaire. Primarily influenced by Émile Fabre's entomological volumes, its main thesis is, "We are animals . . . and when we make love, it is definitely what the theologians call *more bestiarum*." All sexual tastes, all so-called perversions and cruelties, said Gourmont, are in nature: "In love, all is true, all is just, all is noble the moment it is a matter of play inspired by the procreative urge." Dimorphism, based on sexual differences, is the rule of life; the reproducing female is the important member of the couple, and the female of the human species is no exception—although physically and mentally she is inferior to her partner. For civilization to persist, dimorphism is essential: "The sole aim of the couple is to free woman of all care that is not purely sexual, to permit her a more perfect accomplishment of her most important function." In society, her most important function is to attract the male. Thus she is beautiful; her arms are sexual attributes, whereas man's are only tools.

I deduce from several passages in *The Putrescent Enchanter*, especially those concerning Lesbian flies, bats, and dragonflies, that Apollinaire knew well *Physiology of Love* when he wrote his novel. He gives us a key to the manner in which the book—and his short stories—should be analyzed in the following revealing passage from a letter to Madeleine:

. . . I read today the news of the death of the entomologist Fabre whose books I used to enjoy tremendously for his studies on insects taught me to know men and if I had the leisure for it I should like them to be studied in my romanesque work as minutely as precisely and as amorally. . . . But I occasionally used to amuse myself by changing in Fabre's pages the names of insects into names of men and women, which gives those pages a terrifying aspect of overly real humanity *à la Marquis de Sade*. . . . (October 14, 1915).

This behavioristic view of human nature is combined by both Apollinaire and Gourmont with Nietzsche's dichotomy of Ariadne and Dionysos, the passive and active, female and male poles of the universe.

In the last chapter of *The Putrescent Enchanter*, man is characterized as an active idealist, bestial and aspiring; he is a drift of pigs with its swineherd who is either earthbound reaching for the sun, or walking on the sky longing for the earth—and turning his back on it; he is consciously creative, "a field with its harvester." Woman is the opposite, an unconscious, passive realist who expresses herself either as aimless beauty ("useless spring") or turmoil, "the restless ocean, blood shed." Her best prediction is child-birth. Viviane, the Lady of the Lake and Merlin's *femme fatale,* reveals herself to be neither the phantom of Rémy de Gourmont's earlier Decadent works nor the enchantress of legend, neither Psyche nor Medea, but an ordinary woman. She is merely *organically* different from the male and thus inaccessible to her lover. "We are at a distance," she says, "but at a distance before and behind so that man is in the center of our remoteness, he prefers to try to grasp us in order to make love." Solomon and Socrates, summoned to confer the aggregate of man's wisdom in matters of love, can speak only in terms of carnal satisfaction, heterosexual and homosexual. Viviane at heart detests men and admires the female consort of Lilith, the Lesbian dragonfly. Ideal love is dead: "Circe came . . . into the forest the evening of the death of the enchanter" (version of 1904). In spite of their protestations, Merlin and the Lady of the Lake are surrounded by copulating animals. The opening question of the book, "What will become of my heart among those who love one another?" becomes a cosmic irony of fate.

Then how and why, Merlin asks, did a woman enchant and bury him? Viviane remains silent (she speaks, but is censored by the author, in the 1904 version). Merlin has not been able to get her with child. Her dancing, her fertility, and the creative blossoming of spring come to an end at the end of the book amid scenes of Lesbianism and menstruation.

If the impotence and hopelessness of romantic love is the subject of *The Putrescent Enchanter,* conjugal fecundity and the re-population of France are advocated in *The Breasts of Tiresias* (*Les Mamelles de Tirésias*). This dramatic farce was first sketched out in 1903, at a time when France's underpopulation was much discussed by intellectuals. It was natural that the illegitimate Apollinaire should have been interested in marriage and children; he asked each of his loves to marry him, with the possible exception of Lou. What were less obvious were the reasons for his obsession with repopulation. Some critics and friends have considered *The Breasts'* propaganda a Jarryesque joke not to be taken seriously. Let us look at the record.

The anarchist poems had forecast post-revolutionary fecundity. In 1901, the year Apollinaire asked Molina da Silva for his daugh-

ter Linda's hand, his hero of *What to do?* criticized duels for "de-
populating instead of repopulating." The next year he heard Isaac
Laquedem maintain that the sole beauty of women was a pregnant appearance ("The Passerby of Prague"), and he himself
praised the fecund beauty of German girls ("The Rose of Hildesheim," 1902 version). In "The Thief," the pagans admitted being
moved by pregnancies and used them to attack the Christian doctrine of aseity. In *The Heresiarch and Company,* Gaetan Gorene
overcame the sterility of his wife by the grace of science and the
. . . of his priest ("A Monster of Lyons"); the ubiquitous Dormesan conceived three children of his mistress while she was in
Paris and he in Chicago, Jerusalem, and Melbourne; and Pertinex
Restif, the incestuous ragpicker of "The History of a Virtuous
Family, a Basket, and a Gallstone," got his sister pregnant with "a
beautiful pearl" for a belly. In 1906, the young Don Juan impreg-
nated his two sisters, his aunt, and a peasant girl, accomplishing
thereby his "patriotic duty, that of increasing the population of
my country." In *The Assassinated Poet,* Croniamantal's mother
preached that the duty of women was to have children and listened to a Vatican priest tell her that France was being depopulated by anticlericalism ("yes, *baronnesse,* it is proved"). She also
went to a naturalistic play whose plot concerned a woman without ovaries who became pregnant thanks to love and surgery. Farther on in the same book there was the recipe for an antihygienic
powder for having many children to be spread on bedsheets. In
1915, during the war, Apollinaire was proud of his cat giving a
good example of repopulation, praised his fiancée's large family,
and planned to have many children by her ("nothing is more prolific than Polish blood"). In the *Mercure de France* he seriously
counseled a policy of giving the military salute to pregnant
women. He had at least one book on determining the sex of children in his library. And finally, he wrote throughout his life a
novel about a decadent European Lesbian who emigrated to Salt
Lake City as a Mormon convert, a woman whose sterility and
dilettantism he contrasted to the magnificent fecundity of the
Mormon women:

. . . Like swelling rivers, the women were flowing in from every
street, and now everywhere they looked the emigrants saw nothing but

women, and almost all of them were pregnant. . . . And, little by little,
there were so many pregnant women that there appeared to be nothing
in Union Square but their enormous bellies moving like the little waves
of a lake on which little heads made ugly with childbearing were floating like corks.

(The Seated Woman).

"I claim that the farcical (and Surrealistic) drama of Monsieur
Apollinaire is whether he will it or no, a polemical work (*une
pièce à thèse*)," wrote a reviewer of *The Breasts of Tiresias* in
1917, in an article that the playwright called "interesting and judi-
cious." In truth, he was using farce à la Aristophanes to stuff his
ideas; and those ideas were essentially the ones of the philosophers who influenced him in 1903. Nietzsche, for example, had
written that the solution of women was maternity (he had also
advocated the whip) and hymned the sacred fire of pregnancy
(*Dawn*). Rémy de Gourmont, who attacked what he called "the
folly of repopulation"—usually relegated, he said, to poor families
by impotent administrators—also attacked malthusianism, free
love, and the opposite of free love, Anglo-Saxon feminism (puri-
tanism) (*Épilogues*). Feminism, he wrote, if successful, would
move civilization toward human parthenogenesis, a beelike society with a Queen Mother, female workers, and drones; complete
sexual promiscuity, on the other hand, would turn the world into
chaos, destroy the couple, and lead to even greater subjection of
the weaker female than in the past. The basis of society and of all
higher animate nature is the couple: woman is liberated when she
is free to cultivate at leisure her reproductive attributes; while her
male counterpart, animalistically promiscuous, must sustain her in
this freedom while indulging at times in a freedom of his own, in
the joys of "temporary polygamy," the safeguard of marriage
(*Physiology of Love*).

In *The Breasts of Tiresias*, Apollinaire satirizes feminism in the
person of his female protagonist Theresa, who exchanges her
pneumatic symbols of maternity for a beard, names herself Tiresias, and leaves her husband in order to become a "deputy law-
yer senator" and a "mathematician philosopher chemist." But
Apollinaire, in a supreme Oedipal statement, goes Rémy de Gourmont one better: his male hero, the abandoned husband, becomes

[131]

the Father, the phoenix, the phallus, and France—and the conqueror of death—in one mighty act of will by giving birth to "40,049 children in a single day." Has Apollinaire abandoned the couple? Not in the least: a repentant Theresa returns to her husband at the end of the play, ready, as the dramatist wrote in his own review, to do the double!—now that she has shed her beard, donned her breasts, and is back home again where she belongs. Eve unchained would thus transcend herself by following her husband's Promethean example; never would King Ixion ride higher!

We find, therefore, that Apollinaire carried a pregnant Eve symbol on his quest for the Superwoman and in his flight from the sanguinary womb: and he finally bequeathed her and her progeny to France for the cause of French culture and his own immortality. Over the passionflowers and the venomous plants hung the ripe fruits he loved, part of the beauty—and irony—of autumn. They were like the breasts and the body of woman in full maturity. His most admiring description of Eve was of her portrait in the magnificent painting on the ceiling of the Sistine Chapel: "When Michelangelo painted the resplendent Eve of the Sistine, he gave her the splendor of creative forces, breasts of abundance, copious, saturated, breasts that were to nourish a Race, a whole Race . . ."

For three years after Annie's departure, however, he was far from both male parthenogenesis and female fertility. He believed that he could no longer love. His onanistic tendencies and black humor broke into clandestine print in the incestuous fantasies of *The Exploits of a Young Don Juan,* and especially in that apocalypse of copulating beasts *The Eleven Thousand Rods,* with its numberless episodes of sadism, masochism, fetishism, saphism, transvestism, urolagnia, coprolagnia, coprolalia, necrophilia, poedophilia, gerontophilia, and zoophilia erotica, and with its close understanding, as Robert Desnos pointed out, of the essentially modern role played by masochism and the whip (*On Eroticism*). Typically, Apollinaire was extending his death of love to the rest of society; in the only thoughtful passage of the book, he carried Gourmont's cultivated dimorphism as far as Sodom and Gomorrah. One of his characters comments:

The New City

. . . Masturbation is a very laudable action, since it permits men and women to get used to their approaching definitive separation. The customs, the spirits, the clothes, and the tastes of the two sexes are becoming more and more distinct. It is about time we recognized this fact, and if one wants to dominate on earth, it would appear to me to be necessary to take into account this natural law which will soon impose itself.

(Chapter VII).

Apollinaire wanted to dominate, to be king. He later wrote to Lou after he had taken his vow of chastity, that it was a joy to dominate his carnal desires "in order to dominate others some day" (letter of April 14, 1915). In the next few years, he became the loveless poet-god of "The Brazier," the chaste Templar of "The Betrothal," and the solitary enchanter of *Onirocritique*. This last work was published in 1909 as an epilogue to *The Putrescent Enchanter;* its *leitmotifs* are, "But I was conscious of the different eternities of men and women," and "Two dissimilar animals were coupling." In surrealistic prose the lone poet wanders through a dreamlike chaos left by the splitting apart of the universe into two eternities, until, as the two animals melt away to shades, he becomes the ultimate man in harmony with the empty cities, the rivers, and the undefiled mountain snows.

In his prefaces to erotic classics like *The Memoirs of Fanny Hill* (1910), Aretino's *Ragionamenti* ("*Dialogues*") (1909–12), and Sade's works (1909), Apollinaire, now in love with Marie Laurencin, became a polemicist for free erotic experience, that is to say, the greatest range of erotic possibilities within and between the two separate eternities of male and female. *The Eleven Thousand Rods* had been a Sade-like compendium of erotic vices, revealing great knowledge of the subject on the part of its young author both through personal experience and through literature, and had contained a number of insatiable Juliettes. Now he advocated the sixteenth- and eighteenth-century cult of the flesh, of "sublime obscenity," as against the limited range of sexual freedom advocated by puritanical apologists for free love in the twentieth century. Their Eros had become "a statue of a little naked, sick god, his bow unstrung, a shameful object of curiosity, a subject of medical and retrospective observations" ("Andréa de Nerciat"). Sade, on the other hand, the creator of the new Juliette-with-wings-to-renew-the-universe, was the great libertarian of sex, as well as an important precursor of Lamarck, Spencer, Nietzsche, and Krafft-Ebing. His ideas were best expressed in "that *opus sadicum* par excellence" *Philosophy in the Boudoir.*

In this chaotic but fascinating treatise, the ideal woman is sketched out by Sade in terms reminiscent of those used by Fabre to describe certain female insects. Her only desire would be to be made carnal love to from morning till night. She would be unmarried, she would live in a state house of prostitution—there would be male houses for her, too—and she would be completely *free,* "with no restraints but her penchants, no laws but her desires, no morality but that of nature." Her children, if any, would be brought up by the state. Virtue and vice being nothing but relative social terms for natural phenomena and love being nothing but desire, incest, sodomy, crime, and murder, as well as egoistic altruism, humanity, fraternity, and charity, would all be permitted. Inequality is the rule of nature; one should profit by any superiority one is lucky enough to have. The anarchistic rule of the strongest will finally dawn; men and women will grow in strength, primitive beauty, and godliness; "charming sex, you will be free."

Apollinaire's New Woman did not entirely fit this portrait, but she was partly formed by it. He mainly compromised Sade's ideas with those of Rémy de Gourmont (and Proudhon's belief in the family) in his advocacy of as much erotic freedom as possible within the limits of monogamy, "the licentiousness which is the health and safeguard of marriage." He lauded Aretino's sonnet sequence on love's positions: "Variety is the only arm we possess against satiety. And the man [Aretino] who, directly or indirectly, furnished love with a pretext never to become stale should be honored by all married people." Apollinaire saw Juliette as the mistress of both Eve and Mary; he would later instruct his virgin fiancée Madeleine in the same ideas.

Two years after he lost Marie Laurencin, in the summer of 1914, he was attempting to enlist in the French forces, driven by a need to fight with the angels on the right side of what he considered to be the Armageddon of Esthetics (Art against the Huns). He was also spurred on by an inner need to become at last the hero of his mother, that proud, tyrannical Pole who had chivalraic ancestors going back to Ryurik, the first king and legislator of

Russia. "Count Guillaume Albert Wladimir Alexandre Apollinaire
de Kostrowitzky" his service record read; he wondered at times if
he were not another Napoleon, starting out like that Corsican in
the artillery; and he hoped that the war would finally bring about
the liberation of Poland and the return of his titled estates (letters
to Lou). What was his pleasure, therefore, to find himself with a
new, noble mistress, a member of one of the most illustrious families in Europe, with the same name as a famous ancestress, Louise
de Coligny, daughter of Admiral Coligny, wife of Prince William
the Silent. To climax his joy, he found that she was also Juliette in
person.

The extraordinary ladder of erotic love they climbed together in
the space of a few months is described in minute detail in the
Poems to Lou and the more than two hundred (unpublished)
letters he sent her from his basic-training camp and the front;
suffice it to say here that their erotic range was remarkably wide,
and included sodomy, one of the ultimate stages of sexual liberation for Apollinaire as it was for Sade. Heterosexual sodomy,
accompanied by essential flagellation—binding the two eternities,
Xerxes and the sea, together by the whip—was a supreme triumph to him of "pure and perverse love," "mythic, carnal, absolute," a way through the valley of the shadow of death to life (she
was not entirely convinced). He had said earlier that love sought
to destroy dualism, that there could not be two freedoms. Now as
Lou was a microcosm of the female principle, the archetype of
Helen, Mary Magdalen, and Messalina (letters of December 18,
1914; February 3, 1915), and as he was a microcosm of all creation, "the head of creation" (May 3, 1915), so their union was
godlike and sacred and contained everything in the universe. He
was the flagellating sun (January 27, 1915), she the Marvelous
Rose (Poem XI); "Vice never enters into sublime loves" (Poem
XIV).

Yet he soon found the defect in the absolutely free woman
when she left him for other microcosms; and he pathetically repeated after she had gone his ideas on the essential importance of
the couple (April 25, 1915). She had been a rebound from Marie
Laurencin; now a young Algerian English teacher took her place
and rose to the rank of ideal goddess, phantom of clouds, and
mother of letters and poems. Apollinaire created Madeleine al-

[135]

most entirely out of his imagination (he had met her briefly on a train), just as he was doing everything in his power to create esthetic significance for the war; but he never found another woman who so well embodied his philosophy of Eros Transcendent as his Lady Ashley, the Lady known as Lou.

Nevertheless, he wrote a volume of letters to Madeleine from the front (*Tendre comme le souvenir*—"Tender as Memory") and made her his "Roselily," his Magdalen ("Madeleine" in French), his Eve, and even his slave, in short, his fiancée. Reality, after a visit to her home in Oran and after his head wound in March 1916, inevitably dispelled the mirage. He never fully recovered either from his wound or from his loss of Lou, even in new love and marriage to Jacqueline Kolb, "the pretty redhead" of the last poem in *Calligrammes*. His final writings are full of bitter misogyny, from the transvestism of his stories ("The Pins," "Cinderella Continued, or the Rat and Six Lizards," "The Adventuress," etc.) to the paranoiac denunciations of *The Seated Woman*. A final pessimistic if more rational attitude can be found in his second play, *Color of the Weather,* produced a month after his death, in December 1918.

Color of the Weather is a résumé of the dark side of his philosophy on love. It picks up for the last time his first positivistic trinity, History, Science, and Philosophy, and allegorizes it in the three key personages of the play, Ansaldin the rich man, Van Diemen the scientist, and Nyctor the poet (scene i). Escaping from reality, represented by the terrible beauty and suffering of war, they flee to the Antarctic against the poet's better instincts and there immolate each other over the figure of a beautiful woman frozen in ice. The play ends on the ironic comments of a dead soldier's fiancée and mother contrasting their hero's sacrificial struggle for life with the egotistical and idealistic battle for a phantom peace and beauty.

In 1914, Apollinaire had been excited by his discovery of Rimsky-Korsakov's *Golden Coquerel* as danced by the Ballets Russes; in 1918 he called it a subversive revolutionary work which showed that sexuality was the strongest force in life, transcending patriotism and religion (*Europe Nouvelle*, August 17). The old legend is basically the same as that of *Color of the Weather*: a king, a magician, and the king's two sons, trying to forestall war, kill each other for love of a phantom Oriental beauty. Apollinaire's play is a modern, science-fiction account of the fatal implications of the Symbolist pursuit of the Ideal;[16] but his dogmatic intent of proposing a different kind of love to take its place, one committed to duty, to life, and to France (the fiancée and the mother) is belied by the flat prosaicism of the play's tone, and the discouragement felt in many of its lines ("Farewell farewell all must die"). With *The Seated Woman* one of Apollinaire's most pessimistic works, it is modern and realistic in its prophetic doubts about science's ability to save the world from catastrophe; but its disparity in tone and idea keeps it from being a successful work of art. Nevertheless, as a revelation of the underside of his Symbolist philosophy— Anteros' side—and a counterpart to the prolific optimism of *The Breasts of Tiresias,* produced the year before, the play is a tribute to the poet's idealogical integrity. The more characteristic philosophy of *The Breasts of Tiresias* predominates in his total *ethos,* however, and provides the basis for the three successful manifestoes of revolutionary estheticism written at the end of his life, "Victory," "The Pretty Redhead," and "The Hills" (discussed below).

In summary, Apollinaire's New Woman rose full-blown out of his positivistic pantheism and his early idealism. The biological separation of the sexes paralleled the division of the world into anima and animus, Ariadne and Dionysos, the Lady and her Knight, the Madonna and Christ. His lifelong quest could be termed the desire and the pursuit of the whole; he knew like modern psychologists (and theologians) "the eschatological proposition that mankind will not put aside its sickness and its discontent until it is able to abolish every dualism." [17] Eros was the connecting link between the two separate eternities of man and woman, "love which fills like light/ All the solid space between the stars and planets" ("Marriage of André Salmon"). When, as it recurrently happened, Eros turned into Anteros and led the poet to a woman of straw, he substituted for her other animae of his inner vision, revolution, nature, memory, the Muse, the Madonna, Eve, will, desire, and the modern world—or, in his nihilistic, onanistic works, himself, Lilith, the bitch-goddess, or a fatal illusion. Eros was also Dionysos and Pan; their Psyche was Ariadne-Juliette, an illusory twin image, a guide and an inspiration, Eagle, Mole, and

Panther. Their child was art. Apollinaire owned the Abbé d'Au-
bignac's fascinating seventeenth-century treatise on comparative
mythology, *Satyrs* (1627). This work pointed out that Pan's symbolism went all the way from Theocritus' god of noonday rutting
(used in "A Monster of Lyons") to the Platonic Celestial Face
Itself, the incarnation of the Word (*la Parolle*), the Orphic
Whole (*le Tout*). Apollinaire made the shepherd-god into the
creative spirit of the universe, piping now sphinxes, women, and
stars, now paintings and words, into new worlds.[18] His own flock
of words, "following into the myrtle groves/ Eros and Anteros in
tears" ("Victory") could change the faces of children and renew
the universe:

The word is sudden and it is a trembling god . . .

Victory above all will be
To see well from afar
To see all
Nearby
And may all have a new name ("Victory")

IV *The New Poet: Ideas of 1914–1918*

Apollinaire's lyrical acceptance of World War I and his role in it
of artillery sergeant and infantry lieutenant was in keeping with
his character and ideas. He had foreseen a blood purge of nations
since his adolescence; he knew the dangers of the antipoetic
forces loose in the technological age; and he had felt early in his
life the world's need for the hegemony of French art to save it
from barbarism. He was always one to be in the forefront of every
movement he endorsed. His early poetry had been among the
most medieval and Decadent, his anarchistic tracts the most violent, his anticlerical stories the most satirical, his Rhenish lyrics
the most Romantic, his pornographic writings the most erotic, his
Symbolism the most messianic, his Futurism the most destructive,
and his "poem-conversations" the most modern of our times; it
was natural that his war poetry was to become among the most
heroic. He knew the secret of giving himself fully to a cause; and
his main weapon, in war as in peace, was his personal example,
his myth. The shift from errant poet to knight-errant poet was

correspondingly easy. The soldier had been a leading symbol of poetic adventure in *Alcools,* and the simplified and intensified life in wartime with its easy blacks and whites and great surface reserves of emotion waiting to be exploited gave extra significance to his favorite verbs *sing, dance, look, love, weep,* and *die.* He knew that mere photographic reporting of love and life grew charged with emotion when it came from under a bombardment on the front; his hundreds of poetic dispatches to friends and periodicals used the simplified, impressionistic cosmopolitanism of his prewar muse to keep ahead of exploding events.

In letters to Lou, Madeleine, and a literary correspondent, Jeanne-Yves Blanc, he discussed the new esthetic to come out of the war. Fernand Fleuret, Blaise Cendrars, and he—three poets who had adopted a simplified, telegraphic syntax to keep pace with external reality[19]—constituted the only trinity in French poetry that had "true talent and lyricism" (letter to Lou, January 7, 1915). Literature was moving back to the principles of language, he said, taste and classical restraint were changing rapidly and returning to *life* which was the governing principle of art.[20] Who were the great forgetters, he asked, the Christopher Columbuses who could *forget* a continent in order to make greater discoveries? He was certainly one himself, the "Don Juan of the thousand and three comets" on a cosmographic search for new forces ("Toujours"—"Always"). Out of the poet's explorations would arise an epic muse which would be neither that of esoteric Symbolism nor imagistic impressionism, but rather one of esthetic humanism mirroring a secular religion of honor, duty, and heroism.[21]

Most of his war poems incorporate these ideas and testify to his exuberant, if oversimplified, picture of himself as a troubadour, crusading knight, and lover, singing war's marvels to his loves, his *amors de lonh,* and his friends on the home front. At their best—in "The Night of April 14," for example—they present a unique appreciation of life and love in the most harrowing situations:

The heavens are starred by the shells of the Boche
The marvelous wood where I live throws a ball
The machine gun plays a demisemiquaver air
But have you got the word
                    yes! the fatal word
To the battlements to the battlements Leave your shovels there

Like a forlorn lost star in search of its seasons
Heart bursting shell you were whistling your romance
And your thousands of suns have emptied the caissons
That the gods of my eyes are filling in silence

We love you O life and we aggravate you

The shells were wailing a deathly love
A love that is dying is more tender than others
Your breath swims in the river where the blood will **dry**
The shells were wailing
                             Listen to ours sing
Purple love hailed by those who are going to die

The springtime all humid the night light the attack

It's raining my soul but it's raining dead eyes

Ulysses how long to get back to Ithaca
Lie down on the straw and dream a fine remorse
Which pure effect of art is aphrodisiac

But
      organs
                in the wisps of straw where you sleep
The hymn of the future is paradisiac

At their worst, they comprise the excessively conceptual, patriotic
war poems of forgotten anthologies:

> Take my verses O my France Future Multitude
> Sing what I sing a pure chant the prelude
> Of the sacred hymns the beauty of our time
> Will inspire you with more pure more sublime
> Than those that this evening I am striving to sing
> In honor of Honor and the beauty of *Devoir*
> ("Song of Honor")

It is ironical that Apollinaire's esthetic of *The Eleven Thousand
Rods* (unintentionally rediscovered in *The Seated Woman*) would
have served him better to portray war in terms that we more readily accept as accurate after World War II. Occasionally, however,

he let down his guard and let slip a few lines that avoid the weight of war's ulterior motives:

> How many you can kill
> By God (*Ma foi*)
> Funny you don't feel anything
> By God
> A chocolate bar for the Boche
> By God Fire
> A Camembert cheese for the Boche's house
> By God Fire
> Every time you say fire! the word changes out there
>   into flying steel
> By God
> Cover
> By God
> Kra
> They're answering back the dirty
> Funny language by God ("Peu de chose"—"Not much")

Especially when he joined the infantry from the artillery did he become aware that the war was no medieval joust between Saint Guillaume and the dragon. The following fragment, an inadvertant cry of distress out of the bloody trenches, is more valuable as poetry and truth than much formal rhetoric:

> Harden yourself old heart to the cries
> The wounded make in their agony
> Men lice of the earth vermin tenacious

The war poems of *Calligrammes*, the *Poems to Lou*, and *Poems to Madeleine*, then, constitute no epic *Iliad* or *Song of Roland*, a form of literature that will probably never return; but they do make up a remarkable modern romance. Apollinaire was closely acquainted with the Freudian connections between love and war, the connection between love and hate and the phallic release of artillery fire; and he finally broke his vow of chastity to take advantage of the erotic opportunities which are the main weapons of recruiting sergeants. Living for the most part like the Marquis de Sade through a period of enforced abstinence, he released his pentup desires in a flood of erotic letters and poems that make up one of the most unique war records in literature. Here is an example, written on the front, to a young woman he knew only by correspondence (Madeleine):

> My mouth will have the ardors of Gehenna
> My mouth to you will be a hell of sweetness
> The angels of my mouth will reign in your heart
> My mouth will be crucified
> And your mouth will be the horizontal bar of the cross
> And what mouth will be the vertical bar of that cross
> O vertical mouth of my love
> The soldiers of my mouth will assault and carry your entrails
> The priests of my mouth will cense your beauty in its temple
> Your body will toss like a region during an earthquake
> Your eyes will then be full of all the love that has
>   accumulated in the eyes of humanity since it began
> My mouth my love will be an army against you . . .
>
>   ("Fourth Secret Poem")

His dream of the new city of the future was equally aphrodisiac-paradisiac. A whole new civilization, he prophesied, with a new humanity would rise phoenix-like out of the ashes of France. It would constitute a multiplication of Eros, a more Dionysian dance even than the one he danced in Paris in the spring of 1914 [22] or with Lou at the beginning of the war in Nice and Nîmes. There would be an increase in sensuous enjoyments, voluptuousness, bacchic games, and fleshly perfection.[23] The world would drive with more speed and dynamism into new ranges of experience; explorers would move into the abysses of earth and sky; and mankind would find "all the joys":

> Women Games Factories Commerce
> Industry Agriculture Metal
> Fire Crystal Speed ("War")

He, the poet, would be the supreme architect of this new world:

> It is I who begin this thing of the
> future ages

> It will be longer to realize than was the
> fable of flying Icarus
>
> I bequeath to the future the history of
> Guillaume Apollinaire
> Who was at the war and everywhere else . . .
>
>   ("Wonder of War")

He would replace Christianity—Christ having lived and died in vain, since He had failed to bring peace to the world—with his soldier-poet's religion of pagan love and, especially, the new Beauty, consisting of "Grace Virtue Courage Honor which are/ Nothing but the same Beauty" ("Song of Honor").

Back in Paris after being wounded in early 1916, he continued to sketch out his vision in his poetry. Apocalyptic elevation as in "The Brazier" would raise the rest of the world to the poet's heights:

> . . . there is still a brazier up there
> Where they are shooting down smoking stars
> And those who rekindle them demand of
> You to raise yourselves up to those transcendent flames
> And flame in kind
> O public
> Be the inextinguishable torch of the new fire
>   (Prologue to the *Breasts of Tiresias*).

The tombs had already been opened by the war in a great resurrection ("To Italy"); a beast resembling Leviathan or the dragon-Antichrist of Revelation would appear in the heavens bringing with it "things so subtly new that they will fill space . . . as if the sky began to speak a thousand different tongues" ("Profondeurs" —"Depths"). The Lucifer of the past was being shot down by Saint Michael in a dogfight of airplanes over Paris ("The Hills"); man was flying now higher than eagles, and a fabulous merchant of prodigious stature and unbelievable opulence was displaying extraordinary wares. Gigantic shepherds were abroad, driving great word-browsing flocks; and the poet felt in himself new beings of great dexterity bringing forth a new universe ("The Little Auto" [24]).

Apollinaire more carefully defined the messianic poet in his critical writing of 1916–18. Man's new faith would be in himself and in his species rather than in God,[25] and his new religion of will, duty, and honor would take the place of the old superstitions:

Religions promised rewards in the other world, sociologists promise individuals happiness in this one; we must suppress all that so that men henceforth find happiness only in themselves through the satisfaction of duty accomplished and honor safeguarded. We shall arrive at this through education without weakness or error.
(*The Seated Woman;* Apollinaire's spokesman is speaking).

The poet would be a member of the free elite as before, but he would have to be exceptionally steadfast before the increasing danger of the reactionary democracies of the future ordering men about in "great docile flocks." [26] Moreover, he was at a new disadvantage, having fallen behind the scientist in progress and influence. In fact, scientists had forged so far ahead since 1908, that "mathematicians have the right to say that their dreams, their preoccupations surpass by a hundred cubits the crawling imaginations of poets." Just as the poet's ancestors invented Icarus—and as Apollinaire himself invented a kind of human androgenesis in *The Breasts of Tiresias*—the poet must *will* the truths of the future:

Those who imagined the fable of Icarus . . . will find others. They will carry you along alive and awake into the closed, nocturnal world of dreams. Into the universes palpitating ineffably over our heads. Into those universes closer and farther from us which gravitate at the same point of infinity as the one we carry in ourselves. (*The New Spirit and the Poets*).

[Theresa's] husband relies completely on will. And as a matter of fact, we won't know the limits of will for a long time to come. Will is the most powerful lever for a nation as for an individual, and we couldn't possibly overdevelop its boldness. (*Sic*, June 1917).

Thus he must *prophesy*, prophecy being nothing more than the clairvoyant perception of mankind's possibilities. Fortunately, on his side he has the discoveries of the past to guide him, the artistic masterpieces and, particularly, the great ethnic patrimony of France, its classical order, morality, duty, honor, and patriotism. These virtues will orient him in his reasoned yet adventurous, *free* explorations into the future and the unknown. Terrible suffering and pain will be his lot on this road of self-sacrifice and martyrdom before the uncomprehending antipathy of the world; but his reward will be the joyful reality of the future. "The poet is one who discovers new joys, however painful they may be to endure" (*The New Spirit and the Poets*).

What would be the new poet's techniques? Here Apollinaire's muse moves farthest away from the absolute estheticism of 1908. He speaks for the first time of *inesthetic* poetic exploration of reality and virtue (*bonté*) for the sake of pure reality, truth without art. The new art *"is not a decorative art, nor is it an impressionist art"* (Apollinaire's italics); its artists are not only men of beauty, they are also and primarily men of truth. The world has seen the end of dilettantism (*Sic*, October 1916). The artist would use, as he did in 1913–14, all the genres, all the arts and all the machines—like the phonograph and the cinema—in his effort to include in his great synthesis "the entire world, its noises and appearances, thought and human language, song, dance, all arts and all artifices." Inevitably it will be *surprising* to the old world, still living in the past. It will be far from Naturalism and Naturalism's deceitful photography (*"trompe l'oeil"*) of a slice of life; it will be rather what he called in 1914 *surnaturalisme* ("supernaturalism") and what he christens in 1917 for the first time *surréalisme* ("super-realism" or "surrealism"), that is to say, a *translation* of reality. If this translation is more truthful than beautiful, still it may yet bring about a new beauty ("who would dare to say that, for those who are worthy of joy, what is new is not beautiful?"). It will contain the new universe of joy, lyricism, knowledge, virtue, and the marvelous in advance. Apollinaire in the final poetic manifesto of *Calligrammes*, "The Pretty Redhead," ringingly speaks for himself and for his poet-companions as he describes this universe to the traditionalists:

We want to give you vast and strange domains
Where mystery in flower is offered to him who would pick it
There are new fires colors never seen

A thousand imponderable phantasms
To which we must give reality
We want to explore virtue that enormous country where all is still
We can also pursue or bring back time
Pity for us who are always fighting on the frontiers of limitlessness
    and the future
Pity for our errors pity for our sins . . .

He is under the sign of his final Muse, a graceful goddess of reason:

> O Sun it's the time of ardent Reason
>   And I await
> To follow her forever the noble tender form
> She assumes so I can love her only
> She comes and attracts me as an iron the magnet
>   She has the charming air
>   Of a pretty redhead ("The Pretty Redhead")

V *"The Hills"*

A hill was the most appropriate symbol Apollinaire found for the superior poet-prophet, the man who sees farther than other men into the worlds of order and adventure, the past and the future. A hill himself, he spoke down to mankind and summed up his lifetime esthetic, orienting it toward the new reality.

> Certain men are hills
> Who rise above men and see
> The future from afar
> Better than the present
> Clearer than the past . . .
>
> I say what life truly is
> Only I can sing like this
> My songs fall like seeds
> Keep quiet you who sing
> Don't mix the tares and wheat ("The Hills")

With "The Betrothal" one of his two major prophetic poems, "The Hills" may be mentioning the experience of its predecessor and similarly placing itself under Picasso's aegis in two mysterious stanzas:

> Another time I begged
> But only got a flame
> Which burned me to the lips
> I couldn't speak my thanks
> Torch inextinguishable
>
> Where are you then my friend
> Who turned so far in yourself
> That only a gulf remained
> In which I have thrown myself
> Down to the colorless depths[27]

As in the 1908 poems he sacrifices his past—which now includes his young manhood—to the future; and he foresees the end of the old beauty, which he terms "that of proportions." The following stanza, which reminds one of the pure, immobile beauty at the end of *Color of the Weather*, is perhaps a picture of the death of the legendary beauty sought by the Symbolists:

> A vessel arrived in port
> A great pavilioned ship
> But the only soul we found
> Was a beautiful lady in red
> Lying assassinated there[28]

"The Hills" resumes the experience of "The Brazier"

> Often I have soared so high
> So high farewell all things
> Phantoms and fantasies

and that of early Symbolist poems

> No more will I admire
> That boy who mimics fear

to pass beyond

> The dance in the depths whirls on
> I have killed the fine orchestra leader
> I am peeling for my friends
> The orange of which the savor
> Is a marvelous fireworks

The poet has a Rimbaud-like self-sufficiency:

> I stop myself to watch
> On the incandescent lawn
> A serpent glide myself
> Who am the flute I play
> And the whip to punish others

As in his last critical works, he speaks of semiscientific explorations into the subconscious, into the powers of will and the meaning of suffering, all for the sake of new prodigies and a new virtue:

> We will seek in man himself
> More than has ever been sought
> We will penetrate his will
> And its power born without
> Machine or instrument . . .

> Accustom yourselves like me
> To the prodigies I announce
> To virtue about to reign
> To the suffering I endure
> You will know the future too

At the end of the poem, using the magic talisman of poetry, he conjures up a few of those prodigies himself, little secrets which bring all the arts together and embody a *surprising* reality:

> A top hat sits upon
> A table bearing fruit
> By the apple the gloves are dead
> A lady wrings her neck
> Near a man swallowing himself

[148]

He discovers a final trinity, a slave (in the manuscript, an emperor), a car driver, and an ascending lady, and he concludes with his two most universal symbols, the flame and the rose:

> Golden arms support life
> Seek out the secret of gold
> All is a rapid flame
> In the flower of the adorable rose
> Of exquisite perfume

Prometheus in an airplane, he has brought a torch to the poet of the future; he can die content:

> I have finally freed myself
> From all things natural
> I can die but cannot sin
> And that which has never been touched
> I have touched O I have felt
>
> And I have scrutinized more
> Than can possibly be conceived
> Many times I have weighed
> Imponderable life itself
> I can die with a smile

Jacqueline Apollinaire has had these last two stanzas engraved on his tomb.

VI *Epilogue*

The world of suffering, secular morality, and truth foreseen by Apollinaire has come into existence since his death. The Surrealists, denouncing the "assassinated" poet's faith in art and his patriotism while praising his revolutionary explorations into modernism, the dream, and the past, chose the realities of the imagination and international morality over the old Symbolist beauty; and the social consciousness of modern literature has coincided with the collectivization of men "in docile flocks" following World War I. Science has indeed outdistanced art and taken remarkable voyages into truth; and the fact that Apollinaire's new age of lyrical joy has not yet resulted from the voyages of both science and art is perhaps due to a present-day lack of his supreme faith in the individual and in the individual's highest realization through art.

Apollinaire's own voyages into life and art, however, resulted in works which partly combat these tendencies with their successful conciliation of beauty and truth, the individual and society, Christ, Marx, and the modern man. Their synthesis of the Christian, the Hegelian, and the Freudian dialectics in a creative vision of esthetic and social progress which would release man from his psychic and political repressions and send him off on the trail of Eros-Pan-Christ has been a quiet but ubiquitous influence on the world's intellectual integrity ever since the first publication of *Alcools* in 1913. Before 1918, his poems were used as revolutionary tracts in Russia, Germany, Hungary, and Poland; since his death, they have spread over the world in hundreds of translations and appreciations, until, after World War II, his dream of being read by an American Negro boxer, a Chinese empress, a German journalist, a Spanish painter, an Italian peasant, and an English officer in India (letter to Jeanne-Yves Blanc, November 19, 1915) has become almost an actuality. His works at the present time are being studied in Russia, Poland, Portugal, Yugoslavia, Spain, Hungary, and Germany, as well as in Asia (Japanese translations have been appearing since 1928), North and South America, Africa, and Australia; and everywhere they carry the same tidings of a cultural, intellectual millennium about to break forth with a new, transcendent individual creating the future in freedom and love. Bringing a sensitive appreciation of beauty to a chaotic age of anxiety, welding together nymphs and airplanes, roses and electricity, Babylon, Rome, Leningrad, Paris, and New York, they constitute the enchanted "castle of air" of a modern Merlin; it behooves their readers to build this castle in reality, carefully, with science and art, over the precipice of universal destruction.

In the beginning was the Word, said Apollinaire, that is to say, Poetry; if we do not travel toward it in the future we are lost. He knew that scientism in itself, like technological progress and democracy, is harmful to poets, as it is to all men; he said as much in "Orpheus," *Color of the Weather*, and *The Assassinated Poet*. But it is because he recognized the potential of science and democracy —as he recognized their poetic, anthropomorphic origins—that he has become an important prophet of our times. At the end of his life, in "The Hills," he sang of the possibility of a renaissance of Aphrodite and the gods, born once again from matter, from the machine:

> Sign of the times if machines
> Should finally begin to think
> On the beaches of precious stones
> The waves of gold would break
> The foam would be mother again

The poet who invented Icarus invented the airplane; other poets like Cyrano de Bergerac and Jules Verne invented the rocket and the voyage to the moon; who in an age of sputniks and calculating machines could affirm that Apollinaire's vision was unrealistic?

> Higher than eagles goes man
> He makes the sea's joy
> He dissipates in air
> Shadow and dizzy spleen
> Where mind rejoins the dream

Appendices

Glossary of Reference

A great part of Apollinaire's vast network of literary reference and exotic vocabulary has never been explored; much of what has been discovered is scattered through dozens of scholarly articles and books and is thus inaccessible to the average reader. In an effort to begin to fill a gap and provide at least an elementary map for this poorly known territory, I offer the following glossary of the obscurer references and words that have been traced to date by myself and my colleagues. They are from the main creative works *Alcools, The Assassinated Poet, The Bestiary, Calligrammes, The Heresiarch and Company,* and *The Putrescent Enchanter.* For the most part, they are references that do not appear in common dictionaries or encyclopedias, as, for example, in *Webster's International,* the *Columbia Dictionary of Names,* or, particularly, in the nineteenth-century *Larousse,* which Apollinaire used himself and which is the most useful of all reference works for the Apollinaire reader. In order to be as brief as possible, I have attempted to include only the aspects of the references that are relevant to Apollinaire's work. Uncertain or ambiguous references—and there are many—are marked (?).

A

abeille "bee" (*Clair de Lune, CMA, Voyageur*) aural constellation; insect of Apollo.

Abonde (see *Dame-Abonde*).

Adam (see *crâne d'Adam*).

agate (*Passant, Zone*) stone with portraits of kings and gods in medieval lapidaries.

Agla (*Montre, Que faire?*) magic word in occult formulae.

Aguereth (see *Naama*).

alcancie (*Larron, Roi Lune*) "alcancía" (Sp.) a round vessel thrown at festivals in Spain "at the time of the Moors" according to Apoll. (*Chroniques,* May 7, 1910).

Aldavid (*Toucher*) "offspring of David" (Arab.); Messiah.

Amblève (*Ench, Que vlo-ve?*) river near Stavelot, Belgium, with mussel pearls (Fettweiss, Thiry).

âme "soul" (*Ench, Larron*) round in some Pythagorean, Gnostic beliefs (e.g., in Hermes Trismegistus); see poem "Passion" of Apoll.; see *licorne.*

améthyste (*Passant, Simon, Zone*) symbol of the divinity, of crucifixion, in medieval lapidaries, cabalistic works.

amie de Justin Prérogue "mistress of J. P." (*Serviette*) Fernande Olivier; see *Justin Prérogue.*

ancolie "ancoly" (*Clotilde*) flower of melancholy (Her.).

anémone (*Clotilde, Fiançailles*) traditional flower of sickness, abandon, of Venus and Adonis; literally, "windflower" (Greet).

ange "angel" (*Porte*) species of Mediterranean fish.

Apollonius de Thyane (*Ench, Passant, Zone*) Apollonius of Tyana, Pythagorean philosopher, rival of Christ, famous for chastity, mysterious disappearance; see *gymnosophites, pantaure.*

apôtre "apostle" (*Un soir*) Judas Iscariot, who hanged himself on fig tree (folklore).

Archelaus (*Ench*) 5th-century Greek poet and alchemist; (?).

Ardabure (*Ench*) chief of militia at Antioch in 469 A.D.

arveye (*Que vlo-ve?*) "au revoir" in Wall. (Piron).

aubépine "Hawthorn" (*Ench, Merlin*) traditionally, plant over Merlin's tomb.

B

babo (*Que vlo-ve?*) "simpleton" (Wall.) (Piron).

baiser florentin "Florentine kiss" (*CMA, Larron*) lingual kiss (It.) (cf. Diderot's *Bijoux indiscrets,* XLVII).

bandelettes noires et blanches "black and white bands" (*Larron*) Babylonian, Hebrew talismans.

Bandi (*Otmika*) Hungarian name (Warnier).

barcarols (*CMA*) "boatmen" (It. *barcaroli*) (Durry).

bâton "staff" (*Salomé*) attribute of John the Baptist in early Church iconography (Couffignal); phallic symbol.

Befana (*Giov Moroni*) It. fairy of Epiphany, from *Epiphania.*

bègue "stutterer" (*Larron*) Moses (from Ex. 4:10).

Beheime (*P Ass 15*) Heb. for "cow" (note of Apoll.).

belle mais noire, la "the comely but black one" (*Ench, Larron*) the Shulamite from *Song of Solomon* (cf. "Le . . . Poème secret"); the Black Virgin; Cybele (Décaudin); (?).

Appendices

Belo (Roi Lune) Antilles sailor, pure-blood Negro (Pia, *Antilles*).
Belphégor (Larron) pagan god, sometimes Priapus (Durry); productive force.
Benzel (Schinderhannes) German bandit, Bible-lover, in band of Schinderhannes (*q.v.*) (Durry).
Bé-rieux (CMA) Berruyers, Gallic tribesmen (Décaudin).
boiteuse "limping woman" *(Ench, Hôtels)* traditionally an erotic woman; see *La Vallière.*
bouche de Dieu "mouth of God" *(Jolie Rousse, Simon Mage)* angel of Order in cabalistic angelology (cf. "Quatrième Poème Secret").
brasier "brazier" *(Brasier, Mamelles)* symbol of religious martyrdom (Her.); creative force to Apoll.
brouet "broth" *(Larron)* food of Spartans.
brûler le dur (Lettre-Océan) "beat the pavement" (Fr. slang).
bruyère "heather" *(Adieu, Ench)* prophetic "plant of double sight" in Fr. folklore; good luck charm (see letter to Lou, July 26, 1915); magic plant to druids (Pliny); symbol of purity to Greeks, Romans, Celts; see *selage.*

C

Calais (CMA) town of 14th-century incident involving heroic Fr. hostages; subject of famous Rodin statue *Les Bourgeois de Calais.*
Câpresse (Fenêtres) mulatto.
Carabosse (CMA) name of wicked fairy.
centaures (Brasier, Mamelles) centaurs, born of Ixion (*q.v.*) and cloud in shape of Hera; symbol of human-divine poetry, prophecy to Apoll.
chabin, chabine (Fenêtres, Roi Lune) Antilles mulatto (Pia, *Antilles*).
Chancesse (Que vlo-ve?) Tschantchesse, Wall. for *Françoise* (Piron).
chanson d'amour "song of love" *(Automne)* Eichendorff's "Das Zerbrochene Ringlein" (Wolf).
Chapalu (Ench) Capulu, Chapulu, Cath Paluc, Cath Palug, Kapalu, monster cat, enemy of King Arthur; with cat's head, dragon's feet, horse's body, lion's tail, in romance *Bataille Loquifer* (Paris).
chape "cope" *(Larron, Merlin)* ecclesiastical cape; term of blazonry, two rectilinear triangles with isosceles triangle between (Durry); see *triangle.*
châtaignes "chestnuts" *(Rhénane)* funereal fruit of all Saints' Day (folklore); heart with swords in it (Décaudin); see *sept épées.*
chauve-souris "bat" *(Ench)* vampire, Lesbian to Apoll.; perfect, angelic, created by Christ in Arab legend.
Chef du Signe de l'Automne (Signe) Sagittarius the centaur (*q.v.*), man with arrow; (?).

chérubin (*Best, Ench, Rose de H*) winged steers in Jewish *Hagadah,* Assyrian myths.

chevalier de cuivre "copper knight" (*Ench*) often castle guard in medieval romances.

Che vuoi (*À travers l'Europe*) "What do you want?" (It.), greeting of devil in Jacques Cazotte's *Le Diable amoureux;* (?).

chibriape (*CMA*) neologism of Apoll. from *chibre, priape* (Fr. terms for phallus).

chien "dog" (*Cortège, Larron*) diabolical companion of Cornelius Agrippa in tradition; in "Larron" symbol of masturbation, of Diogenes the Cynic (Gk. "dog") (from Diogenes Laertius, VI, 69) (see poem "Vae Soli").

Chypre (see *vin*).

Cichina (*Favorite*) Françoise in It. (Pia, *Apoll.*).

cinyre (*Larron*) Greek harp.

citron "lemon" (*Brasier, Fiançailles*) Mary's fruit; ex-voto, lover's heart to Apoll.

cloches "bells" (*Cloches*) bells of Oberpleis in Rhineland.

Clotilde (*Clotilde*) sainted queen of France, favorite of Marie Laurencin; mythical poetess, Marie Laurencin (Bates); Franco-Italian princess (Steegmuller, *Notes*); (?).

colchique "saffron" (*Colchiques*) poisonous flower, used by Medea.

colombe poignardée "poignarded dove" (*Colombe poignardée*) a Philippine dove with red spot on breast (Rouveyre).

coq de Tanagre (see *Tanagre*).

corbeau "crow" (*Ench, Vend*) scavenger; with eagle, bird of Gallic gods (see *Lugu*).

Cosaques Zaporogues "Zaporogian Cossacks" (*CMA*) Christian warriors of the Ukraine asked by Turkish Sultan (*q.v.*) to join his army in 17th-century according to legend; their violent epistolatory refusal became famous.

Costantzing (*Favorite*) *Costantino* (Pia, *Apoll.*).

cramignon (*Que vlo-ve?*) serpentine Wall. dance with song (Piron).

crâne d'Adam "Adam's skull" (*Zone*) said to be buried at Golgotha, "the place of the skull" (Couffignal).

crapaute (*P Ass 2, Que vlo-ve?*) "girl friend," "fiancée" in Wall. (Piron).

Croniamantal (*P Ass*) ("Croniamental" in MS.) from *Cronos? Craniomental? Croc-n'y-a-mental?* (for this last, see Rouveyre, *Amour*).

cucuphe (*Ermite*) medieval medical bonnet worn by patient.

cyprès "cypress" (*CMA, Fiançailles*) funereal, phallic tree; tree of King Charming, the *oiseau bleu* (*q.v.*).

D

Dame-Abonde (*arbre*) leading good fairy in Fr. folklore.

dauphin "dolphin" (*Best, Émigrant, Larron*) animal of Apollo; classical symbol of joy.

demoiselle "damsel" (*Ench*) "dragonfly" in Fr. prov. dial.; "Lesbian" in Fr. slang; cf. *Poèmes à Lou*, LII.

dendrophores (*CMA*) Roman tree-carriers, usually slaves or poor people, in spring festivals (Piron, *Chanson*); see *pin*.

dernier venu ferme la porte, le "the last comer closes the door" (*CMA*) 17th-century saying, "he who trifles misses his chance."

Désirade (*Brasier, CMA*) island in Antilles; first land Columbus found on second voyage.

diable "devil" (*Émigrant, Ench*) a cuckold to Apoll. (horned); see *diablesse, Lilith*.

diablesse "she-devil" (*Ench*) lover of dragonfly to Apoll. (see *demoiselle, Lilith*).

doge (*Émigrant*) Venetian magistrate who annually wed the sea in Renaissance; symbol of suicide by drowning to Apoll.

Drikkes (*P Ass 16*) deformation of *Dreckig* ("dirty"), Ger. name (Durry); see *Marizibill*.

druides "druids" (*Ench*) refugees in Forest of Broceliande in ancient tales; had powers of shape-shifting.

E

écrevisse "crayfish" (*Best*) symbol of inconstancy (Her.).

Édesse (*Larron*) Edessa, first Christian city of Mesopotamia, Jesus invited to live there (see *roi d'Édesse*); city of first miraculous portrait of Christ.

églantine (*Fiançailles*) Mary's flower.

égypan "aegipan" (*CMA*) small satyr; demon to Middle Ages.

Élie "Elias, Elijah" (*Ench, Passant, Zone*) immortal Hebrew prophet to return with Enoch (*q.v.*) at end of world; one of two olive trees of Rev. 11:4.

éliésaïte (*Heresiarch*) Gnostic disciple of Elijah; (?).

Élinor (*Ench, Sacrilège*) fairy mistress of Gauvain, mother of Giglan (from *Histoire de Giglan*); first name of the Viscountess of Milhau.

Empédocle (*Ench*) Empedocles, a Pythagorean mystic, said to have thrown himself in crater of Mount Etna over a woman (thus "Volcanique"), immortal in other legends.

Enoch (*Ench, Passant, Zone*) immortal Hebrew prophet, to return at time of Antichrist with Elijah (see *Élie*); olive tree.

épées (see *sept épées*).

épervier "falcon" (*Automne Malade, Échelon*) bird associated with fairies in folklore and medieval romance; symbol of sun, Ra, Horus, Apollo; Pluto in Rodin's symbolism.

Épileptique (see *Merlin*).

épurge "spurge" (*Fiançailles*) plant used by beggars to make artificial wounds.

équevilles (*Histoire d'une famille*) Lyonese jargon for "junk" (Pia, *Antilles*).

ermite "hermit" (*Ermite*) ninth Tarot card, carries staff and lantern; see *papesse.*

Ernest (*CMA*) Herzog Ernst of German folklore (Bates); symbol of ardor (*Ernst* in Ger.—Lawler).

Escavalon (*Ench*) King Alain's country in prose *Lancelot;* also found in *Meraugis*, Chrétien de Troyes, etc.

étoile de six branches "six-branched star" (*Zone*) star of David; Greek cross or star; chrismon; Hebrew hexalpha; see Rev. 22:16.

Éviene (*Ench*) variation of *Viviane* (*q.v.*), from *Aivienne* (OF).

F

fantôme de nuées "phantom of clouds" (*Fantôme de nuées*) Hera in cloud shape, mother of centaurs (*q.v.*); the poetic vision to Apoll.; see *Ixion.*

Faltenin (*Lul de F*) phallus (from *phallum tenens*) (Louis); see *Lul.*

far tiz (*Madeleine*) "to give the fig" (Arab.) (Chevalier).

Farwaschen Ponim (*P Ass 15*) "dirty mouth" (Heb.) (note of Apoll.).

fauste (*CMA*) "favorable" (Lat. *faustus*).

Fenêtres "windows" (*Fenêtres*) title of Orphic paintings of Robert Delaunay.

Ferdine (*Zone*) mulattto in Effe Geache's pornographic novel *Une nuit d'orgies à Saint-Pierre* (Pia, *Antilles*).

Finngal (*Matelot d'Amsterdam*) from Ossian's Fingal; (?).

fopoïte (*P Ass 12*) from *faux poète* ("false poet") (Pia, *Navire*); (?).

fornarine (*Ermite, Passant*) erotic woman to Apoll.; neologism from name of Raphael's mistress, La Fornarina.

Fortunatus (*Passant*) character in popular 15th-century German novel with magic purse and hat.

Frajle (*Otmika*) "Miss" (*Fraulein*) in Hungarian (Warnier).

Frau Sorge (*Femmes*) "Madame Care" (Ger.), title of poem by Heine (Durry); name in Goethe's *Faust,* II.

Appendices

G

ganique (see *mouches ganiques*).

Gauvain (*Ench*) sun-knight (*Perceval,* prose *Lancelot*); *chevalier des demoiselles* (*Meraugis*); searcher for Merlin (*Vulgate Merlin, Brut*) (Paris).

gazelle (*CMA*) companion of Shakuntala (see *Sacontale*), hunted by King Dushyanta in first act of Kalidasa's play.

gemmipare (see *oiseaux gemmipares*).

genévrier "juniper tree" (*CMA*) tree symbolic of protection and refuge (Her.).

gerce (*Lettre-Océan*) Fr. slang for "girl" (pejorative) (Schmits).

gibelin (*CMA*) "Mountain-like" (Arab.); neologism formed by Apoll. from Mount Gibel (Etna), place of Vulcan's forge (Bates, Piron); Ghibeline (Lawler, Décaudin).

Giovanni Moroni (*Giov Moroni*) Apoll. at Rome (Décaudin) with his foster parents (Davies); see *Moroni.*

giroflée "gilly-flower" (*Fiançailles*) a cruciform or cross-shaped flower.

giroflier "clove tree" (*CMA*) tree symbolic of Christ's crucifixion (cloves-nails).

gnou "gnu" (*Larron*) Chaldean *rimi,* sacred antelope-buffalo, symbol of power; (?).

grotte "grotto" (*Ench, Lul*) home of Christ, Merlin, Sirens, Thaïs in legend; erotic symbol.

grusiner (*Que vlo-ve?*) "sing" in Wall. (Piron).

grusiner one saquoue (*Que vlo-ve?*) "fix you" (lit. "sing something") (Wall.) (Piron).

guivre "wyvern" (*Ench*) beast turned into princess by kiss in romance *Bel Inconnu;* common emblem in Her.

gymnosophites "Gymnosophists" (*Ench*) Indian sages, hosts of Apollonius of Tyana (*q.v.*).

H

haleine tiède "warm breath" (*Lul de F*) traditional poisonous breath of Sirens.

Hambourg (*Best*) home of famous animal dealer Karl Hagenbeck (Guthrie-Diller).

Hanoten ne Kamoth bagoim tholanoth (*Synagogue*) "He gives vengeance to the nations, punishment to peoples" (Hebrew, from Psalms) (Breunig).

Haute-Rue "High Street" (*Marizibill*) Hohe-Strasse, street in Cologne frequented by prostitutes in 1901 (Décaudin).

hawai (see *sol*).

Heisterbach (see *moine*).

Hélène (*Ench, Que vlo-ve?*) wife of Menelaus, quite old when abducted by Paris according to cock Pythagorus, a character in Lucian's *The Dream.*

Hélinor (see *Élinor*).

hématidrose "hematidrosis" (*Ermite*) bloody sweat (medical term); Christ's sweat in Garden of Olives; symbol of menstruation to Apoll.; cf. *Poèmes à Lou,* XLI.

Hermès (*CMA, Que vlo-ve?*) Greek god, phallic roadside idol (Louis); magician (Bates).

Hérodiade (see *Salomé*).

Hésus (*Ench*) Esus, god of Gallic trinity with Taranis, Teutatès (*qq.v.*).

hibou "owl" (*Ench, Ermite*) bird of Minerva, Lilith (*q.v.*); symbol of Christ in Edgar Quinet's *Ahasuérus.*

hilare "mirthful" (*Merlin*) "benevolent" when related to moon, Diana.

houhou (*Lettre-Océan*) sound of whistle (*sirène*); 17th-century term for prostitute; see *sirène*.

I

ibis (*Best*) sacred bird, eater of corpses, mummified by Egyptians; pun on "you will go" (Lat.—cf. Hugo's poem "Ibo"—Durry).

Isabelle Lefaucheux (*P Ass 11*) character in Rétif's *M. Nicolas* (Pia, Navire).

isocèle (see *triangle*).

Ixion (*Vend*) king in Greek myth who embraced a cloud in the form of Hera, engendered centaurs (*q.v.*); symbol to Apoll. of poet embracing his vision to create poetry; see *fantôme de nuages.*

J

Jacob Born (*Schinderhannes*) Jacob Porn, companion of Schinderhannes (*q.v.*), hanged with him in 1803.

Jean-Baptiste (see *bâton, mouches, Saint-Jean*).

jeu de la grande oie "game of the great goose" (*Ermite*) coitus (from 17th-century Fr. slang).

Justin Prérogue (*Serviette*) Picasso, who had but one napkin when living in Montmartre with Fernande Olivier.

K

kief (*Lundi Rue Christine*) form of hashish.

kikiriki (*Rhénane*) cock's cry in German (*kikeriki*).

kolo (*Danseuse, Otmika*) "round dance," common group of Serbian folk dances.

kordax (*P Ass 12*) obscene dance in ancient Greek comedy.

L

labrint (*Que vlo-ve?*) "labyrinth"; *o labrint* "in a fix" (Wall.) (Piron).

Lac Lomond (*Ench*) originally "smooth lake"; thought to be 360 feet deep in Apoll.'s time (Chalmers, *Caledonia*, VI, 857).

laps "lapse" (*Merlin*) forced apostasy (Durry); *laps d'amour* pun on *lacs d'amour*, term of blazonry.

larron "thief" (*Larron*) Jesus Christ; poet; Apollinaire (Durry).

larron de gauche "thief on the left" (*Larron*) Gestas, the impenitent thief of the Passion (Nicodemus 1:10).

laurier "laurel" (*Cortège, Fiançailles, P Ass*) bitter-tasting plant sacred to Orpheus, Apollo; pun on name Laurencin.

La Vallière (*Hôtels*) limping mistress of Louis XIV; see *boiteuse*.

Léonard Delaisse (*Serviette*) Mécislas Golberg, who died of tuberculosis in 1907.

Léviathan (*Ench, P Ass 17, Synagogue*) Talmudic beast to be killed by God, eaten by faithful at end of world (Breunig, *Synagogue*).

libellule (see *demoiselle*).

liberté (*Fenêtres*) name of Parisian newspaper; see *temps*.

licorne "unicorn" (*CMA, Ermite, Larron*) the flesh; the soul; zodiac sign of Virgin under which Apoll. was born.

ligure "Ligurian" (*Larron*) "musical" (Celtic) (see letter to Lou, Dec. 25, 1914); pun on medieval talisman formed from lynx urine which symbolized angelic qualities.

Lilith (*Ench, Ermite, P Ass 7, 15*) "owl" (Heb.—see Isaiah 34:14); first mother, wife of Adam, wife of Beelzebub, lives in Red Sea, howls (folklore); symbol of menstruation, Lesbianism to Apoll.; see *diable, diablesse, Mer Rouge, Naama*.

Linde (*Ench*) Lindus, city of roses on Isle of Rhodes, built by Telchins; city in which Apollonius of Tyana (*q.v.*) disappeared, according to Philostratus (VIII, 30).

Loreley (*Loreley*) adaptation from Clement Brentano's "Loreley."

Lorie (*Ench, Colombe poignardée*) fairy love of Gawain in *Rigomer*; love of Apoll. (?).

lotte "burbot" (*Fenêtres*) sacred fish of Tanit, goddess of moon (see story "Le Cubisme culinaire").

lucioles (see *mouches de la Saint-Jean*).

Lugu (*Ench*) Lug or Lugus, Gallic Mercury or Apollo; "crow" (Celtic; the site of Lyon, *Lugudunum*, was said to have been first indicated by crows).

Luitpold (*CMA*) regent of Bavaria 1821–1912, "tutor" of mad regent Othon and King Ludwig II.

Lul (*Carte Postale, CMA, Lul de F*) phallic symbol (Flemish for "phallus"), sword; Apollinaire; (?); see *Faltenin.*

M

Macarée (*P Ass*) "happy," feminine name from Rétif's *M. Nicolas* (Pia, *Navire*); son, priest of Apollo, son of Aeolus, in Greek mythology.

maclotte (*Ench, Marie*) "tadpole" in Wall. dialect (Guthrie-Dillon); Wall. folk dance; religious festival dance (cf. art. of Apoll. in *Rev. d'Art Dramatique,* Aug. 1903); Marie Laurencin skipping rope (Décaudin).

Madoine (*Ench*) fairy at castle of Morgane la Faye (*q.v.*), mistress, enchantress of Laris in story *Claris et Laris.*

mages (see *rois-mages*).

mains coupées "cut-off hands" (*Marie, Rhénane, Signe*) dead leaves, like those of oaks in Stavelot, Belgium (Décaudin); (women with amputated hands are often associated with trees in European folklore).

Maison des morts (*Maison des morts*) open morgue in Munich's old North Cemetery (Décaudin).

Manala (see *Naama*).

Mara (*Otmika*) "Mary" (Slav) (Warnier).

Marco (*Otmika*) from Marco Kraljevic, Slav folk hero (Warnier); (?).

Mareye (*Colombe poignardée*) Marie Dubois, Apoll.'s Belgian love.

Marizibill (*Cox-City, Marizibill, P Ass 16*) "Mary-Sybil" (*Marie Sibyll*) popular name at Cologne; see *Drikkes, Haute-Rue.*

M.D. (*À travers l'Europe*) Maurice Denis, religious artist, friend of Apoll.

Meicabl (*P Ass 15*) "devil" (Heb.) (note of Apoll.).

menhir (*Ench*) phallic god in European folklore.

Merlin (*Ench, Merlin, P Ass*) *in history:* epileptic Celtic bard, prophet; *in mythology:* Prometheus, Orpheus, Hercules; *in Breton legend:* son of a virgin princess and a dove, hunts serpents' eggs (cf. *P Ass 12*), a druid, a shape-shifter, spring-maker; *in romance:* son of a priestess, son of a virgin and a devil (serpent), son of Satan, is baptized, immortal, teaches and loves Morgane (*q.v.*), teaches Viviane (*q.v.*) to make springs, is lover of 100-year-old woman, is enchanted, entombed by Viviane, goes to Jerusalem in *Robert de Borron,* goes to Rome in *Livre d'Artus,* is the Antichrist, a divine prophet (Villemarqué); *in Edgar Quinet's Merlin l'enchanteur:* son of Satan, represents French genius, humanity, marries Nature-Viviane, engenders son, destroys Hell, leads nations to freedom.

[162]

Mer Rouge "Red Sea" (*CMA, Ench, Larron, P Ass* 7) home of Lilith (*q.v.*); symbol of sterility, menstruation to Apoll. (see *Poèmes à Lou,* XLI).

Mia (*Colombe poignardée, P Ass* 8) love of Apoll. at Monaco (?).

moine de Heisterbach (*P Ass 12, Sacrilège*) miraculous sleeper in legend of Heisterbacensis Caesarius.

Morgane la Faye (*Ench, Giov Moroni, Merlin*) enchantress, traditionally either young and beautiful or old and ugly, temptress of knights in her castle Sans Retour on Mount Gibel (Etna); student, mistress of Merlin (*q.v.*); dispenser of mirages (*fata morgana*); symbol of lust, death, night, art to Apoll.

Moriane (*Ench, P Ass 1*) Mauritania, Africa, country of the Moors in medieval romances *Brut, Morien,* etc. (Paris).

Moroni (*Giov Moroni*) famous Mormon angel; from *mort au nid* to Rouveyre; see *Giovanni.*

mouches "flies" (*Ench, Musicien, Santé, Tourbillon de mouches*) sterility symbols, Lesbians to Apoll. (cf. prose poem "Pablo Picasso"); see *quinconces, Saint-Jean.*

mouches de la Saint-Jean "flies of Saint John" (*CMA*) fireflies (called *mouches de Saint-Jean* in Belgian folklore); see *Saint-Jean.*

mouches ganiques (*Best, Que vlo-ve?*) invisible flies used by Lapp sorcerers to torment evildoers (Gourmont); from Norwegian *ganne* "to hex."

murènes "Muraenas" (*CMA*) species of eels, to which Vedius Pollon, a Roman gastronome, fed slaves according to Pliny, Seneca, Tertullian, etc., also Victor Hugo (Piron, *Chanson*); subject of painting by Gustave Moreau.

myrthe "myrtle" (*Maison des morts*) plant of Limbo.

N

Naama, Lilith, Aguereth, Manala (*P Ass 15*) demon mothers, dominated by Solomon, governesses of four seasons in Hebrew lore (Couffignal).

nageur "swimmer" (*CMA, Lul de F, Vend*) lover, poet; Apollinaire (cf. *Onirocritique*).

navire pavoisé "pavilioned ship" (*Collines*) magic, unmanned boat of folklore, medieval romance, Symbolist poetry; see works "Le Printemps" and *Onirocritique.*

noir et blanc "black and white" (*Émigrant, Larron*) ancient Oriental color talismans; see *bandelettes.*

noms six par six "names six by six" (*Vend*) number of names of Apoll., Croniamantal.

Noubosse (*CMA*) neologism of Apoll. for pudendum (Lawler,

Davies); from *faire la nouba* and *se donner une bosse* "to go on a spree" (Greet).

noyer "walnut tree" (*Signe, Simultanéités*) blazon of persecuted innocence (Her.).

O

oblong (*Cortège, Larron, Lul de F*) shape of light, fire, vision; of Apoll.'s face.

oiseau bleu "blue bird" (*Fiançailles, Tzigane, Un oiseau chante*) Roi Charmant ("King Charming"), changed into bird *couleur du temps* in story "L'Oiseau bleu" by Mme d'Aulnoy; see *cyprès, Truitonne.*

oiseau de Bénin "Benin bird" (*P Ass*) Apoll.'s name for Picasso (Benin: African country noted for fetishes, barbarism).

oiseau de la quintaine "quintain bird" (*Fiançailles*) phoenix; phallus; cock in religious feast-day jousts (Bates); Christ; (?); see *quintaine.*

oiseau tranquille "tranquil bird" (*Cortège*) one of several footless birds that nested in mid-air according to Oriental, medieval accounts (bird of paradise, hummingbird, etc.); (?).

oiseaux gemmipares "gemmiparous birds" (*Larron*) birds born of buds, issued from fruit in medieval travel literature, cabalistic writings; (?).

olivier "olive tree" (*Ench*) tree of Minerva; see *Élie, Énoch.*

ombre du soleil "shadow of the sun" (*Photographie*) from *ombre de soleil*, term of Her.; (?).

Ordre (see *bouche*).

Orkenise (*Ench*) town visited by Lancelot in *Le Livre de Lancelot del Lac.*

Orphée (*Best, Larron, Poème lu au mariage*) Orpheus, symbol of poet martyred by women (rose again in Orphic mysteries).

orphelin "orphan" (*Vend, Voyageur*) adj. for "disinherited," "abandoned," "deprived" (archaic).

otelle (*Lul de F*) blazon in shape of peeled almond, spear head, cicatrized wound; erotic symbol to Apoll.; (?).

P

pahule (*P Ass 1*) Wall. for "calm," "peaceful" (Piron).

pain "bread" (*Ench, Ermite, Larron, P Ass 2, Sacrilège, Vend, Zone*) symbol of the flesh, resurrection, Christ; hospitality.

Pâline (*CMA*) name of sword, neologism of Apoll. from *pâle* and *câline* (Lawler); (?).

Appendices

Pallas (*Larron*) goddess of femininity, reason, geometry; name from Gk. for "virgin," "maiden"; see *triangle.*

Pan (*Brasier, Chant du horizon, CMA, Ench, Musicien* (?), *Un monstre d'envie*) shepherd of flock of sphinx (*q.v.*), symbol of poetry, art, love, death to Apoll.; god of noonday rutting (Theocritus); see *pâtre.*

pantaure (*Larron*) the *pantarbe*, a magical magnetic stone shown to Apollonius of Tyana (*q.v.*) in India (Philostratus, III, 46).

paon pythagorique "Pythagorean peacock" (*Larron*) bird of Pythagoras' transmigration.

papesse "popess" (*Cox-City, Ermite*) the legendary antipopess Joan (9th century); second Tarot card, a seated woman (see *ermite*); a Catholic woman; (?).

pasquèle (*P Ass 1*) Wall. folksong (Piron).

passiflore "passionflower" (*Ermite, Fiançailles*) religious, erotic symbol.

pâtre "shepherd" (*Brasier, P Ass 12*) Pan (*q.v.*); Picasso in *P Ass.*

pattes (*Histoire d'une famille*) Lyonese cant for "old rags" (Pia, *Antilles*).

Peau-rouge "Redskin" (*Fantôme de nuées*) American Indian; Latin Quarter bohemian (cf. *Flâneur des deux rives*, ch. 1).

péket (*Que vlo-ve?*) cheap brandy, gin in Wall. (Piron).

pentacle (*Brasier*) five-sided astral figure, man, the microcosm-macrocosm, Pan, God, in magic; see *quinconces.*

phénix "phoenix" (*CMA, Zone*) symbol of poetic, erotic renewal, death-birth to Apoll.; Christ in medieval bestiaries; flew to pyre accompanied by world's birds in Latin legends; see *oiseau de la quintaine.*

Pie X (*Infaillibilité, Zone*) Pius X, the anti-modern pope (1903–14).

pierre d'un coq "cock's stone" (*Larron*) the *alectorian* or *cock's stone*, found in cock's maw; a *bezoar* or amulet in ancient times, often worn on necklace; virility symbol; see *Tanagre.*

pigeonnier "pigeon loft" (*Loin du pigeonnier*) Apoll.'s apartment in Latin Quarter.

pihi (*Fenêtres, Zone*) fabulous Chinese bird with one eye, one wing, flew in couples, male to right, female to left.

pimus (*Porte*) legendary Chinese fish with one eye, one fin, swam in mixed couples.

pin "pine" (*Vent nocturne*) tree of Atys into which he was metamorphosed, carried in spring fertility festivals; phallic symbol; see *dendrophore.*

Polydamne (*Ench*) wife of Egyptian Thoon, taught Helen (*q.v.*) how to make *nepenthe.*

pont des Reviens-t'en "bridge of Return" (*CMA*) opposite of *pont de Nul Retour* of medieval romance; term invented by Apoll.; (?).

pontifes "pontifs" (*Liens*) "bridge-builders" (from Lat.).

Port-Aviation (*Zone*) airport at Javisy-sur-Orge south of Paris in 1912 (Guthrie-Dillon).

postkotznida (*Otmika*) common dance around Sarajevo, Yugoslavia (Warnier).

probloque (*Lundi Rue Christine*) "proprietor" (Fr. slang).

Psylles (*Collines*) the Psylli, African people who perished battling the South Wind when it dried up their reservoirs (Heroditus); snake charmers, diviners to ancients.

puiseurs d'eau "water drawers" (*Larron*) Chaldean priests who used water from sacred Euphrates for divining.

pupille de mon oeil "pupil of my eye" (*Fiancée posthume, Zone*) term of endearment (same as "apple of my eye") from Deut. 34:10.

pyrauste (*CMA*) "fire-lighter," moth that lived in fire (Pliny).

Q

quadruple triangle (*Simon Mage*) cabalistic talisman (as △ or ⊠); early Gk. nimbus for Christ; symbol of absolute divinity in Christian iconography.

quarantaine (*Fiançailles*) "age of forty" (Durry) "forty in number" (Davies); "Lent"; (?).

quarante de Sébaste "forty of Sebastus" (*CMA*) sainted Christian soldiers frozen and burned by Romans in Asia Minor in 4th century (Holy Day: March 9).

quinconce "quincunx" (*Ench, Salomé*) magic five-starred pattern, associated with erotic death dances of flies, Salome (*q.v.*) by Apoll.; see *mouches, pentacle*.

quintaine (*Fiançailles*) the quintain or jousting target, sometimes a ring; female erotic symbol; see *oiseau de la quintaine*.

quinze signes du jugement dernier, les "the fifteen signs of the Last Judgment" (*Ench, Passant*) early Christian and medieval list of 15 miraculous happenings at end of world, earthquakes, burning oceans, etc. (Bede, Saint Augustine, etc.).

R

rampioule (*Que vlo-ve?*) "bindweed" in Wall. (Piron).

R.D. (*Tour*) Robert Delaunay, Orphic painter of the Eiffel Tower; see *Fenêtres*.

ribambelle ursuline "Ursuline procession" (*Cortège*) Saint Ursula and her 11,000 virgin companions said to have been massacred by the Huns in Cologne in the 3rd or 5th century.

rival (*Lul de F, Merlin*) "fellow dweller on the same bank" (OF).

roi d'Édesse, le "the king of Edessa" (*Larron*) Abgar V "the Black" (7 B.C.–50 A.D.) considered first Christian king by ancients; invited Jesus to Edessa (*q.v.*) according to 4th-century legend.

rois-mages de Cologne "Magi of Cologne" (*Cortège, Ench, Rose de H*) relics of Three Wise Men said to be in Cologne Cathedral, also in church of Hildesheim.

romarin "rosemary" (*Maison des morts, Rhénane d'automne*) funereal flower; flower of remembrance.

roseau "reed" (*Larron*) mock scepter given to Jesus (Matthew 27:29); Christian symbol of humility.

rose des vents "rose of the winds" (*Clair de lune, Merlin*) compass; moon; *derrière* (cf. "ton derrière de miel et de lumière," *Tendre comme le souvenir*, Nov. 26, 1915).

Rosemonde (*Best, Palais, Rosemonde*) Rosamond Clifford, "the Rose of the World," mistress of Henry II of England, said to have dwelt in a labyrinthine palace at Woodstock and to have been killed by the jealous queen, Eleanor of Aquitaine; pun on German for "rosy mouth," *rosen Mund* (Greet).

Rotsoge (*À travers l'Europe*) "red wake" or "red trail" (Ger.), perhaps a nickname for artist Marc Chagall; (?).

Roue "wheel" (*Tour*) huge Ferris wheel near Eiffel Tower before World War I.

roux "russet" (*Histoire d'une famille, Larron, Marizibill, P Ass 8*) color of King David's and Christ's hair in Byzantine art, Hebrew prophecies, apocalyptics works, etc. (Couffignal); traditional color of evil Jew's hair (diabolical) in Mysteries, Shakespeare, Marlowe, etc.

S

Sacontale (*CMA*) Shakuntala, "guarded by birds," Indian queen, heroine of Kaladasa's 5th-century play of the same name; see *gazelle*.

Sainte Fabeau (*CMA*) invented name for sword, from *beau phallus* (Davies); (?).

Saint-Jean, la (*CMA*) June 24, the nativity day of St. John the Baptist when fireworks, firebrands are lighted; see *mouches de la Saint-Jean*.

Salomé (*Danseuse, Salomé*) Salome, favorite symbol of immortal, fatal woman to 19th-century authors; same as *Hérodiade;* died in river with head on plate of ice in medieval legend (Krug) and in 7th-century Apocrypha (*Letter of Herod*).

Salomon (see *Naama, Zamir*).

saquoue (see *grusiner*).

sardine (*P Ass 17*) fish big enough at Marseilles to block harbor according to boast of Marseillais (Shattuck).

Schinderhannes (*P Ass, Schinderhannes*) famous 18th-century German robber, enemy of Jews, executed in 1803 (Décaudin).

Schultz (*Schinderhannes*) companion of Schinderhannes (*q.v.*), hanged with him in 1803 (Durry).

scorpions (*Ench*) animals that sting themselves to death when ringed with fire (Migne, *Encycl.*).

scurriles (*Larron*) "rowdy jokes" (archaic Fr.) traditional in Roman triumphs.

Sébaste (see *quarante*).

sel "salt" (*Larron*) traditional symbol of hospitality.

selage (*P Ass 10, Ench*) selago, magic plant of druids (Pliny); see *bruyère*.

sept ans "seven years" (*Collines*) prophesied period of suffering; from legend of Joseph in Egypt (Couffignal); (?).

sept epées "seven swords" (*CMA*) swords piercing Mary's or Christ's heart in Christian tradition (from Luke 2:35); see *châtaigne*.

sept femmes "seven women" (*Nuit rhénane*) the seven bathers of a Rhine legend of Oberwesel combined with legends of green-haired nixies (Décaudin).

serpents qui s'entr'aiment "serpents making love" (*Larron*) basic creation myth (Indian, Greek [Zeus and Persephone], Druidic, etc.); homosexuals ("69"); Tiresias' serpents; (?).

Sicile (*Vend*) Sicily, place of disastrous earthquake of Dec. 28, 1908.

Signe d'Automne "Sign of Autumn" (*Signe*) autumn figure in zodiac; (?); see *Chef*.

signe du troisième mois "sign of third month" (*Fiançailles*) Virgo the Virgin, zodiac sign of third month of summer under which Apoll. was born.

signes du jugement dernier (see *quinze*).

silence (*Larron*) Harpocrates, sometimes an erotic god (Durry).

sirènes (*CMA, Fiançailles, Émigrant, Ench, Lettre-Océan, Vend, Zone*) Sirens, woman-birds, enchantresses of the straits of Messina; erotic women, prostitutes in Fr. slang; "boat whistles"; see *haleine, houhou*.

six par six (see *noms*).

Socrate (*Ench, Larron*) Socrates, symbol of homosexual love to Apoll. (see *Chroniques,* May 4, 1911).

sol hawai (*Que vlo-ve?*) "sur le pouce"—lit. "sur le boyau"—"on the run" in Wall. (Piron).

songe matinal "morning dream" (*Ench, Hérésiarque, Juif latin*) dream that is always veracious, according to Apoll. (see first version of "Juif latin").

sphinx (*Brasier, Ench*) symbols of wisdom; see *Pan*.

statues suant "statues sweating" (*Larron*) phenomenon noted by Cicero, among others.

Sultan (*CMA*) Turkish Sultan, either Mohammed IV (1642–91) or Ahmed III (1673–1736) (Borschak); see *Cosaques*.

synagogue (*Synagogue*) building at Unkel near Honnef in Rhineland (Breunig).

T

Tanagre (*Larron*) Tanagra, Spartan town famous for its fighting cocks; see *pierre*.

Taranis la femelle "Taranis the female" (*Ench*) member of Gallic trinity with Esus (Hésus), Teutatis (*qq.v.*) according to Lucan, thus female god to some 19th-century Celtic scholars (e.g., John Rhys); Gallic Jupiter, Thor.

taureau "bull" (*Larron*) virile male force; Mithra (Durry); Marduk, Baal, Dionysos, etc.; (?).

Tchatcha (*Que vlo-ve?*) Wall. word for a kind of blueberry marmalade (Piron).

Telchines (see *Linde*).

temps "times" (*Fenêtres*) Parisian newspaper; see *liberté*.

Téremtété (*Otmika*) "made by the Devil" (Hung.) (Warnier).

Teutatès (*Ench*) Gallic Jupiter, Mars, Mercury, or Pluto; see *Hésus, Taranis*.

tiz (see *far tiz*).

todis à vinde (*P Ass 1*) "always for sale" in Wall. (Piron).

Tour "Tower" (*Tour*) Eiffel Tower; phallic symbol; see *Roue*.

tremblement de terre "earthquake" (*Lettre-Océan*) earthquake on French Riviera in spring of 1887.

Trèves (*Vend*) Trier, ancient capital of Gaul (see letter to Lou, May 2, 1915).

triangle isocèle "isosceles triangle" (*Larron*) female erotic symbol (cf. "Deuxième poème secret"); symbol of Pallas (*q.v.*); symbol of reason, geometry (Durry); see *chape*.

trismégiste (*Best, Crépuscule, Vend*) "thrice powerful," popular epithet among Symbolists, occultists, etc.

Tristouse (*P Ass*) woman's name from medieval romance, opposite of *Joyeuse*.

Truitonne (*Histoire d'une famille*) ugly, evil princess in Mme d'Aulnoy's story "L'Oiseau bleu"; see *oiseau bleu*.

Tseilom Kop (*P Ass* 15) "baptized head" (Heb. invective) (note of Apoll.).

Tyolet (*Ench*) hero of Breton lay of same name, has gift of calling animals by whistling.

U

Urgande la méconnue "Urganda the unrecognized" (*Ench*) sorceress in *Amadis de Gaul* (cf. prefatory poem to Cervantes' *Don Quixote*).

V

Vendémiaire (*Vend*) "vintage month," September in French Revolution calendar.

vent du sud (see *Psylles*).

vêtue "clothed woman" (*Un soir*) word for heretic in 13th-century Fr.; Eve; Annie Playden; (?).

vieil ange "old angel" (*Ermite*) angel in Luke 22:43 (Couffignal).

vieille femme "old woman" (*Merlin*) Morgane (*q.v.*), old and lecherous fairy; 100-year-old woman Merlin makes love to in *Prophéties de Merlin;* (?); see *Merlin*.

Vierselin Tigoboth (*P Ass* 2) "Grumpy Your-basket's-dripping" in Wall. dial. (Piron).

vieux Rhin "old Rhine" (*Synagogue*) Father Rhine of German legend (Orecchioni).

vin de Chypre "Cyprus wine" (*Palais*) Eucharistic wine in Apoll.; from *Cypri botus*, medieval symbol of Christ; (?).

Viviane (*Ench, Merlin*) Viviane, Niniane, the Lady of the Lake, who enchanted, entombed Merlin (*q.v.*); see *Éviene*.

Volcanique (see *Empédocle*).

Y

Yette (*Colombe poignardée, P Ass* 9) Mariette, perhaps one of Apoll.'s first loves (Décaudin).

Z

Zamir (*Brasier*) Shamir, fabulous worm or stone used by Solomon to cut stone for Temple of Jerusalem (Jewish-Arabic folklore, *Talmud*).

Zélotide (*Ermite, P Ass* 3) name from Boccaccio's *Fiammetta* (Lawler); name common to 18th-century French novels.

Zone (*Fumées, Zone*) area around Paris, ended at Avenue des Ternes in 1912 (Durry); term for plane in Orphic paintings; name (in

plural) of a projected review of Apoll. (Onimus-Blumenkranz);
name of region in Alsace; military terrain; (?).

Zun (*Lettre-Océan*) Henri Barzun, with whom Apoll. quarreled in
1914 (Schmits).

Sources of References

Bates, Scott, *The Esthetics of Guillaume Apollinaire.*

Borschak, Elie, "La Lettre des Zaporogues au Sultan," *Rev. des Études
Scientifiques,* XXVI (Paris 1950), 98–105.

Breunig, L.-C. "La Synagogue," *Flâneur des deux rives,* No. 4.

Chevalier, J.-C., "Quelques remarques sur un index de Calligrammes,"
Rev. des Lettres Modernes, 69–70 (Spring 1962), 40–53.

Davies, Margaret, *Apollinaire.*

Décaudin, Michel, *Le Dossier d'Alcools.*

Durry, Marie-Jeanne, *Alcools* (3 vols.).

Fettweiss, Christian, *Apollinaire en Ardenne.*

Fonteyn, André, *Apollinaire Prosateur,* Paris (Nizet), 1964.

Gourmont, Rémy de, *Chez les Lapons,* Paris, 1890 [a source of
mouches ganiques].

Greet, Anne Hyde, *Guillaume Apollinaire, Alcools,* notes.

Guthrie, Ramon and Diller, George E., *Prose and Poetry of Modern
France,* N. Y. (Scribner's), 1964.

Krug, Justine, *Les Références à la Mythologie dans L'Oeuvre de Guillaume Apollinaire* (Sorbonne thesis), 1951.

Lawler, J.-R., "Les Sept Épees," *Flâneur des deux rives,* No. 3.

Louis, René, "Lul de Faltenin," *Flâneur des deux rives,* No. 2.

Onimus-Blumenkranz, Noëmi, *Apollinaire témoin des peintres de son
temps.*

Orecchioni, Pierre, *Le Thème du Rhin dans l'inspiration de Guillaume
Apollinaire.*

Paris, Gaston, *Romans en vers du cycle de la table ronde,* Paris, 1888
[a major source for *L'Enchanteur pourrissant*].

Pia, Pascal, "Apollinaire aux Antilles," *Quo Vadis?,* July-Sept. 1954.

————. "Mon beau navire ô ma mémoire," *Carrefour,* Jan. 6, 1960.

Piron, Maurice, "Les Wallonismes de Guillaume Apollinaire."

————. "Sur quelques passages de *La Chanson du mal-aimé,*" *Rev. des
Lettres Modernes,* 85–89 (Autumn 1963).

Rouveyre, André, *Amour et poésie de Guillaume Apollinaire,* Paris,
1955.

Schmits, G., "Lettre-Océan," *Savoir et Beauté,* XLIV, 2–3 (1964),
2691–2698.

Shattuck, Roger, *Selected Writings of Guillaume Apollinaire,* New
York, 1950.

Steegmuller, Francis, *Apollinaire, Poet Among the Painters.*
————. Notes to William Meredith's *Alcools* (N. Y., 1964).
Thiry, Marcel, "Note sur Apollinaire en Ardenne," *Savoir et Beauté,*
    XLIV, 2–3 (1964), 2703–2710.
Villemarqué, Hésart de la, *Myrdhinn,* Paris, 1862 [a major source of
    Merlin information for Apollinaire].
Warnier, Raymond, "Un conte slave d'Apollinaire, 'l'Otmika,'" *Filo-
    logija,* No. 3.
Wolf, E. M. *Guillaume Apollinaire und das Rheinland.*

Appendix B

Erotic References

Apollinaire believed that all life, death, and art proceeded from
Eros: life was Love and Love was "not only French art but Art itself,
universal art" (*Chroniques,* Jan. 26, 1911). Poetry in its basic sense
meant *creation* to him and was by definition an orphic translation of
the erotic unity of the universe: it constituted a basic pun between the
creative Word and its created World. His poems are therefore puns,
pantheistic microcosms of the fuller reality; and they are filled with
erotic wordplay designed to draw the reader into that reality. A great
many of the allusions in this wordplay are not readily apparent to the
common reader. The following list of bona fide, unequivocal erotic com-
parisons culled from Apollinaire's complete works is, therefore, one
more key to an obscure body of prose and poetry. I have compiled this
list in the knowledge that most of the terms are common enough in a
literary heritage which includes Aristophanes, Rabelais, and Shakespeare; and I sincerely believe that, as Apollinaire wrote in *The
Amorous Devils,* they could shock only cads and pedants.

Phallus.—American Peninsula; arrow; baby; bird; bitt; bow; bowling
pin; branch; bread; bridge of flesh; broom; candle; cannon; cock; col-
umn; cutlass; cyclops; distaff; Eiffel Tower; factory chimney; fountain; head; instrument; jujube; key; king; knife; lance; lily; mast; member of triad; menhir; meter stick; milestone; monument; nightingale;
orphan; pen; pencil; pendulum; pestle; pin; pine tree; piston; plough-
share; resurrected flesh; rifle; Robin's flute; rod; Saint Vitus; sausage;
science; serpent; spring; staff; stake; sugar stick; sun; tail; thing-
amabob; thorn; tool; toothpick; totem pole; tower; trunk of tree; unicorn; virility; wand; weapon; yard.

Testicles.—Agates; beggars' sacks (*besace*); bells of Notre Dame;
fruits; globes; heads; pinecones; rollers; rolls; witnesses; Zeppelins.

Sperm.—Balm; burning offering; cervical matter; gold; nuts; pine cone seeds; sap.

Coitus.—Beast with two backs; game (of great goose; of navels); ideal combat; to celebrate, ride, visit, wound, a woman.

Woman's body (general).—Alp; altar; asp; book to be read in bed; canal (becoming sea); cloud; crown of laurel; dough; dove; Eldorado; flock with the staggers; flower; forest; frog; fruit; garden (in four seasons); geyser; gulf; jasmin; life; light; lily; mare; musical instrument; night; ocean; orchard; palace; panther; paradise; pearl; plain; promised land of Canaan; quiver; region in earthquake; rose; rosebush; sea; serpent; ship; sky; soap; spring; star; sun; Switzerland (with Mont Blanc, Mont Rose, Righi); temple; tower; tower of ivory; tree; tuberose; vessel; vine; victim (sacrificial); whistle.

Breasts.— Angels' buttocks; Balas rubies; bananas; bread (consecrated); bridge (double of roses; of snow in the sun); cannon balls; cheeses; cream cheeses; cups; cupules; doves; eglantine; flowers; fruits; half-globes; hillocks; lily; meringues; moon and hill; moons; oranges; pearls; persimmons; pigeons; pimentos; prickly pears; rosebuds; roses; sheep; shells (bursting; hard); snowballs; star; tangerines; tennis balls; vine-leaves; wineskins. *Nipples.*—Bees; berries (strawberries; arbutus berries); buds; coral tips; flowers; rose candy drops; roses.

Derrière.—Ace of spades; amphorae; angel (breathing; blowing); angels (two chubby); balloon (captive); balls; cavern; clouds (of setting sun; with star); cyclops; dawns (white); door (eighth, ninth of body); earth (yellow); egg (soft-boiled); eiderdown (of rosy snow; of Mezidon; of Cupid); eminences; face (posterior); foundation; fruits (candied); globes; hills (of silver, of cream); honey and light; lozenge; mappemonde; melon; moon; mound; mound of butter; path (narrow of Sodom); pear; pearl; pearls (two mountains of); quarters of moon; rose; rose of the winds; rosette; sweet potato; volcanic crater; watermelon.

Pubic hair.—Barbed wire; beard (jolly, of frivolous god); black sheep; buckler of Occidental hypocrisy; bush; crown of thorns; Eldorado; fennel; forest (virgin; in winter; of Erebus; of Dodona); fleece; Golden Fleece; incense burner; lace; lawn; mane; mop; moss; paint brush; parsley; sacred wood; sheaf; submarine garden; tendrils of vine; thyme; triangle (of the divinity; isosceles). *Armpits.*—Grottoes (shady; with stalactites); hot houses (with hellebore; moss; plants; vanilla; scorpions).

Pudendum.—Abyss; American tropical isthmus; apricot; bar of cross (vertical); beak; Bellona; broom holder; butcher shop; cage; cat; country of Tender; crack; divinity; domicile; dugout; door (eighth, ninth of body; of living coral); Empyrean; engine; fig; flesh (secret); garden; grenade; grotto; isosceles triangle; kettle; leaf; lock; lozenge; marmot; mortar; mouth; mussel; nutcracker; pall; passionflower; piston; quetsche; retreat; roll; rose; rosebush; sacred bordello; sea shell; temple; thing (female); trench; Venice (the sex of Europe); volcanic crater; wheel; whistle; wound; "Y." *Clitoris.*—Bud; button; finger; fire in forest; pea; star. *Vaginal mucus.*—Cyprine; foam of the sea; geyser; hippomanes; liquor of love; pap; spring.

Notes and References

Chronology of Alcools

1. Possible dates: 1905, 1906, and 1908, when Apollinaire took his vacation in the Low Countries (Michel Décaudin, *Le Dossier d'Alcools,* Paris 1960, p. 172). I have placed the poem in the 1908 period because of its optimistic symbolism, and because it resembles in theme and imagery a story about Holland, "Jacob Stole a Rose" by Gustave Kahn, that Apollinaire read and admired in the summer of 1908 (*La Phalange,* Nov. 15, 1908).

2. Marie Laurencin wrote in her memoirs that she loved French queens and heroines, beginning with Ste. Clotilde (*Le Carnet des nuits,* Paris, 1956, p. 17). She herself was an anonymous poetess like the nineteenth-century "Clotilde de Surville" whose poems are in Apollinaire's library. "Clotilde" resembles certain poems of the 1911–12 period in prosody and symbolism. All these reasons have caused me to place it here among the poems of the Marie cycle.

Chapter One

1. *Dictionnaire complémentaire de l'Académie française* (Paris, 1846). This reading is supported by a suppressed line from the manuscript, "Thou must put Hell and darkness (*ombre*) in thy voice" (Décaudin, *Dossier,* p. 172).

2. Suggested by Robert Couffignal in his *Apollinaire et la Bible* (unpublished thesis).

3. Couffignal.

4. *Intransigeant,* Jan. 25, 1910. See poem "Ocean Letter" (*Calligrammes*) and Camille Flammarion, *La Fin du monde* (Paris, 1894, p. 197).

5. Saint Jerome seems to have been a favorite of Apollinaire. Among many references to him, two are of special interest:

[Speaking of the importance of the belt in dancing:] "The dance has always been considered one of Satan's pomps by Church Fathers, completely unjustly in my opinion—and in this connection I shall recall that Saint Jerome, who was an authority on the subject, used to place the power of the fallen angel close to the belt." (*La Grâce et le maintien français*, p. 57).

[Speaking against Charles-Henry Hirsch]: "In reality, everything that has to do with poetry irritates M. Charles-Henry Hirsch. He would like to imitate the angel who beat Saint Jerome because he read a work of poetry." (*Phalange*, March 15, 1908).

6. Fonds Jacques Doucet, Bibliothèque Sainte-Geneviève, Paris, in MS of *Le Poète assassiné*. Although Apollinaire told Madeleine that he lost the manuscript of *La Gloire de l'olive* (letter of Sept. 14, 1915), a great part of the work can easily be reconstructed from crossed-out sections on the MS. What he lost, therefore, may have been an amplified copy of the original.

7. The letter dated 1899 by Toussaint-Luca in his *Guillaume Apollinaire* (Paris, 1954, pp. 27–28) where the poet describes his reading of socialist papers, actually dates from the summer of 1901: the letter includes a reference to a work of Émile Bruni which appeared at the end of June 1901.

8. Stanza 16 ("The bearded water drawers . . .") was in part taken from M. Karppe's article "Mélanges assyriologiques et bibliques" in the *Journal Asiatique*, X (July–Aug. 1897), the black-and-white bands from pp. 83–84 and the water drawers from p. 78. Karppe also discusses a line from Psalm 11 on the Red Sea crossing: "The sea saw it and fled" (Apollinaire has the sea "open like an eye" in st. 15), the Chaldean *rimi* or sacred buffalo-antelope (Apollinaire's gnu?), and the symbolism of Jehovah as fire and the sun. The main point of the article is to analyze the Pentateuch in terms of Chaldean belief and custom.

9. Rubens Duval, "Histoire politique, religieuse et littéraire d'Édesse," *Journal Asiatique*, Sept.–Oct. 1891, chapter 5.

10. Pointed out by M. Couffignal.

11. Décaudin, *Dossier*, p. 152.

12. Toussaint-Luca. This letter must have been written in Jan. 1899 when Max Régis was visiting Henri Rochefort in Monaco, an event alluded to in the letter.

13. The word *surhumain* was italicized in the first published version of the story (*Revue Blanche*, June 1902).

14. Apollinaire copied the angels and their qualities from Moïse Schwab's *Vocabulaire de l'angélologie* (Paris, 1897); see my article on this source and others in the *Revue des Lettres Modernes* (1965). Couffignal gives a list of the Biblical sources (pp. 19–20).

15. L. Turgan, *Histoire de l'aviation* (Paris, 1909); Baeder and Dubouchet, *Dictionnaire illustré de la navigation aérienne* (Paris, 1913); etc.

Notes and References

16. L. A. Paton, *Les Prophécies de Merlin* (N. Y., 1927), II, p. 192 ff.

17. Couffignal, p. 120.

18. Décaudin, "Compléments à un dossier," *Revue des Lettres Modernes*, 69–70 (Spring 1962), p. 58.

Chapter Two

1. Pascal Pia, *Apollinaire par lui-même* (Paris 1954), p. 30.

2. *Tendre comme le souvenir*, July 22, 1915.

3. One of the first uses of the name *Tristouse* (the heroine's name in *The Assassinated Poet*), was in a legend about a king who coveted his daughter when informed he could marry only someone who resembled her dead mother; the girl cut off her hands to terminate the resemblance and changed her name from Joyeuse to Tristouse (Hermann Suchier, *La Manekine*, Paris, 1884, I, introduction). The Grimms and Perrault printed versions of this tale, and Apollinaire referred to it in the second chapter of *The Putrescent Enchanter*. The *manekine* or "girl with the cut-off hands" is found throughout European folklore and in Symbolist literature and is often associated with trees (she sits in them). Her hands, therefore, make natural symbols for autumn leaves, an image Apollinaire used in "Rhenish Autumn," "Sign," and "Marie."

4. "Anteros arrives at first, that brother of love who resembles him, but he soon flees to leave place for the little born blind boy who rules us all" (*Phalange*, July 15, 1908, p. 82).

5. "Le Roman du Mal-Aimé," *Table Ronde*, Sept. 1952, p. 117.

6. Apollinaire cited many of these sources in his 1904 article on Anatole France's novel *Thaïs* (*Mercure de France*, July).

7. See Décaudin, *Dossier*, p. 105.

8. Décaudin, *Dossier*, p. 171.

9. René Louis, "Encore 'Lul de Faltenin,' " *Flâneur des Deux Rives*, No. 2 (June 1954), p. 11.

10. L.-C. Breunig, "Lul de Faltenin," *Revue des Sciences Humaines*, Oct.–Dec. 1956.

11. *Reliques of Ancient English Poetry*, ed. Thomas Percy (1847), II, 156, st. 6, 11. 21–24.

12. André Rouveyre, *Amour et poésie d'Apollinaire* (Paris, 1955), pp. 183–86. See Appendix A, *Rosemonde*.

13. Bibliotheque Sainte-Geneviève, Jacques Doucet Collection, Paris.

14. *Revue Littéraire de Paris et de Champagne*, Feb.–Sept. 1906 (cited in full by Décaudin, *Dossier*, p. 230).

15. Décaudin, *Dossier*, p. 205.
16. Décaudin, *Dossier*, p. 202.

Chapter Three

1. Charles Maurras, *Barbarie et poésie* (Paris, 1925), reprint of article of July 21, 1901.
2. The first quotation is from "The Napkin of the Poets," the second from "The Pretty Redhead." The literary influences on Picasso have not been thoroughly traced. For the period in question, the best critical works treating of Picasso's ideas to my knowledge are Alexandre Cirici-Pellicer, *Picasso Avant Picasso* (Geneva, 1950) and Anthony Blunt and Phoebe Pool, *Picasso, The Formative Years* (London, 1962).
3. Gwendolyn Bays, *The Orphic Vision, Seer Poets from Novalis to Rimbaud* (Lincoln, Nebraska, 1964), chapter 1.
4. *Les Diables amoureux*, p. 75 (from introduction to *L'Oeuvre de Crébillon le fils*, 1911).
5. Jeanne Humbert, *Sous la cagoule* (Paris, n.d.).
6. In *El Imparcial* of Madrid; reprinted in Ventura Garcia Calderon's *Une enquête littéraire: Don Quichotte à Paris et dans les tranchées* (Paris, Centre d'études franco-hispaniques de l'Université de Paris, 1916).
7. *La Grande France*, April 1903, p. 244.
8. Erich Meyer, "La poésie française contemporaine," trans. Guillaume Apollinaire, Jan., April 1903.
9. Noëmi Onimus-Blumenkranz, *Apollinaire témoin des peintres de son temps*, thèse pour l'école du Louvre (Paris, 1960 [?]), pp. 124–26. This is the first critical work to analyze in detail Apollinaire's crusade for a synthesis of the plastic arts.
10. L.-C. Breunig, J.-C. Chevalier, critical edition of *Les Peintres Cubistes* (Paris, 1965), introduction.
11. L.-C. Breunig, "Apollinaire et le cubisme," *Rev. des Lettres Modernes*, 69–70 (Spring 1962), p. 19. My translation.
12. Marcel Adéma, *Apollinaire*, trans., Denise Folliot (N. Y., 1955), p. 154.
13. *The Cubist Painters*, chapter 1; first printed in a catalogue to a Fauvist exposition in June 1908 (in *Chroniques d'art*, pp. 56–58).
14. *Phalange*, Aug. 1908, p. 162; Jan. 1909, p. 640; *Pan*, Oct. 1908, p. 260.
15. *Cubist Painters*, ch. 1; "Jean Royère," p. 164; *Phalange*, Aug. 1908, p. 161.
16. *Vers et Prose*, June–July–Aug. 1908, p. 124; *Phalange*, Jan. 1909, p. 640; Sept. 1908, p. 63.

17. "Henri Matisse," pp. 103–7; *Phalange*, April 1909, p. 910.

18. *Le Dernier Cahier de Mécislas Golberg* (Paris, 1908) pp. 220–23, reviewed by Apollinaire in *La Phalange*, March 1908.

19. *Cubist Painters*, ch. 1; Toussaint-Luca, pp. 259–60; see also "Jean Royère."

20. *Phalange*, Aug. 1908, p. 161.

21. Quoted by Christopher Gray in his *Cubist Aesthetic Theories* (London, 1953).

22. *Cubist Painters*, ch. 1.

23. Mallarmé in *Les Dieux Antiques* relates the Ixion legend to the solar cycle.

24. "Jean Royère"; *Cubist Painters*, ch. 1.

25. *Phalange*, Nov. 1908, p. 462; *Chroniques*, p. 51 (May 1, 1908).

26. "Jean Royère"; *Phalange*, April 1909, p. 154; *Symbolist Poetry*, p. 180.

27. Toussaint-Luca, pp. 259–60; Adéma, *Guillaume Apollinaire, le mal-aimé* (Paris, 1952), p. 94; *Phalange*, April 1909, p. 910; *Cubist Painters*, ch. 1.

28. *Chroniques*, pp. 54, 59, 62 (1908–9).

29. *Phalange*, Nov. 1908, p. 463; "André Salmon"; "Jean Royère"; "Henri Matisse"; *Chroniques*, p. 60 (Nov. 1908).

30. See Décaudin, *La Crise des valeurs symbolistes* (Paris, 1960). Charles Morice emphasized the divine mission and the autonomous creation of the poet in his influential Symbolist manifesto *La Littérature de tout à l'heure* (1889). Orpheus, Ixion, and the flame were used everywhere as symbols: see, for example, the *Ixion* of Fagus (1903), the *Lettres à Alexis* of Golberg (1904), and the "Théâtre muet" of Rémy de Gourmont (in *Le Pèlerin de silence*, 1896). The "Théâtre muet" presents striking similarities to "The Brazier."

31. *Chroniques*, p. 146 (Feb. 14, 1911), p. 265 (Oct. 14, 1912), and p. 272 (Feb. 1913); see also p. 253 (June 30, 1912) and *Cubist Painters*, ch. 7. According to Georges Hilaire in his *Derain* (Geneva, 1959), Apollinaire introduced Derain to Picasso (p. 42). Derain was present at the genesis of "Les Demoiselles d'Avignon" and had been an admirer of African art since 1901. His "conversion" took place in 1905 and consisted of a new, "divine" conception of light without shadow in which colors became all-important (Gaston Diehl, *Derain*); Apollinaire wrote in 1912, "Today all shadow has disappeared" (*Chroniques*, p. 211). Fire was one of the Fauvists' main symbols.

32. See Derain's *Lettres à Vlaminck* (Paris, 1955) in which he describes his search for the absolute, his reactions to Nietzsche, his solitude, his early anarchism (which "destroyed the world every night to

reconstruct it every morning"), and his disgust with women and humanity. He pictures the latter in 1907 as voluntarily committing suicide.

33. *Les Marges,* May 1909.

34. Cf. the second chapter of *The Putrescent Enchanter.* In chapter 10 of *The Assassinated Poet* Picasso is a shepherd and his paintings are his flock. For Apollinaire's Pan symbolism see chapter 5, section on "The New Woman," of the present study.

35. Jeanine Moulin and Margaret Davies find an Icarus-like check here. To them the line would mean, "I should rather remain attached to life than be consumed by fire" (or sphinx worms to Miss Davies) which would indicate a feeling of inadequacy before his aims on the part of the poet. See also Durry, III, 168, for similar ideas. The manuscript ends with the ambiguous line, "Strangers it is too cold to lie out under the stars."

36. As the poem about All Saints' Day ("Rhenish Autumn") dedicated to *Toussaint*-Luca. See Décaudin, *Dossier,* p. 41.

37. Adéma, *Apollinaire,* p. 104.

38. Apollinaire possessed one of Picasso's paintings which showed a woman with her eyes closed "remembering" in a blue mist ("Head of a Woman," 1903).

39. This pun is found also in *The Assassinated Poet* (chapter 10), "Cortege," "Anvers," and, perhaps, "Tree." Cf. the lyrical evocation of Marie's treelike paintings in the *Soirées de Paris* for Nov. 15, 1913 (reprinted in *Il y a*).

Chapter Four

1. *Le Figaro,* Dec. 5, 1910.

2. Letter to Henri Martineau in *Le Divan,* June 1913, p. 267.

3. André Billy, *L'Évolution actuelle du roman* (Paris, 1911), p. 75; first published as newspaper articles in 1910.

4. "To have a bud on one's rosebush" (line 11) meant *to menstruate* in the seventeenth century (F. Vosselmann, *La Menstruation,* Paris, 1936, p. 74).

5. A careful examination of *Les Huit Paradis* by Princess G.-V. Bibesco (Paris, 1908) which Apollinaire reviewed for *La Phalange* of March 15, 1908 (pp. 858–59) reveals that the whole of "Ispahan" with the exception of the last four lines is a poetic transposition of the chapter "Ispahan." A reminiscence of Mme Bibesco's "flock of sphinx" (*troupeau de sphinx,* p. 156)—veiled women—may have provided part of the image in the last section of "The Brazier," published two months after Apollinaire's review.

6. Manuscript; in *Dossier,* p. 212.

7. Cited by N. Calas in "The Rose and the Revolver," *Yale French Studies*, Fall-Winter, 1948, p. 111.

8. The passages about the two sailors. The origin of this image may be a photograph of Guillaume and his brother in sailor suits (Décaudin, *Dossier*, p. 133). An illustrated manuscript reproduced in the catalogue of the Milan Apollinaire exposition of 1960 shows that the poet envisoned two stalwart battle companions. A curious coincidence: Rémy de Gourmont in *Un volcan en éruption* (1882) tells of two sisters found in each others' arms at Pompey, the oldest of whom wore two iron rings and had fallen on her side, the youngest of whom wore her hair in a braid!

9. In May 1911 (Couffignal, p. 142).

10. Some critics and several English and American translators have believed that this passage refers to the ascension of Christ, as in the lines immediately preceding it, in which case the *le* of the French would mean "Him" rather than the "it" of my translation. It would seem, however, that the references to Jesus rising "better than aviators" and to the "first airplane" (whereas the flights of Icarus, Enoch, and Elijah preceded that of Christ) would eliminate this possibility. Apollinaire wrote a few months later, "We are going higher now and don't touch the ground any more" ("The Musician of Saint Merry").

11. "The night withdraws like a lovely mulatto girl"; Marie's frizzy hair made some believe that she was part Creole (she was illegitimate like Apollinaire) (Francis Steegmuller, *Apollinaire, Poet Among the Painters*, N. Y., 1963, p. 160). This may explain the references to mulattoes in "Windows" and "The Betrothal."

12. *Paris-Journal*, May 24, 1914.

13. Even the ferret and the hedgehog of "The Traveler" may not be real animals at all, but women—like the ferrets, moles, panthers, tigresses, etc., elsewhere in Apollinaire's writings.

14. Pierre Guiraud, *Index des mots d'Alcools de Guillaume Apollinaire* (Klincksieck, 1953).

Chapter Five

1. Décaudin, *Dossier*, p. 224. Fagus, a friend of Apollinaire, published an almanac of poems in 1903 with some titles from the Revolutionary calendar.

2. Pierre Orecchioni, *Le Thème du Rhin dans l'inspiration de Guillaume Apollinaire* (Paris, 1956), p. 120.

3. Jacques Naville, "A propos d'une lettre de Guillaume Apollinaire à André Gide," *Mercure de France*, June 1957, p. 327.

4. Cendrars' great poem is often cited, to the contrary, as a major influence on "Zone." The two poets met in 1912, and the two poems

are remarkably similar, with many almost-identical lines and situations. Cendrars said repeatedly that he wrote his poem in New York in April 1912, and critics usually date "Zone" the following summer, after Marie Laurencin had definitively left Apollinaire. Yet I submit that internal evidence shifts the weight of evidence in the opposite direction.

Both poems are narrated, seemingly spontaneously, in the first person by a sad, sick, and lonely poet walking through a big city, discussing the past, the poor, and refugees from society as he goes. Both poets evoke the powerful figure of Christ. Both speak of their exotic voyages, both describe Jewish ghettoes. Neither goes into a church as he desires. Cendrars sees immigrants in flop-houses; Apollinaire watches emigrants at the Saint Lazare Station. In "Easter in New York" Jewish women are "polluted" "at the back of bars"; in "Zone" they are "bloodless" at the back of shops. "Easter" ends with a description of the rising sun as Christ's head "covered with spit"; "Zone" ends with the rising sun as a bloody stump of a neck.

Now, most of this subject matter had been used before 1912 by Apollinaire in poems and stories from "The Passerby of Prague" to "The Bethrothal"; emigrants, Jewish ghettoes, rambles through cities by night and day, churches, Christ's presence or absence, Christ as the sun, prostitutes, dirty streets, the poor, etc., were all essential to his Muse. He had used similar poetic techniques in "The Betrothal" and "The Song of the Poorly Beloved," both poems much admired by Cendrars. Cendrars, on the other hand, had written nothing before "Easter" but "The Legend of Novgorod" (which no critic or poet has ever seen) and some sophomoric love poems, Séquences, which contain none of "Easter's" symbols, subjects, themes, or techniques.

I believe, then, that Cendrars was either first influenced by Apollinaire's works before writing his poem and influencing "Zone" in turn; or, more likely, that he wrote his poem after seeing a draft of "Zone." There is nothing but a shifting body of oral evidence to prove either that Cendrars actually wrote "Easter" in April 1912 (he was a notorious yarn-spinner and later changed some details of his original story), or that Apollinaire wrote all of "Zone" after that date. The latter had been having problems with Marie for some time before the June parting; he had also been depressed—and religious-minded—ever since his incarceration at the Santé prison the preceding September.

5. Félicien Fagus also combined the Ixion myth with a divine child-savior (*Ixion*, Paris, 1903).

6. *Chroniques*, Oct. 1, 1910.

7. See letter to Picasso of Sept. 4, 1918 (in *Cahiers d'Art*, 22e année

Notes and References

[1947], pp. 142–143), in which Apollinaire speaks of Picasso's and his own classical preoccupations.

8. *Le Flâneur des deux rives*, No. 4 (Dec. 1954), pp. 1–2.

9. Henri Kahnweiler, *Juan Gris* (Paris, 1947), pp. 251, 313.

10. *Mercure de France*, Jan. 1962.

11. L.-C. Breunig, J.-C. Chevalier, *Les Peintres Cubistes*, p. 115, nn. 3, 4, 7, 8.

12. Cited by Pierre Cabanne in *L'Épopée du cubisme* (Paris, 1963), p. 86 (in introd. of Breunig, Chevalier to *Les Peintres Cubistes*).

13. Letter of July 4, 1913 (in *Le Flâneur des deux rives*, No. 4, p. 4).

14. In the Apollinaire Museum of Stavelot, Belgium, there is a letter of Dec. 24 from Nîmes which is probably to Delaunay: "Greetings to you, Robert, to your wife, to your paintings. Write me often. I embrace you." For a thorough discussion of the relationship between the two men, see Breunig, Chevalier, introd. to *Les Peintres Cubistes*.

15. When Apollinaire arrived at the front during the war, he wrote Paul Guillaume (April 18, 1915), "Here I am entirely in the rank of man-target as in Chirico's portrait" (*Les Arts à Paris*, Jan. 1923).

16. The last act is reminiscent of the last chapter of Gide's Symbolist *Voyage d'Urien* (1893), and of Rimbaud's prose poem "Being Beauteous."

17. Norman O. Brown, *Life Against Death* (N. Y., 1959), p. 52.

18. Besides *The Putrescent Enchanter*, "The Song of the Poorly Beloved," "The Brazier," *The Assassinated Poet* (ch. 10), and "The Musician of Saint Merry," see "The Nine Doors of Your Body," "The Second Secret Poem," and "Song of the Horizon in Champagne" for more evocations of Pan. Apollinaire's great interest in group dances and processions relates to this theme.

19. Fernand Fleuret, an erudite Symbolist poet, had written three-line short stories in newspapers.

20. Letters to Madeleine Aug. 3, July 1, 1915; letter to Jeanne-Yves Blanc Oct. 30, 1915.

21. Letter to Jeanne-Yves Blanc Nov. 19, 1915; letters to Madeleine May 20, July 1, 1915.

22. See article in April 1, 1914, *Mercure de France* (*Anecdotiques*, p. 153).

23. "Mandolin Carnation and Bamboo," "To Italy," "War."

24. See my article *"Les Collines*, dernier testament d'Apollinaire" (*Revue des Lettres Modernes*, Nos. 69–70, 1962, p. 25) for internal evidence that "The Hills" and the noncalligraphic part of "The Little Auto" were written in the 1916–18 period. In the proofs of *Calli-*

grammes at the Sainte-Geneviève Library in Paris, the two poems and "The Pretty Redhead" (1917) are in script in the same ink on the same kind of paper, as if added to the other poems which are in print; and the title "The Hills" is inserted between "Landscape" and "Tree" on the table of contents.

25. *Mercure de France*, Nov. 1, 1915 (*Anecdotiques*, p. 204).

26. Introduction to *Les Fleurs du mal* (1917); in *Les Diables amoureux*, p. 259.

27. Apollinaire, like other poetic critics (e.g., Cocteau) habitually used terms relating to abysses and depths when referring to Picasso's paintings.

28. Red is a color often associated with the magic unmanned boats of folklore, Romance, and Symbolist poetry. In the *Huth Merlin*, for example, one of these boats is pavilioned with "drap de soie aussi vermeil comme une escrelate," and in Régnier's "La Galère," which probably was a source of Apollinaire's "Spring," the galley has scarlet sails. Our poet's unmanned golden vessels at the end of *Onirocritique* (cf. Mallarmé's "golden galleys," Rimbaud's "golden vessels," etc.) have scarlet sails.

Selected Bibliography

WORKS

In English

Alcools, trans. Anne Hyde Greet. Berkeley-Los Angeles (U. of Calif. Press), 1965. Bilingual edition of *Alcools;* with extensive, perceptive notes. Many excellent translations. Foreword by Warren Ramsey.

Alcools, trans. William Meredith. N. Y. (Doubleday), 1964. First complete translation in English of Apollinaire's main work. Prosaic, literal, many mistakes. Bilingual edition. Brief introduction and notes by Francis Steegmuller.

The Assassinated Poet, trans. Matthew Josephson. N. Y. (Broom), 1923. Lively if somewhat dated version of the long *novella* that opens the second collection of stories.

The Breasts of Tiresias, trans. Louis Simpson. *Odyssey,* Dec. 1961.

The Cubist Painters, trans. Lionel Abel. N. Y., 1949. Introduction by Robert Motherwell. Excellent translation. Good bibliography.

The Debauched Hospodar. Paris (Olympia Press), 1953. Literal translation of *Les Onze Mille Verges.*

The Heresiarch and Company, trans. Remy Inglis Hall. N. Y. (Doubleday), 1965. Adequate if unexceptional translation; many inaccuracies.

The Memoirs of a Young Rakehell. Paris (Olympia Press), 1953. Literal translation of *Les Exploits d'un jeune Don Juan.*

Selected Writings, trans. Roger Shattuck. N. Y. (New Directions), 1950. Important poems, stories, criticism. Bilingual edition. Some good translations, many errors. Excellent critical introduction by translator.

In French

Oeuvres poétiques, ed. Marcel Adéma and Michel Décaudin. Paris (Gallimard, Éditions de la Pléiade), 1956. The best and most complete edition of the poetic works. Contains *Le Bestiaire* (with Dufy's woodcuts), *Alcools, Vitam Impendere Amori, Calligrammes, Il y a, Onirocritique, Poèmes à Lou, Le Guetteur mélancolique, Poèmes à Madeleine, Les Mamelles de Tirésias, Couleur du temps, Casanova,* and poems from letters, unpublished papers, and prose works. Introduction by André Billy. Chronology of poet's life and published poetic works. Thorough notes, bibliography.

Anecdotiques, ed. Marcel Adéma. Paris (Gallimard), 1955. Articles written for the *Mercure de France* from 1911 to 1918. Notes, index.

Chronique des grands siècles de la France. Vincennes, 1912. Popular, anecdotic history of France, from the Middle Ages to Napoleon, for young people. Illustrated.

Chroniques d'art (1902–18), ed. L.-C. Breunig. Paris (Gallimard), 1960. All art criticism not contained in *Il y a* (see below) or *Les Peintres cubistes.* Notes, bibliography, index.

Contemporains pittoresques. Paris (Éditions de la Belle Plage), 1929. Reprint of articles on Moréas, Gourmont, etc., written for *Les Marges.*

Diables amoureux (Les), ed. Michel Décaudin. Paris (Gallimard), 1964. Prefaces to erotic classics (*Le Marquis de Sade, Le Divin Aretin,* etc.) published from 1910 to 1918. A work that Apollinaire intended to bring out. No index.

Enchanteur pourrissant (L'). Paris (NRF), 1921. The second edition, less rare than the first of 1909 and with a few changes by the author. Woodcuts by André Derain.

Enfer de la Bibliothèque nationale (L'). Paris (Mercure de France), 1913 (in collaboration with Fernand Fleuret and Louis Perceau). A critical bibliography of erotica at the French National Library. Interesting notes.

Épingles (Les). Paris (Éditions des Cahiers Libres), 1928. Three of the better short stories written from 1916–18, "Les Épingles," "Chirugie esthétique," and "La Plante."

Esprit nouveau et les poètes (L'). Paris (Jacques Haumont), 1946. Reprint of article published in *Mercure de France,* Dec. 1, 1918.

Exploits d'un jeune Don Juan (Les). Philadelphia (?), 1944. One of many clandestine editions of this pornographic work. Banned in France.

Femme assise (La). Paris (Gallimard), 1948. Novel on Mormons. First published in 1920.

Fin de Babylone (La). Paris (Bibliothèque des curieux), 1914. A potboiler, historical novel written in collaboration with René Dalize.

Selected Bibliography

Flâneur des deux rives (Le). Paris (Gallimard), 1928. Articles from *Mercure de France* and elsewhere arranged to show picturesque, literary aspects of Paris.

Grâce et le maintien français (La). Paris, 1902 (communicated by Mme Onimus-Blumenkranz). A study of the style and references of this dance manual signed Molina da Silva shows that it was definitely written by Apollinaire as he claimed himself in a letter of 1902. Much of it was copied from classic manuals like Rameau's *Le maître à danser* (1748). Of interest for a few literary allusions, some humor, and personal anecdotes.

Hérésiarque et cie (L'). Paris (Stock), 1948.

Il y a. Paris (Messein), 1949. Contains important articles "Jean Royère," "Alfred Jarry," "Paul Fort," "Henri Matisse," "Henri Rousseau," "Kees Van Dongen," the calligram "Pablo Picasso," and art criticism not collected in *Chroniques d'art*. Also contains important poems, reprinted in *Oeuvres poétiques*.

Lettres à sa marraine, 1915–1918, ed. Marcel Adéma. Paris (Gallimard), 1951. Letters written to Jeanne-Yves Blanc.

Onze mille verges (Les). Holland, 1948. Banned in France.

Peintres cubistes (Les), ed. L.-C. Breunig et J.-C. Chevalier. Paris (Hermann), 1965. Excellent critical edition with manuscripts, notes, introduction, comparative texts. No index, however.

Poésie symboliste (La). Paris (L'Édition), 1908. Apollinaire's lecture of April 1908 on young poets.

Poète assassiné (Le), ed. Michel Décaudin. Paris (Club du meilleur livre), 1959. Best edition, but with incomplete notes.

Que faire?, ed. Noëmi Onimus-Blumenkranz. Paris (La Nouvelle Édition), 1950. Ghost-written novel of 1901. Excellent notes by Mme Onimus-Blumenkranz, although more of the novel is written by Apollinaire than she believes. The preface by Jean Marcenac is the only discussion to date of science-fiction themes in Apollinaire.

Tendre comme le souvenir. Paris (Gallimard), 1952. Almost 200 letters written to Madeleine Pagès in 1915–16 on literature, war, love. Introduction by Mlle Pagès.

Théâtre italien (Le). Paris (Michaud), 1910. A history and anthology of Italian drama; some translations (e.g., *Colombine, soldat de l'amour*) done by Apollinaire.

Trois Don Juan (Les). Paris (Bibliothéque des curieux), 1914. A book written for money patched together out of the *Don Juans* of Molière, Byron, etc.

Oeuvres complètes, ed. Michel Décaudin. 8 vols. Paris (Cercle Français du Livre), 1966. Contains most of the above works, journalism, correspondence. Notes, facsimiles.

Literary Periodicals Edited by Apollinaire
  Le Festin d'Ésope, Nov. 1903–Aug. 1904 (no May issue).
  La Revue Immoraliste, April 1905.
  Les Lettres Modernes, May 1905.
  Les Soirées de Paris, Feb. 1912–Aug. 1914.

CRITICAL STUDIES

In English

Adéma, Marcel. *Apollinaire,* trans. Denise Folliot. N. Y. (Grove Press),
  1954. A translation of *Guillaume Apollinaire le mal-aimé* (see below).
Balakian, Anna. *Surrealism: The Road to the Absolute.* N. Y. (The
  Noonday Press), 1959. Contains a chapter in which Apollinaire's
  modernism is excellently summarized.
Bates, Scott. *The Esthetics of Guillaume Apollinaire,* Madison, Wis-
  consin (unpublished doctoral dissertation), 1954. Discussion of
  main works and ideas. A compendium of Apollinaire information
  before 1954.
Breunig, L.-C. "The Chronology of Apollinaire's *Alcools,*" *PMLA,*
  LXVII, 7 (Dec. 1952), 907–23. A basic scholarly text, brought
  up to date by Décaudin (*Dossier*) and the present study.
Davies, Margaret. *Apollinaire.* London (Oliver and Boyd), 1964. Good
  critical study arranged on biographical lines.
Golding, John. "Guillaume Apollinaire and the Art of the Twentieth
  Century," *The Baltimore Museum of Art News,* XXVI; 4, VII, 1
  (Summer–Autumn 1963). Short summary of Apollinaire's career
  as an art critic by an authority on modern art.
Shattuck, Roger. *The Banquet Years.* N. Y. (Harcourt, Brace), 1955.
  Delightful journalistic and critical account of four artists, Henri
  Rousseau, Alfred Jarry, Eric Satie, and Guillaume Apollinaire, and
  their creative age.
Steegmuller, Francis. *Apollinaire Poet Among the Painters.* N. Y. (Far-
  rar, Straus), 1963. Pleasant, mostly accurate biography. Some new
  biographical material from Rome and Monaco.

In Other Languages

Adéma, Marcel. *Bibliographie générale de l'oeuvre de Guillaume Apol-
  linaire.* Paris (Chez l'auteur), 1949. Basic bibliographical source.
  Rare.
————. *Guillaume Apollinaire le mal-aimé.* Paris (Plon), 1952. First

Selected Bibliography

accurate biography. Prosaic, factual. A major source of information.

Bergman, Par. *"modernolatria"* et *"simultaneità."* Paris (Minard), 1963. Basic study on Apollinaire and Futurism.

Billy, André. *Apollinaire vivant.* Paris (Éditions de La Sirène), 1923. The leading critical work on Apollinaire before 1950. Somewhat unimaginative but with important documents, anecdotes, and insights. Based on author's close acquaintance with Apollinaire.

Couffignal, Robert. *Apollinaire et la Bible* (unpublished thesis, 1964). Analysis of some of the most important of the 200–odd references to the Bible in Apollinaire's work (60 from Genesis and Exodus, 123 from O.T.; 96 from N.T.). Importance of Catholic education. Apollinaire a prodigal son who never returned to his Father.

Décaudin, Michel. *La Crise des valeurs symbolistes.* Toulouse (Privat), 1960. Comprehensive survey of French literary movements from 1895 to 1914.

———. *Le Dossier d'Alcools.* Paris (Droz), 1960. A major study of *Alcools.* Essential for manuscripts, published versions of poems. Biography of poet, critical study of genesis of *Alcools*, its publication and reception. Important notes, critical bibliography.

Durry, Marie-Jeanne. *Guillaume Apollinaire, Alcools.* 3 vols. Paris (Société d'Éditions d'Enseignement Supérieur), 1956–65. Long study of *Alcools* based on notes for course given at the Sorbonne in 1955. Important biographical and critical insights, sources, analyses. Includes two essays on poet's symbolism, "Ombre-Lumière," " 'Passe et dure sans t'arrêter.' "

Faure-Favier, Louise. *Souvenirs sur Apollinaire.* Paris (B. Grasset), 1945. Letters, memoires from post-*Alcools* period.

Fettweiss, Christian. *Apollinaire en Ardenne.* Brussels (Henriquez), 1934. Description of Apollinaire's stay in Stavelot, Belgium, in 1899, his criminal departure. Influence of this stay on work.

Jannini, P. A. *La Fortuna di Apollinaire in Italia.* Milano (Instituto Editoriale Cisalpino), 1959. Apollinaire and Futurism, other Italian movements. Testimonies of Italian artist-friends of poet.

Lawler, James R. "Apollinaire inédit: Le séjour à Stavelot," *Mercure de France*, 1098 (Feb. 1955), 296–309. A detailed description of "Stavelot notebook." Some errors, corrected by Michel Décaudin in the *Mercure de France* for June 1955.

Moulin, Jeanine. *Guillaume Apollinaire, Textes inédits.* Geneva (Droz), 1952. Biographical study, evolution of poetics. Somewhat outdated but still important for study of influence of Nerval and Rimbaud on Apollinaire.

Onimus-Blumenkranz, Noëmi. *Apollinaire témoin des peintres de son temps* (unpublished thesis for École du Louvre), 1960. History of Apollinaire's esthetic revolution as it applied to the plastic arts. Lists and describes more than seventy portraits of the poet.

Onimus, James, "Souvenirs," *Lettres Françaises*, 392 (Dec. 1951). Account of adolescent friendship with Apollinaire on the Riviera.

Orecchioni, Pierre. *Le Thème du Rhin dans l'inspiration de Guillaume Apollinaire*. Paris (Lettres Modernes), 1956. An updating of Wolf's book (see below). Thorough, but overly cautious. Similarities and (mainly) differences between German Romantic poems and Apollinaire's Rhenish lyrics.

Pia, Pascal. *Apollinaire par lui-même*. Paris (Éditions du Seuil), 1954. A biography, more literary than Adéma's work on which it depends for facts. Very readable, by a member of the Parisian Bohemia.

Piron, Maurice, "Les Wallonismes de Guillaume Apollinaire," *Mélanges de linguistique française offerts à M. Charles Bruneau* (Geneva, 1954), 193–207. Complete dictionary of Apollinaire's wallonisms in the story "Que vlo-ve?" and the first two chapters of *Le Poète Assassiné*.

Rouveyre, André *Apollinaire*. Paris (Gallimard), 1945. Psychological analysis of Apollinaire by former friend and associate. Contains many letters to Lou.

Salmon, André. *Souvenirs sans fin*. 2 vols. Paris (Gallimard), 1955—. Anecdotes by a close friend.

Toussaint-Luca, A. *Guillaume Apollinaire, Souvenirs d'un ami*. Monaco (Éditions du Rocher), 1954. Memoires and letters, covering for the most part the period of adolescence.

Warnier, Raymond, "Apollinaire journaliste," *Revue d'Histoire Littéraire de la France*, LVI, 1 (Jan.–March 1956), 107–22. Valuable discussion of the beginnings of Apollinaire's journalistic career with *La Grande France* and *L'Européen* (1902–4); not always accurate, however.

Wolf, E. M. *Guillaume Apollinaire und das Rheinland*. Dortmund-Husen, 1937. The first university thesis on Apollinaire. Close search into literary and biographical backgrounds of the prose and poetry written out of the Rhineland sojourn of 1901–2. Contains list of German books in the poet's library.

REVIEWS DEVOTED TO APOLLINAIRE STUDIES

Esprit Nouveau (L'), No. 26 (Oct. 1924).

Flâneur des deux rives (Le), Nos. 1–8 (March 1954–Dec. 1955).

Selected Bibliography

Images de Paris, Nos. 49–50 (Jan.–Feb. 1924), 56–57 (Sept.–Oct. 1924).

Présence d'Apollinaire, Dec. 22, 1943–Jan. 31, 1944.

Revue des Lettres Modernes (La), Nos. 69–70 (Spring 1962), 85–89 (Autumn 1963), 104–7 (1964), 123–126 (1965).

Revue des Sciences Humaines (La), No. 84 (Oct.–Dec. 1956).

Rimes et Raisons (1946).

Sic, Nos. 37–39 (Jan.–Feb. 1919).

Table Ronde (La), No. 57 (Sept. 1952).

Vient de Paraître, No. 24 (Nov. 15, 1923).

Index

Index

Index

Index

Index

What To Do? See Que faire?
"Whirlwind of Flies." *See* "Tourbillon de mouches"
Whitman, Walt, 65, 106, 109
Wilde, Oscar, 23
Willette, Adolphe, 114
"Windows, The." *See* "Fenêtres (Les)"
"Women, The." *See* "Femmes (Les)"
"Wonder of War." *See* "Merveille de la guerre"
Wotan, 35

Xerxes, 135

Yeats, William Butler, 51, 84–85
Yette. *See* Mariette

Zeus, 86–87, 168
Zola, Émile, 33–34, 78
"Zone," 22, 26, 32, 35, 45, 100, *101–102*, 103–104, 106, 111–112, 153–154, 156–158, 164–166, 168, 170

DATE DUE

GAYLORD   PRINTED IN U.S.A.